Dinghies to Divas

Dinghies to Divas

or

Comedy on the Bridge

Some memoirs
of a compulsive sailor in
troubled waters

MORAN CAPLAT

COLLINS
8 Grafton Street, London W1
1985

William Collins Sons & Co Ltd
London · Glasgow · Sydney · Auckland
Johannesburg · Toronto

British Library Cataloguing in Publication Data

Caplat, Moran
Dinghies to divas.
1. Sailing
I. Title
797.1'24   GV811

ISBN 0—00—217237—2

Frontispiece cartoon by Gerard Hoffnung, 1958

First published 1985
© Moran Caplat 1985

Printed and Bound in Great Britain by
T. J. Press (Padstow) Ltd, Padstow, Cornwall

To Diana, who has heard it all before, and the children and grandchildren, who haven't.

Contents

Illustrations

facing p. 126

Early rehearsal for *La Calisto*, 1970. (*photo by Guy Gravett*)
Planning meeting, 1972. (*photo by Guy Gravett*)

facing p. 127

At the Rosehill Theatre, 1952. (*photo by George Konig*)
With David Hockney, 1974. (*photo by Guy Gravett*)

Acknowledgements

I begin with an apology to those whom I have not mentioned. This neglect is not a measure of my disregard or ingratitude but due to lack of space and the fact that I have resolutely tried to avoid writing a history of Glyndebourne in my time. Spike Hughes and Wilfred Blunt have done the subject proud and we have had, for the Golden Jubilee year, *Glyndebourne – a celebration* to embellish the records. This, then is a small exercise in autobiography, not complete, not guaranteed to be accurate as to detail. Dear reader, you are welcome to what you may discover between the lines.

Most operas and many books have alternative titles and I have adopted the name of Bohuslav Martinů's opera for mine because it admirably describes my view of my life. I apologize to him for the theft and for never having put on his opera despite the wish, more than once, to do so.

My most affectionate thanks go to Victoria Walsh, who has wrestled with the manuscript for over a year. Having been my invaluable secretary for a number of years, she could at least make a stab at reading my hand and guess what I was trying to say.

I am grateful to Diana Avebury for egging me on and aiming me in the right direction and to Philip Ziegler who has been a calm and polishing influence.

Barcombe
28 November 1984

ONE

In the castles

I was conceived on a night very early in January 1916 in a coast-guard cottage at Reculver, that Roman fort with the remains of a great Norman church superimposed which stands on the bleak coast of north Kent at the western end of the marshes dividing the 'Isle' of Thanet from the 'mainland'. No doubt the weather was typical of the place and season, a hard northerly on-shore wind – cold, grey, but dry, though the salt in the wind made everything damp.

My father was a Frenchman, twenty-four years old, slim then, later to become rotund, bespectacled, verbose in a heavily accented way – a charming style which he was never to lose. He was an architect by chance rather than training. His damaged back precluded military service, but his passionate dislike of the Germans, learnt from his grandfather's experience of the Franco-Prussian war, had led him to volunteer for any service. The one he found himself in was that of Sea Scout master, in charge of a teenage patrol of the coast between Birchington to the east and Herne Bay to the west.

Christened Armand Charles Victor Roger (though after coming to England he always used the anglicized name of Roger), he was born in La Ferté Alais, a little market town some thirty miles south of Paris near Fontainbleau. His father was François Armand Jules Victor, a notary in the town and at the age of thirty-four a respected citizen with keen sporting (mainly shooting) interests. His mother was an elegant girl of twenty-two, born Blanche Thérèse Madeleine Percheron (without any resemblance to, or as far as I know any connection with, a cart-horse).

Both of them died, presumably of some epidemic, when my father was four years old, and he retained no clear memories of them or of his life in La Ferté Alais. At that crucial age he found himself in the care of his paternal grandparents in Alençon, or rather in Damigny, a nearby village. His grandfather was a heavily bearded and locally respected figure, a man who won national awards for viniculture, a veterinary surgeon who looked after race-horses, a *gourmand* and no doubt *'un snob'*. He claimed, and I have done nothing to disclaim it, that the Caplats were directly descended from Charlemagne (not a particularly rare claim in France) and that had it not been for *La Terreur* he would have been Duc de Damigny, Vicomte d'Alençon.

When he was eighteen my father was sent by his grandfather to learn English at a private language-school in Herne Bay. A year later his grandfather died and he stayed on, first to complete his course and then, having identified with the social life, and the Hingston family in particular, to become a draughtsman in a local architect's office. My French great-grandmother went to live in Paris with a 'companion' who dominated the old lady and appropriated many of her belongings. When the French railways suffered their great financial collapse most of what was left of the Caplat fortune went with them. All that my father collected on the death of his grandmother were a few bits and pieces of furniture and pictures of no great value. Despite long legal battles in France he acquired little or no money and no property, the odious companion having apparently feathered her nest most effectively.

My mother was an attractive girl, a year younger than my father, a bit dumb and dizzy (though not a blonde) and partially deaf from an ear infection said to have been caught smelling the flowers in Highgate cemetery in early childhood.

Her family was very different from my father's but also a little less than humdrum. My English grandfather was, by my childish recollection, a tall austere figure, a pillar of the Congregational church in Herne Bay, 'something' in Lloyds and shipping in the City – a senior clerk perhaps – who invested his savings in three newly built semi-detached villas in prime residential areas in the fast developing Herne Bay on the commuters' line from Cannon Street to Ramsgate. These he named Kinfauns, Braemar and Tantallon, not as might be supposed after the castles but after the Union Castle liners which bore the same names.

Like others of his family he aspired to painting – marine subjects in particular – but, unlike the rest, he did so notably badly. His picture of the R.M.S. *Kinfauns Castle* proceeding through the Suez Canal (which he had never seen) was a masterpiece of naïve non-art.

Amongst other weaknesses, which did not include drink, tobacco or women, was a penchant for military bands. I well remember as a small boy going to many such concerts given in the cast-iron bandstand on the Downs at Herne Bay, holding the hand of my tall grandfather and being tremendously impressed by his easy way with the splendidly uniformed bandmasters who, baton still in hand, were regularly nobbled by him for serious discussions literally way above my head, after the final encore of *Poet and Peasant* or the Rossini selections.

The most impressive piece to me, which appeared regularly in the programmes, was a trumpet serenade, in which the solo trumpet was echoed by another trumpeter in an illuminated upstairs bedroom window of the Queen's Hotel which then stood opposite. This was to be brought back vividly to me years later when on one late summer evening in Corfu a brass band in a similar bandstand in the capital of that island played the same piece. Sure enough the equivalent hotel window was illuminated, but this time to reveal not the trumpeter, who had obviously got the wrong room number, but a nude lady of ample proportions who was enjoying the night air and the animated scene below.

My maternal grandmother, on the other hand, was the opposite of pompous; she was a forceful, compact figure, strict to the extent that promotes awed affection. She was a firm teetotaller but inordinately fond of Stone's Ginger Wine, which she stoutly maintained was non-alcoholic. She had married my grandfather on the rebound after a romantic disappointment and regretted the fact. Born Eliza Shaw, she was one of four sisters who claimed to have been the four most beautiful sisters in Edinburgh, where they had a somewhat rugged upbringing on the wrong side of town with a drunkard father. She and two of the others made respectable marriages; the fourth did not marry but never wanted for male company, and I suspect took rather more than the others after her father.

My maternal grandfather's family – he was christened John Cincinnatus Hingston because he was born in Cincinnati, whereas his brother was christened James Australis Hingston for similar reasons – were by Victorian standards a Bohemian lot.

Ebenezer Edward Peron Hingston, my great-grandfather, was born in 1823, the son of a builder. In his teens he began attending lectures at King's College Hospital, London, with the idea of becoming a doctor, but at the age of eighteen he turned his mind to a literary career and soon began to contribute regularly to Chambers's *London Journal* and Douglas Jerrold's *Illustrated Magazine* and had three novels published. In 1849 he became lecturer to the Newcastle-upon-Tyne Polytechnic Institution but after a few months he departed for Egypt and the Holy Land. Fortified by his experiences, he returned to London and took the Egyptian Hall in Piccadilly to give lectures on Egypt and Syria. Apparently he enjoyed full houses for two years.

By the early fifties Ebenezer was associated with 'Professor Anderson – the wizard of the North', a conjuror for whom he, to quote from his obituary in the *Era*, 'invented some of his best illusions depending on an application of scientific agencies' and at the same time 'furnished him with the most attractive programmes ever penned'. He toured with the Wizard in Europe and America and on his return to London became treasurer (box office manager?) of the Lyceum Theatre. At the end of 1855 he and the Professor took Covent Garden Theatre for a season, which culminated in a 'disastrous conflagration' in March 1856.

In 1857 he married Elizabeth Stage, the daughter of another builder, and left with the Professor for a further tour of America and Australia. There he got caught up in the gold diggings, went on to Tasmania and the Society and Sandwich islands and finished up in California as editor of a San Francisco newspaper.

By 1864 Ebenezer was managing Artemus Ward, the comic writer and lecturer, and together they spent six weeks amongst the Mormons at Salt Lake City. On the way they had been captured by Indians and narrowly escaped being scalped; on the way back their sleigh overturned in the Rocky Mountains and they had to walk several miles through the snow 'followed by a troop of hungry wolves'.

In 1866 he brought Artemus Ward to England where he, as my grandfather had, lectured in the Egyptian Hall. Ward died suddenly and 'E.P.H.', as he was known, went as manager to Spiers and Pond's *Hall by the Sea* at Margate. This seems to have been the precursor of the 'entertainment complex' of modern seaside resorts, with concerts, balls, entertainments and 'ices, pastry and other refreshments of the kind . . . made at Messrs. Spiers and Pond's large factory in London being . . . received by railway fresh every day'.

He obviously tired of the seaside and wished to return to the theatre proper, for in 1870 he became Stage Manager of the St James's Theatre, now alas no longer in existence. In 1872 he became Lessee and Manager of the old Opéra Comique in the Strand (where Bush House now is) and presented such works as *L'oeil crevé* or *The Merry Toxophilites* by Hervé, *The Wonderful Duck*, which appears to have had a Dodo as its protagonist, though to whose music I don't know (could it have been Mozart's *L'oca del Cairo*?) and adaptations of works by Offenback (*sic*), *The Bohemians* (*La vie parisienne*) and a new version of *L'isle de Tulipatan* entitled for London *Kissi-Kissi* and for which he, the adaptor F. C. Burnard and the actor Henry Corri were all officially reproved by the War Office for their caricature of the Shah of Persia who had recently been on a state visit to England.

Ebenezer's health began to fail but Spiers and Pond had built the Criterion Theatre in Piccadilly and in 1874 he was appointed their business manager. His indisposition got worse, however, and he was soon forced to retire. A benefit performance was given for him at Drury Lane which raised the large sum for those days of eight hundred pounds.

E.P.H. died aged fifty-two in June 1876, the cause of death being given as '*Degenerentio Spinalis* 3 years. Apoplexy 6 days'.

To return to my father, he must have seemed a bit of a catch to my mother, despite the fact that he was French. Arriving at the private language-school in Herne Bay with what were then adequate private means, he quickly fitted into her provincial society of tennis and dancing parties. Never a church-goer, though born a Roman Catholic, he took no part in the chapel activities of the Congregationalists. My mother was not religious-minded either; the most important part of Sundays for her was the fashion parade that they provided.

My parents were married in the Congregational church in Herne Bay in April 1915. When my arrival was imminent they retreated from the rigours of Reculver to the comparative luxury of one of the three castles (the two on the sea-front had been taken over by the Services), and eventually on 1 October 1916 my mother gave birth to me in Tantallon.

I was christened Moran Victor Hingston Caplat (the final 't' being silent as in Harlow, as Margot Asquith is supposed to have informed Jean Harlow when wrongly and familiarly addressed by her in Hollywood). My father maintained that the name Moran was French and had been used in the family before. My mother, I think, felt that it sounded rather Celtic and romantic. The name Morgan in Welsh means sea or sea-shore (*morven* is Celtic for a wave of the sea). Moran I have remained ever since, except that at one school I was called Moggy; whether that was because my first boat, a canoe, had that name or whether the canoe was called after my nickname, I don't remember.

I have never met another Moran as a first name; it is of course a

17

fairly common Irish surname and can be found over countless bars up and down that well-supplied country. Nor have I been able to trace any other Caplats, apart from the owner of a bookshop in Blois who said he came from the Midi.

I know less of my birth than of my conception; perhaps that is due to my greater interest in the mechanics of the latter. My first clear memory is of sitting on my father's shoulder to see the celebratory bonfire on top of the Beacon Hill on Armistice Night when I was just under two years old. My next, perhaps the same winter, is of my father coming down the garden path in a heavy tweed coat and matching hairy cap, covered in soft snowflakes like a walking snowman.

The war had made holidays abroad impossible but after the war my parents enjoyed a second honeymoon in Paris, I being left behind with my grandmother. Eventually, as money became tighter, protracted holidays were fewer and fewer. My father did go back to France once or twice after my French grandmother's death but only to try to settle her affairs, and my mother and I stayed at home sharing Tantallon or Kinfauns with my grandparents. My aunt and her husband eventually occupied Braemar, but one of the castles was always let furnished at a good rent in the summer. Kinfauns was the largest of the three and, like Braemar, looked out over the grassy lea, known as the Downs, from the top of the steep cliffs to the Thames estuary. These two therefore let most easily. Tantallon, the least eligible of the three, was for that reason the one most used by us. When no castle was available we would move into a furnished flat in the town. I didn't understand the economics of it all then and certainly do not now. I do recollect, however, that one of the lets of Kinfauns was to Joseph Conrad. He was apparently a heavy smoker of powerful cigars, and on our return to the house all the curtains and loose covers had to be dry-cleaned to get rid of the smell.

Whichever one of the castles I was in, from my bedroom I could see the sea: from Kinfauns a broad prospect from Sheppey to Reculver and out to the Girdler light-vessel and on clear days even the coast of Essex; from Tantallon only a narrow peep, but even that held the occulting beam of the light-vessel at night, and there was a steady procession of coasters, sailing barges, Whitstable oyster smacks and the paddle steamers on their way from Herne Bay pier to Margate pier, over to Southend and back to London.

On clear days, too, big ships and liners and sometimes even square-rigged ships as well as modern warships could be seen in the deep-water channel which the light-vessel marked. With my grandfather's knowledge of, and interest in, their comings and goings, I was kept well informed. He always knew the time of high water at London Bridge, and studied the ship movements in the daily paper. For special events we sat with binoculars in a convenient shelter at the highest point on the Downs and impressed passing strangers by our talk of things nautical.

My grandmother was a good cook in a conventional Anglo-Scottish way, but my mother a poor one. However, my father retained his Gallic palate, and after my grandmother gave up cooking (she got lazy as she got older, and I feel the same thing is happening to me) he hit on a good way of getting one decent meal a week. Down in the town was the Continental Stores, a delicatessen-cum-grocery kept by a splendid Italian called Mr – never Signor – Bosi and his wife. They prepared many of their own dishes, and my father had the bright idea of asking them to cook Sunday lunch for us. An errand boy with a bicycle would appear punctually at our house just before one o'clock and from his basket he would take a large insulated tin box, a kind of hay-box. Out of it would come a delicious *civet de lièvre*, or a boned and stuffed shoulder of veal, or roast beef cooked to perfection, or a leg of lamb properly pink as the French like it.

My father, whose office in Messenger's the architects was almost next to Bosi, would call on him on Friday on his way home to fix the weekend treat, which would include a box of delicious hand-made chocolates from another shop. I do not remember there ever being any alcoholic drink, however, except my grandmother's ginger wine. It seems that the drinking habit never caught my father, despite his time spent in France; he managed to elevate his spirits by laughter and endless talk. I have known him to be so busy talking that he didn't notice he was trying to take soup with a knife and fork. My mother used to put a damper on these meals, and many others less good, by her treatment of the vegetables: potatoes were always mashed and mushy, greens likewise and so heavily laced with washing soda – 'to keep them nice and green, dear' – that they were uneatable. This led to innumerable battles to get me to eat them up and it was many years before I developed the liking for vegetables and salads that I now have.

My mother was a great reader, and being deaf she found a lot of pleasure in books, mostly romantic novels and popular library fiction. For years she got through these at the rate of one a day. I too was encouraged to read from the library, and Henty and Jules

Verne (whom my father considered to be a genius and infallible prophet), Fennimore Cooper, *Worldwide Magazine*, the *Boys' Own Paper*, the *Children's Newspaper* and much else was greedily devoured. Being an only child — my mother flatly refused 'to go through all that again' — there was no one to play with at home, and reading and watching the seascape filled in a lot of time.

My mother knew no French and never made any effort to learn it, and so my father talked to no one in his own language. His attempts to speak French to me met with much ridicule from my grandfather, who couldn't speak French either, and when I giggled at Grandpa's rotten jokes my father gave up in disgust. So, sadly, I missed the chance to be bilingual.

My first school was a mixed kindergarten attached to a girls' school, named The Girdlers after the light-vessel upon which it also looked. The kindergarten was held in the old stable block at the back of the house and was what nowadays is known as a play-school. The teaching was minimal but I did learn to do useful things with my hands and, more important, I learnt what little girls were made of. At the beginning of my second term we were playing some version of ring-a-ring-o'-roses when a new girl next to me started to cry. The mistress, a smart young lady in her early twenties, asked her what the matter was, and receiving the shy but inevitable answer, enquired who would show little Mary where 'it' was. I immediately volunteered. Much to my surprise my gallantry was ill-received. I was hauled out of the class, taken upstairs to what turned out to be the mistress's bedroom, and shut in a cupboard which was full of her clothes on hangers. My cries of fear and annoyance were stifled by the hypnotic effect of the scent and the feel of the clothes around me. The *odor di femmina*, as Don Giovanni calls it, together with the silky softness of what was probably a party or ball dress, quite overcame me and the memory has titillated me ever since.

How long I stayed at The Girdlers I don't remember, but it was long enough for me to be allowed to go to and fro by myself, a mile or so including a steep hill, along roads that even in those days could scarcely be called busy. There were still plenty of horse-drawn vehicles then, tradesmens' carts — milkman, baker, green-grocer — even a two-horse mail coach running regularly from Herne Bay through Herne village to Canterbury and back, carrying passengers and parcels and with the driver blowing his long horn at intervals. The fire engine in its housing opposite my father's office was horse-drawn too and when the fire alarm, a maroon, went up, the horses from whatever vehicles stood nearby were commandeered and the engine careered off in great style. There was a pyromaniac at work in Herne Bay about then and we had a number of spectacular fires. One which I witnessed was in an old farmhouse not far from our house, and the sight of the fierce flames belching out of the windows and the roof falling in amidst a shower of sparks became one of my recurrent nightmares. For a few years after the blaze, when I had been put to bed and the grown-ups were safely downstairs, I used to get up and tour the upper floor, looking behind the doors and under the beds. Exactly what I expected to find, I do not know, but I was convinced that one day I would detect the smouldering beginnings of a conflagration. Then, in the middle of the night when everyone was upstairs and asleep, I would go to the loo. By standing on the seat I could look out of the little window down on to the laurel hedge below. The hedge was outside the kitchen window and in the kitchen was a 'kitchener', a coal-fired cooker. One day, I felt sure, this would burst into flames. If it did, I reckoned I would see the reflected glow on the laurels and be in time to escape. Happily I never had cause to do so, though a fear of fire remains with me to this day.

My next school was to be the most formative of my young life. I moved to a 'dame' school, perhaps one of the last fully to deserve that name. It was called St George's and was situated in a residential road behind the High Street in the centre of Herne Bay. To look at, it was just another Victorian double-fronted villa with a small formal front garden, into which no pupil ever went. The pupils approached it down a narrow alley at the back, just wide enough for one bicycle at a time. A high brick wall with a solid green-painted wooden door in it divided the alley from the playground, which was no more than a small back yard asphalted over. There was nothing much to distinguish it from a prison yard.

Through the back door one entered a dark corridor, smelling of a mixture of cabbage-water and beeswax, with coat hooks along the wall. There was a classroom to the right, that looked out only on to the yard. Up a few steps in the corridor one reached the entrance hall, facing the front door with its stained-glass fanlight. To the right was the second classroom; to the left the mistresses' study. We never went up to the first floor and whatever went on there remained a mystery.

On our daily walks round the block, which were conducted in a crocodile two-by-two, we passed the front of the school. My chief memory is of seeing through the shrubs of the front garden the

21

formal front elevation with its central door and two square windows on either side, both upper and ground floors having net half-curtains which hung from broad, flat, brass rails that were always gleaming with polish on the outside. Behind these there were dark brown velvet curtains. From the inside of the classroom the brass rails were of black iron and the velvet curtains lined with even darker brown casement cloth, though the bobble fringes on the pelmets lent a slight touch of frivolity to an otherwise formal gloom.

Miss May and Miss Gibson were the proprietors and, apart from Sergeant Sharp who took us for drill, P.T. and games, were our only teachers. They were inseparable and lived on the first floor of the school. Miss May was the older, I believe; certainly she was the more commanding, lightly moustached, imposing of mien as of bosom. Miss Gibson was smaller and fluffier, also more gently rounded. Both wore black bombazine high-necked blouses with stiffening bones in the collars, tight leather belts, full dark skirts to the ground, and generally buttoned boots, though occasionally they permitted themselves flat black lace-up shoes and woollen stockings (I presume they were stockings – they might as well have been socks for all the leg that was displayed). But their most distinguishing feature was their pince-nez. Both of them wielded those clip-on gold glasses which hung on a chain emanating from a large black metal button pinned strategically on the left breast. The sound of these being drawn from the button (left hand holding the button down, right hand tugging with a flourish and steering the glasses so that they settled firmly on the nose) and the subsequent letting go, when they would rush back like the retractable seat-belts of today, remains with me yet. Miss Gibson had only one pair, Miss May two, which sometimes to our intense pleasure became entangled with each other.

We, somewhere between a dozen and twenty-two of us, were sometimes taught as one class, sometimes two, as the subject demanded. Scripture for instance was taken by the whole school as the first lesson each day and was conducted by the two ladies together: Miss May instructing, Miss Gibson, the more mellifluous, leading the unaccompanied singing of the hymn. The school was Church of England, with our patron St George set firmly on the right-hand of the Almighty.

We would split into two classes for arithmetic, writing and geography, according to our length of time at the school. The upper classroom with its one large central table doubled as dining hall for our lunch, which was simple, but as I recall it not much worse than

I was used to. The food was cooked and brought in by 'the Maid', suitably attired in cap and apron; a down-market counterpart of Miss Gibson, she dwelt on the attic floor and did all the menial tasks, including filling the coal buckets. The only means of heating the classrooms was by coal fires, which were never allowed to do more than smoulder damply. Sometimes peat blocks were added, which at least had a pleasant smell. The food was distributed by the ladies, always of course with grace before and after. An enamelled mug of cold milk in summer, hot in winter, came in mid-morning.

We used standard copy-books and primers, including Latin and French, which gave me little trouble though I never mastered grammar in any language. We also had 'cards' which we learnt by rote. These were sheets of pasteboard, the contents devised by Miss May and written out in copperplate by Miss Gibson. There was at least one for each subject and they sat in piles on the window ledge of the lower classroom. After the summer holidays we would come back to find that Miss Gibson had lovingly recopied one set or another during her holiday, so as to replace the most dog-eared specimens. Arithmetical tables, the Capes and Headlands of Britain, the Kings of England, are just three that spring to mind. I can still chant some of them: William the First ten sixty-six, William the Second ten eighty-seven . . . Dungeness, Beachy Head, Selsey Bill, St Catherine's Point, The Needles . . .

As adolescence approached, sex and boats manifested themselves. There was a piece of wasteland near our house with a large blackthorn tree in the centre whose thorny branches scraped the ground. Underneath it was a secret area that I and a few of my playmates got to know. Another secret place was under the wooden staging of the promenade facing the sea opposite our house – the asphalt path was always slipping away down the eroding clay cliffs and being replaced by sections of wooden planking. Both these places served for experiments in smoking and in determining the differences between the sexes. The smell of Woodbines on our jumpers plus a green and lethargic air gave the former away to the grown-ups; the fact that our underpants were found to be inside out on undressing for bed betrayed the latter.

Looking daily at the sea with all its activity inevitably led to an interest in boats. My nautical career was launched more modestly, however, on a large pond in some wasteland nearby on which we used to play, fishing out newts, tadpoles and sticklebacks. A split-chestnut and wire fence ran across part of it. One day, wishing to get away from the bank, I found a wooden box, something like a wine case, which I duly launched. Then I scrambled into it in my wellingtons and hauled myself precariously out along the fence. The box leaked and soon sank under me, but luckily the pond was not deep and, wet but wiser, I struggled with my precious box back to the shore and eventually to a ticking off and threats of no supper. My next move was to beg some tar from the roadman and caulk the box so as to make it watertight. This worked well enough until I came to get out, when I found that my rubber boots had stuck to the bottom. More trouble at home!

Now I decided that I wanted a real boat to use on the sea. Here my father was firm. I could not swim, and had had little incentive to learn, since although I played on the beach a lot, the sea is shallow at Herne Bay except at high water and the spring tides go a long way out. My father said that I could have a boat when I could swim the distance between two breakwaters, about fifty yards, I suppose, without touching bottom. This I did very soon and my boat was ordered.

My father was no marine architect, and although he became official timekeeper for the Herne Bay Sailing Club at a later date and even used to contribute reports on the weekend racing to the *Herne Bay Press*, he never, so far as I know, set foot in any vessel smaller than the Dover–Calais ferry. The carpenter he persuaded to build the boat was no shipwright either. The result was an elongated coffin with a sharp prow. The front three feet were canvased, and the after two feet were a solid deck. There was a bung-hole with a cork bung, and a hefty two-ended paddle. The whole thing was heavily built of deal, painted a startling red and black, and called *Moggy*.

It was not long before the labour of paddling began to pall; a modification to provide rollocks on outriggers and a pair of primitive oars proved no more effective and also obliged me to proceed facing backwards, which I found unsatisfactory. So the great transition began – to sail.

Moggy was not very different in miniature to a Thames barge, slab-sided and flat-bottomed. She hadn't the barge's bluff but sea-kindly bows or her neat stern, but these had taken centuries of evolution and we were just beginning. Up went a simple unstayed mast, and sails were ordered from my mother. No sailmaker she; an indifferent seamstress, a botcher of darns, though a tireless trimmer of hats and cushions, she nevertheless tried, out of unbleached calico, to produce the right shapes, each cut from a

single piece of cloth. Again inspired by the barges which were a
daily spectacle in the middle distance, I eschewed the complications of gaff and boom and went straight for a spritsail.

With this primitive rig, plus an equally primitive rudder hung
on curtain-rod fittings over the stern, I was able to proceed, facing
forward, in a leisurely way along the foreshore to east or west in the
prevailing southerly off-shore breezes. Unfortunately the breeze
rarely blew equally favourably in both directions, so it was back to
paddling or rowing to get home. *Moggy* and I had to learn how to
go, if not close to windward, at least a little better than at right angles
with an awful lot of leeway. Again from the barges, lee-boards were
borrowed as an idea. In time I devised bigger and better sails and
tougher rigging. Eventually poor old *Moggy* demonstrated that she
had reached the limit of her development by capsizing and involving us both in the need to be rescued by the 'trips-round-the-bay'
motor boat, clinker-built, counter-sterned and beautiful, with the
equally beautiful though locally unpronounceable name of *Psyche*.

The *Psyche*'s owners were a father and son named Sayer. The
old man had been to sea either in the Navy or the Merchant Service; the younger, then in his thirties, had been in the Navy in the
First World War. Besides taking trips round the bay, they went out
to and round the Girdler light-vessel some five miles off shore.
This I particularly enjoyed. Sometimes I paid sixpence for the
trip round the bay – a shilling for the longer tour – sometimes, if
there were not too many paying passengers, I was taken for
nothing. I also sat at the Sayers' feet ashore and listened to their
tales of derring-do. *Psyche* was kept in sparklingly clean condition,
and repainted annually. There were smart canvas cushions for the
passengers. Father and son, and everyone else in the neighbourhood, called her the 'Psitchy'.

My other mentor in these matters was Bill, the boatman at the
Sailing Club. Bill was a real old reprobate, a bachelor come ashore
from years as a deck hand in square-rigged ships. He knew nothing
of the art of sailing but he could steer and splice ropes, both hemp
and wire, and do a number of fancy ropework knots and mats.
Although I have let the knack get rusty, what he taught me was,
like riding a bicycle, something one never quite forgets. He smoked
shag tobacco which he kept in a pouch made, he assured me, from
his own caul. He had been born with a caul and for that reason was
convinced that he could never drown; nor did he, except perhaps
in beer, of which there was a constant strong aroma compounded
with those of tobacco and Stockholm tar as well as poor attention

to washing and laundry. He was fond of quoting: 'Every 'air of me 'ead a rope yarn, Every drop of me blood Stockhollum tar', and he also claimed in his naval days to have been 'up the Yeller River and down the Yangtse Kiang'. I never enquired fully about this, but believe it to have had something to do with the Boxer rising. I too have always believed that I shall not die by drowning, for I was born with partially webbed feet – that is to say two toes on each foot, though perfectly mobile, are joined by a web of skin, like a duck. So far it has worked.

One of the outstanding memories of those halcyon childhood summers was the annual shrimping expedition. On a balmy summer's day – they all were, of course – I would go with a few other children and their parents along the beach from Herne Bay to Reculver some two and a half miles, armed with shrimping nets and stout sticks with iron hooks on the end. The tide had to be just right, spring tides at the ebb with the flood just beginning, and we would push our shrimping nets along the sandy, slightly muddy bottom. A specially big 'professional' net was borrowed for the adults to use, and we carried haversacks slung on our backs to take the catch. Further inshore other members of the party armed with the sticks would rake round under the bigger rocks for lobsters, of which we usually caught a few.

Reaching Reculver in the late afternoon we would go round to the east of the Norman towers to another row of coastguard cottages, which stood at that time with grassy gardens sloping steeply down to the beach itself. In one of these lived an old woman who had looked after my father and mother during the war and who now made a little pin – or gin – money by providing modest teas to summer visitors. Her guests sat at a big, weathered wooden table, on benches planted in the rough grass of her salt-swept garden with its shrubs distorted by the wind. Having been alerted by some sort of bush telegraph that we were on our way, she would already have a large kettle of sea-water on the boil, into which went all the shrimps. In what seemed a magically short time we were seated round the table set with huge plates of warm brown shrimps (it is the deep-water ones that are pink when cooked), mugs of tea or bottles of fizzy lemonade – the kind of bottle with a captive marble for a stopper – and, an equal treat, an unlimited supply of 'squashed-fly' biscuits (Garibaldi biscuits is their proper name but when young we thought of the currants with which they were so thickly endowed as something more exotic). My father would entertain us with stories of war-time Reculver, of how the garrison soldiers would play knuckle-bones with human relics from the Norman abbey and the Roman fort, in just the same way, he said, as the Roman garrison probably sat on its haunches and played the same game with the bones of earlier generations. A scramble up the ruin as far as one was allowed and then, as the evening began, the walk home, along the clifftop with net and stick on shoulder, the tide nearly up and the sun beginning to go down over Sheppey. Happy days!

When I was twelve, the time came for me to leave Miss May and Miss Gibson. It was decided to send me as a day-boy to Herne Bay College. This was a large red-brick building on the Canterbury road, outside Herne Bay proper and close to the old village of Herne. My preparation at St George's was apparently sufficient for me to be accepted straight into the College by way of some sort of examination, in which the only difficulty I encountered was mathematics. I dare say the standards were not high.

The College was a private school, though it liked to think of itself as a Public School with capital letters. It was a boarding school, and in my time there were never more than one or two day-boys at the College besides myself. I cannot now recall the name of the headmaster or of a single fellow scholar; there were boys from Europe and from the Argentine in particular, I remember. Most of the masters were young graduates, but I can remember only one at all vividly. He taught maths and by some magic succeeded in opening the door of my imagination to the poetry of figures and fractions. I never became academically brilliant in that subject, but thanks to him I ceased to be afraid of it and can still work my mental calculator, if not as fast or as efficiently as the electronic kind, at least quickly and on the whole accurately. His name was memorable: Colenso Pentecost. A Cornishman with a marked regional accent, he wore a hairy tweed jacket with leather elbows. He had a badly pock-marked face and was always called 'Scabby' Pentecost. He was most respectfully feared and went on to become the headmaster of an important private school.

My education followed conventional lines and was generally unexciting. I particularly enjoyed the engineering. There was a workshop with lathes and other machinery, a forge and a good instructor. Periods spent there were always pleasurable, and the smell of newly turned metal and hot soapy water used as a lubricant was as characteristic as that of the smell of singed hooves in a smithy. Chemistry provided some amusing moments too, though the smells created there were less salubrious.

I still took little interest in games. In summer I had better things to do on the water and I managed to get a special dispensation to use official games time for sailing, at which I steadily improved.

The Officer's Training Corps, or O.T.C., was the hardest grind. It seemed to be obligatory to be a member unless you were proclaimed physically unfit; the boring squad drill, blancoing of equipment, wrapping of puttees round one's shins, and countless other bits of what is nowadays called 'bull', were only slightly alleviated by the rifle range and field days, the latter involving a lot of bussing and debussing, scrambling through hedges, wilfully mishearing commands and, with a bit of luck, being able to fire a blank cartridge towards the backside of some unsuspecting sheep. Days spent at the Canterbury depot of the Buffs were unmitigated hell. Square-bashing under the command of professionally sadistic company sergeant majors, uneatable 'canteen' food (the thin pale-yellow custard in particular remains a nightmare), interminable lectures, all conspired to convince me that a soldier's life was not for me.

So, for relief, to extra-curricular activities. There is that old alliterative joke about the Northern Isles, that in the summer there is fishing and . . . . ing and in the winter there is no fishing. Well, in the summer there was sailing and in the winter there was no sailing. There was, however, 'the pictures', at this time still silent with a redoubtable lady hammering a piano in a hole – pit would be too polite a word – under the screen. Entry was cheap even by the standards of my modest pocket money, condensed milk was the most satisfactory form of sustenance, and an empty tin could be sent rolling down the steeply raked concrete floor, banging on the cast-iron seat standards as it went, to add an unnerving accompaniment to the piano. Sometimes one could lure a female companion into the back rows; 'nobody one knew', of course, but there was a regular supply of young assistants at the local Woolworth's who could be persuaded to meet a College boy at the entrance and sit with him in a clumsy and relatively innocent embrace. A few sticky kisses – the condensed milk and Woolworth's lipstick proved a particularly glutinous combination – would be the limit of the affair, followed by a parting in the dark, each to leave by different doors, with no more to follow than a knowing exchange of glances at the next encounter in the 'threepenny and sixpenny store'.

TWO

On the boards

I cannot be certain what sparked off my interest in the theatre. When it began, in my teens, I had no idea that my great-grandfather had been an active and intermittently successful theatre manager. Still less had I any musical leanings. My grandfather's military band concerts had been the height of my musical experience except for a visit to a performance, professional I think, of Messager's *Véronique* in the pretty wooden theatre at the shore end of Herne Bay pier shortly before it became yet another victim of the local pyromaniac. I vastly enjoyed this little operetta. I was taken to see *Treasure Island* at the Strand Theatre in London, and the thrill of the curtain rising silently on the darkened stage, the drunken singing of 'Yo ho ho and a bottle of rum', and the light slowly coming up on the interior of the inn was, and is, unforgettable.

I suppose I had inherited some of my great-grandfather's showmanship. In my teens, rising to my feet quickly at the end of a boring morning class, I felt a sharp pain in the genitals. On inspection I found that I had been stung by a wasp. Between lunch and afternoon school I made quite a decent little pile out of twopence a peep at the enormity of the result. I was a natural show-off. I can remember doing one-man shows of a bloodthirsty nature on the narrow stage provided by curtaining off part of the glazed veranda known as 'the extension' at Tantallon. The loo which adjoined this made a dressing room, or rather a dressing-up room, and provided the only entrance on to the five foot by five foot stage. The 'turns' lasted only seconds and the audience room was limited to four, two standing and two seated.

When I was fifteen, I went with a school party to a performance of *Twelfth Night* by the Ben Greet Players in the chapter-house garden at Canterbury. Suddenly I was stage-struck. I began to read plays, particularly Shakespeare, and regularly to attend performances by Harry Hanson's Court Players in the King's Hall at Herne Bay.

During those few years I was truly adolescent, with all the

29

attendant complications. I did little at school but managed to pass School Certificate with three distinctions. My father put me off becoming an architect. He said that, unless I was to be a genius, which somehow he doubted, the future looked bleak; individuals were going to have less and less chance and one would just have to join a big firm and be part of a team with little room for original thought. He himself was an original thinker and there are several houses in Herne Bay that still carry his, to me, very individual style.

I worked for pocket money as a labourer on building sites, carrying a hod of bricks or mortar up ladders to the bricklayers on the scaffolding. I learnt to tie the knots of scaffolding (it was all done with wood and rope in those days), to mix cement and mortar (the latter still being made up of lime and sand) and plaster with cow hair as its binding ingredient. I became an iron-fighter, which was the title given to those who set the rods and bent the ties that became the armature of the newly introduced reinforced concrete.

All this was leading nowhere. I had already toyed with the idea of becoming a jockey but was clearly not of the right build. I had a brief experience as an apprentice marine engineer in the General Steam Navigation Company's yard at Deptford. For a few weeks I stuck it out, lodging in Lee Green and cycling to work in the dark February mornings as well as pedalling the sixty-odd miles home at weekends. I was teased by my more experienced workmates for not being a cockney, though my accent was distinctly Kentish, and I was taunted and deliberately aroused, as were others of the younger members of the work force, by the gang of fearsome female cleaners of all ages who swarmed over the Thames Estuary pleasure steamers which were in the yard for their winter refit. Finally, while working by candlelight on the plumbing in the cold and echoing ladies' lavatory of the paddle steamer *Golden Eagle*, I was laid low by bronchial flu. I wheezed in my digs in a state of great despondency until my father came to rescue me, took me home and succeeded in getting my apprenticeship to the General Steam Navigation Company annulled.

As that spring of 1933 grew into summer I lazed at home, sailing and being dissolute, without any purpose and no doubt to the despair of my parents. On an impulse I wrote to the Royal Academy of Dramatic Art in Gower Street for their prospectus and applied for an entrance audition. At that time I had never, except for my juvenile attempts in the 'extension', appeared before the public as an actor; I had not taken part in any amateur theatricals, nor had I acted in any school plays. I do not exactly remember now what was asked of me at the audition – I think it was one set-speech to be memorized, one self-chosen speech, which for me, because of *Twelfth Night* in Canterbury, had to be 'Make me a willow cabin at thy gate', and something to be sight-read.

I arrived at R.A.D.A. knowing no one, having made a journey I was to make many times thereafter – by train from Herne Bay to Cannon Street and then by bus to Gower Street. Having waited with others in a classroom I was then catapulted on to the brightly lit stage of the little theatre, facing a black void in the depths of which an oblong box of dim light silhouetted the four or five heads of the panel. Here I suffered, not for the first and certainly not for the last time, the shock of being in an instant out on my own with nothing but luck and instinct to guide me.

I launched into *Twelfth Night*, was asked for the set-speech and then was told to retire and wait. Some of those who had been waiting earlier had disappeared, which gave me alternately the hope that I was on a short list and the fear that the best had already been selected. Soon I was recalled to read something – I think from *The Tragedy of Nan* by Masefield – and then was told by a silhouetted head with a kindly masculine voice that I had passed. I caught the train home in a state of bliss and found my parents surprised but proud.

Now came the problem of paying the fees. I had not been sent to R.A.D.A. by any education authority or other body, I had been out of school for a year or two, had no personal earnings and my parents were just about scraping along. My fairy godmother turned up in the shape of a chicken. During the war my father had kept chickens to provide food and eggs for the family but successfully enough to show a small profit. This profit he had invested in War Bonds in my name and the sum resulting was just sufficient to pay my fees at and fares to R.A.D.A. for several terms.

I was hard put to make ends meet but I lived free at home, had only to have one meal out, lunch, and allowed myself one shilling and ninepence a day to cover that, bus fares and 'incidental' expenses. In the canteen at R.A.D.A. a small meat pie was fourpence, and by swamping it in ketchup, which was free, and having a two-penny cup of coffee, I could get by and even save something to help meet other expenses. Walking from Cannon Street to Gower Street saved twopence; fourpence if one did it both ways. The great treat was lunch in Bertorelli's in Charlotte Street, where for ninepence one could have a *demi-ravioli*, a generous half portion which, together with a roll and a good shell-shaped scoop of butter for another threepence, fourpence for good coffee and twopence for the waitress, could usually be afforded once a week.

I managed occasionally to stay the night in London in someone else's digs. One enterprising fellow-student, whose parents paid the rent of a small mews flat but otherwise kept him short, did well by sub-letting a chair or a corner of the floor at twopence a night and, more profitably, by holding a bottle party once a week for which he provided the premises but retained the money returnable on empties. Staggering, hung-over, to his local with a suitcase full would perhaps make him late for class but might net him as much as four or five shillings. The wear and tear on the flat was, however, considerable.

Harry Plunkett Green was already in his late sixties or seventies when I sat at his feet, or rather across from him in a small room at a little table on which he would place his gold pocket-watch and the day's *Times* folded at the leader page. His mission was to eradicate from my speech the pinched vowels of the Kentish side of the Thames Estuary. To this end, dressed even on the warmest day in his hairy tweeds, he would for a strict twenty minutes, three times a week, work on my reading of *The Times* leader, never commenting on its subject but untiringly working on my diction and pronunciation. It has occurred to me since that he could have been of great assistance in making the name *Morning Cloud* for a famous yacht somewhat less of an embarrassment to its owner.

I missed one whole term through scarlet fever. It was a vicious attack which, in those pre-penicillin days, led to a stay in the isolation hospital at Herne Bay, a grim institution in which I seemed to be the only patient. A resultant infected gland in my neck kept me there as a solitary patient for several weeks.

Before rejoining R.A.D.A. I got my first professional engagement. Harry Hanson gave me a small part in *White Cargo* with the Court Players. As payment I received a white evening scarf of artificial silk with black fringed ends.

In my final term I was, for my passing-out play, given the part of the lion in *Androcles and the Lion*. Bernard Shaw himself turned up on a number of occasions to supervise. This was an awe-inspiring experience but I remember his patience and kindness (and his glasses of milk), and it is his interest no doubt which led to the *Daily Telegraph* saying in its notice: 'Of Moran Caplat's powers it is difficult to judge, but his leonine capers certainly qualify him for immediate success in pantomime', while the *Manchester Guardian* called me 'the jolliest of household pets'.

Probably it was not difficult in those days to get jobs; certainly I always seemed to be in work despite the fact that television had not got going. I went from repertory company to films to B.B.C. radio drama to West End runs, living, it now seems, a happy itinerant life with few if any responsibilities.

From R.A.D.A. I went directly to Margate Rep – a sort of J. B. Priestley *Good Companions* experience. It was run by Pat Nye, whom I was to encounter again in 1946 as Chief Wren at Greenock on the Clyde. She was an ample lady in every respect, enthusiastic, efficient and dominating. If she had a penchant for the fluffier end of the female juvenile actress spectrum, she also had a healthy gusto for theatre as theatre and well-salted performances. She was in fact the reverse of what her male counterpart might have been: precious.

Apart from the beauty of the little Theatre Royal and the archaic backstage conditions I have scanty memories of performances, but there in Margate I saw my first ghost.

We, all of us members of the company, were living in a mid-Victorian terraced house in a little street not far from the theatre. There were a few steps up from the street to the front door, over a basement area without separate entrance. On the front door level to the left was the dining room which was shared by all the inmates, behind it a bedroom occupied by the leading man. A short flight ahead led to the 'mezzanine', in effect a wooden shanty that had been tacked on to the back of the house at an early date to provide a lavatory and bathroom.

Above the 'mezzanine' the narrow staircase reversed to two more rooms. The small front one was mine, the back one being occupied by a senior female member of the company. From this floor a precipitous stair led to the attic occupied by a male colleague.

One Friday night after the performance, we had our supper, probably of stuffed sheep's hearts washed down with whatever pay-day allowed us to afford, and retired to our several rooms. Some time in the night, inspired by the sheep's hearts, the stuffing therein or a bit too much of Shepherd Neame's bottled ale, I felt the need to visit the mezzanine. Drowsily I lit the candle in the enamel holder beside my bed and descended the stairs. Without becoming any less drowsy I seated myself, put the candle on the shelf and went into a kind of coma. Re-awakening a minute or two later I put out my right hand to search for some of the quartered sheets of *Tit-bits* which were stacked on a shelf and found I was not alone. My hand went straight through a small dark man of late middle-age who seemed to be occupying virtually the same space as myself though I could see him like a sort of double image. He was looking directly ahead with an intense expression, surely normal in the circumstances, and he had a prominent Adam's apple over a high celluloid collar with a nondescript tie knotted loosely below the big brass collar-stud. This experience roused me from my somnolence and when I looked harder he wasn't there. Grateful for, if not soothed by the *Tit-bits*, I took up my candle and returned to bed.

Probably I would have dismissed this as a dream or even forgotten it entirely, had it not been that at breakfast the next morning (lumpy porridge, soggy toast and strong tea) the actress who occupied the room behind mine said to the fellow in the attic above: 'I say, Bish, did Mrs Mills put anyone else into your room last night?' 'No!' Bish replied, a note of horror in his voice. 'Well I didn't think he looked like a friend of yours. In the middle of the night when I went down to the lav I had to stand aside for a little old fellow coming up the stairs. He went on up to your attic. Who on earth was he?' 'You must have dreamt it,' Bish said.

A few days later on my departure for Croydon, braving the hitherto unplumbed depths of the basement to say goodbye to Mrs Mills, I saw on the wall a photograph of the late Mr Mills, a slight dark man in a high celluloid collar with a large collar-stud below a jutting Adam's apple.

At Croydon Rep I had the experience of playing on the same stage as Donald Wolfit, the first publicly acclaimed star I had encountered. A distinguished Norwegian rejoicing, I hope, in the name of Stein Bugge came to direct Ibsen's early piece, *Catiline*, and a contemporary piece of his own. Wolfit played the major role in both works; the rest of us were little but spear-carriers. The stage at Croydon was small; the proximity to Wolfit in full spate and sweat was a matter of endurance for the olfactory nerves. He wasn't very nice to us either. The Bugge piece gave us an opportunity for revenge, however. In this Wolfit played the part of some kind of political four-letter word man and we, the plebs of the Roman piece, were journalists and photographers who at one point had to mug, or rough-up, the protagonist. On the last night we managed to de-bag Wolfit entirely. In fairness I must say he took it in good part.

Money was tight; three pounds a week was a good salary, eight pounds riches, but you could take a girl out to dinner in Durand's little restaurant in Dean Street for ten shillings, including a bottle of wine and sometimes including a cockroach or two which fell from the ceiling into the salad. Durand's kept me going during a hard winter at the Little Theatre: it provided a superb bowl of onion soup with all the bread and glutinous cheese that you could desire for sixpence. I had recurrent tonsilitis, and continued to do so until I had my tonsils removed at the age of forty-one, but the onion soup kept me quacking.

Marguerite Steen, the novelist, with the help of Matheson Lang, turned one of her Spanish books into a play. He, one of the great actor-managers, put it on and directed it. It had a rewarding principal role for him as the retired matador, father of three sons. I was the youngest, a would-be poet and reluctant bull-fighter who in the end, after the death of his eldest brother in the ring, was made to follow in his father's and brother's footsteps. I learnt two new skills during the run of this play; one was to make some of the classic passes with the cape, lessons for which were given me by a waiter in the basement of the Barcelona restaurant, and the other to tie a double-ended bow tie without looking in the mirror. There were four acts and in each I had a different suit and bow tie, so I became quite adept.

I learnt another lesson too. One evening in Aberdeen I strayed from my dressing room to talk to a girl in another one. In consequence I failed to hear the call boy (there was no intercom system in the provinces in those days) until he came hammering on the door and told me that I was 'off' – that is to say that I was late in making my entrance to the stage. When I rushed to the wings I realized that Lang was busily 'gagging' with the leading lady and had been doing this for a minute or two. I shot on to the stage, the leading lady exited after a few lines, and I was left to play a short scene with my father. Lang looked at me mercilessly and then proceeded to give me all my cues just wrong and to make quite different moves while at the same time conducting the scene correctly as far as the audience was concerned. I was kept in a sweat of fear trying to fit my responses to his words and my moves to his. Finally he went off, I had a few words with another character and then exited in terrible apprehension of retribution to come. Making my way through the darkness of the wings to my dressing room I found my arm trapped by the crook of a walking stick and myself dragged face to face with the great man who was waiting behind a stack of scenery. All he said was, 'I don't think you'll be "off" again, will you?' I never was.

Marguerite Steen was living with Sir William Nicholson the

great painter and he provided the designs for *Matador*, as far as I know the only designs he ever did for the theatre. On a number of occasions we went on a Sunday to Arundel, where Sir William sat on the banks of the river Arun and painted or I rowed them both about in a hired boat. A few years ago in Christie's I saw one of his paintings done at that time and there am I at the oars. The sun always shone, the meadows were always full of buttercups.

When I announced one day that I had made up my mind, no doubt influenced by some of my Bloomsbury friends, to go to Spain and fight on the Left in the civil war, they rounded on me and told me in no uncertain terms that, from their considerable experience of Spain, the best hope for that unhappy country was with the Right. Unnerved and surprised I took the correct decision and didn't go at all – an experience lost but possibly my life saved.

A film was to be made by London Films, in conjunction with a German company, of Edward Whymper's first ascent of the Matterhorn and its tragic dénouement. The Alpine scenes were to be directed by Luis Trenker, the star and director of the classic film *The White Hell of Pitz Palu*. There had to be two casts, one English and one German-speaking. Robert Douglas was to be the English Whymper and Luis Trenker would himself play the part of the Italian professional climber Jean-Antoine Carrell, Whymper's rival, in both versions. Joan Gardner was to play his girl-friend. The English cast lacked a young actor to play the part of Richard Hadow who, joining the climb with his tutor the Rev. Charles Hudson, caused the fatal accident on the way down by slipping and dragging Hudson, Lord Francis Douglas and a Swiss guide with him. The rope to which all seven climbers were attached broke just below Whymper's position on it and he and two other guides survived. The great controversy then arose: did the rope break or had Whymper cut it? Whymper was exonerated but only after much argument.

This was not the only time in my life when telling a half lie, wishing it were the whole truth, has been to my advantage. I went to Pinewood, had a screen test and was asked whether I knew anything about climbing and if I had a good head for heights. Remembering scrambling on the clay cliffs of north Kent after jackdaws' eggs, I said I could climb a bit. My work as a bricklayer's labourer on scaffolds led me to claim that I had an excellent head. I was engaged. After a hectic fitting for a suitable tweed knickerbocker suit, which I wish I still had today, I was despatched to Zermatt.

Eight weeks of adventurous bliss followed. It was summer, and

36

we chugged up to Zermatt on the single-track rack-railway. After a day or so there the whole unit moved on to a hut under the Kleiner Matterhorn on the slopes of Monte Rosa. Here we lived, going out daily on foot to find the snow line. Most of the dramatic stuff, the detailed climbing shots, the fatal fall and so on, was shot on the Kleiner Matterhorn at points that could be reached after a few hours' walk. We had no lights or generators, cameras were assisted by large silver-paper screens to concentrate the light where needed and the German phrases that I first learnt were *'Die Sonne kommt'*, which was the cry that heralded the appearance of the sun from behind a cloud, *'Butter bitte'*, which seemed to be the only way of getting a little bit of butter with one's black bread and honey at breakfast, and *'Sheiss, leck mein arsh'*, which was Trenker's favourite expression whenever anything went wrong.

But we did climb the Matterhorn, by the standard route it is true, and the shot of Whymper's party rudely kicking snow down on the rival Italian party led by Carrell who had failed on the other side was actually made on the summit. On subsequent crossings of the Alps by air I have looked down on that summit with a happy sense of *déjà vu*.

Joan Gardner was very attractive and I much longed for her; one hot afternoon on the slopes alone with me she boldly stripped to her bra, but she felt that she was a little too old and experienced, or, more probably, that I was the opposite, to allow me any further liberties.

A few days after my return from the Matterhorn, thinking myself enormously fit, I suddenly felt so weak when half-way up New Bond Street that I could not walk any further. I hailed a taxi and retired to bed, to learn that I had jaundice; most unfairly, considering the healthy way I had been living. After three weeks I recovered and was soon into autumn and the shooting of the interior scenes of the Whymper film, by then entitled *The Challenger*, at Pinewood. The inside of the inn from which the climbing party had set out had been faithfully reconstructed – a kitchen with a huge fireplace hung all about with cooking gear, bundles of dried herbs and, most important, garlic.

Trenker could only give us a limited number of days' filming to complete the English version and it so happened that the day he turned up to act his love scene with Joan Gardner was a foggy and cold one. Straight from the Alps, Luis arrived on the set, coughing *'Dein Englisch Klima'* and all that. His eyes lit up at the sight of the stage dressings round the chimney. Striding over he took an entire head of garlic and stuffed it into his mouth, chewed it and spat the skin into the fireplace. Joan Gardner threw a fit and the whole day's shooting was called off.

The Trial of a Judge was Stephen Spender's first play, put on at the Unity Theatre in Mornington Crescent. Although I did not have any political leanings, the young artistic and intellectual set with whom I was involved looked leftward and I had no second thoughts about accepting the part of a young Communist airman. The play's subject was the vain attempt of a judge to be impartially just under a Fascist régime. The notice in the *Manchester Guardian* read: 'Even more moving was a brief performance by Mr Moran Caplat as a Communist savagely slain. His death speech had true lyrical simplicity . . .' So moving was I, apparently, that when, after the war, I went to the American Embassy in London to get a visa to visit New York I was refused as they had a record that I was a Communist. Eventually they were obliged to agree that I had never been a member of the party other than in that brief theatrical association.

I was fortunate enough at this time to meet Tod Slaughter, another great travelling actor-manager of his day. His métier was in melodramas of the type of *Sweeney Todd* and *Murder in the Red Barn*. He gave me two pieces of advice that have remained with me. The first has a similar text to a famous *New Yorker* cartoon: 'Never underestimate the power of a woman.'

Tod, in his late sixties, said to me, just twenty-one: 'Always listen to a woman's advice, however hard it is to take. I had a marvellous play offered to me once. I saw a great part in it for myself as well as a small cast and easily tourable scenery so I took it and rehearsed it, producing it myself of course, with a rather pretty girl opposite me, though my wife said she was no actress. We got to the first performance but somehow I wasn't satisfied. That night in bed I asked my wife, "What's wrong with it?" She said, "Tod, you're playing him as a man of action and he isn't, he's a dreamer." Do you know, the next day I played him as a dreamer and brought the house down.' What effect his rapid shift of character had on the rest of the cast he did not relate.

His second example was on the art of extemporization. The play had been on tour a long time and the scenery was getting tatty. He had to play a love scene on the deck of a snip, with the sea represented by a painted cloth with stage hands writhing under it to make waves. One night the cloth split and the head of a stage-hand appeared. 'Love scene ruined, laughter from the audience, quick as a flash I cried "Man overboard!", grabbed the lifebelt from the rail and slung it at the head. Hit rather hard on the temple, he sank beneath the waves, astonished audience silent. "Another poor soul gone to its rest", I said, and went on with the love scene.'

Like all the actors I have met, Tod gloried in anecdotes, how original one never questioned, but always presented as happening to him. (I must confess myself to be an actor in this respect if in no other.) He told a story of an eastern melodrama which he toured. The most elaborate scene had a semicircular rostrum on which every available male in the company, and some supers, were required to be seated on three-legged stools round the perimeter dressed only in loin cloths and a great deal of brown body make-up. In the centre of the semicircle they placed the doyen of the company, an aged actor who now toured as a dresser. The curtain rose on the scene with its crescent of inscrutable figures. The stage manager walked round the back of the stage and saw that old Walter Plinge's seat had one of its three legs poised on the edge of the rostrum. Unable to alert him directly to the danger he ran to one end of the crescent and hissed to the first man, 'Tell Walter his stool's out.' When the message reached Walter by relay he gave a strangled scream, grabbed his loin cloth and raced for the wings.

My last professional appearance was in the film *A Royal Divorce*. The great French actor Pierre Blanchar was Napoleon and Ruth Chatterton, who was also responsible for the script, Josephine. I played the Dauphin. My acting career had been continually disrupted by my sailing exploits, however, and was to become ever more so.

THREE

Under sail

When I was ten my red and black canoe *Moggy* was the passport to adventurous freedom; in her I could paddle or sail the mile or so off shore that brought me to the Whitstable oyster fleet. Taking a small packet of shag tobacco and some cigarette papers with me as payment I would be invited on board with the canoe towed astern. To dredge up the oysters, whelks and crabs from the shallow waters off Herne Bay the smacks would sail up wind to the selected point (wind and tide had always to be together for this manoeuvre as the smacks had no engines), heave to, put the two big dredges over the side, and allow the tide and wind to carry them for a mile or two to leeward. Then the dredges would be hauled in, their contents tipped on to the deck, the sails would be let draw, and they would sail back to do it all again. The crews of three or four had an occasional boy among them but they were all a good deal older than I was.

On the windward leg the catch would be sorted, oysters too small thrown back, most of the crabs too, starfish killed before being thrown over for the gulls to fish out of the water before they sank. Whelks and winkles were kept, and often two or three hermit crabs living in old whelk shells would be kept too. As soon as the dredges were down again and the smack had resumed its long slow drift to leeward, stone jam jars full of tea with a tremendous amount of condensed milk and sugar would be produced in the fo'c'sle cabin; one man would remain on deck but there was nothing for the crew to do unless a shift of wind caused a problem.

Then the hermit crab contest would be staged. Their shells would be broken off, exposing not only their long, thin, fierce claws but their vulnerable hinder parts which had been protected deep in the whelk shell. The naked crabs, together with one empty whelk shell, were put in a bucket of water and bets made as the crabs battled with each other for the sanctuary of the shell. Sometimes the fight was to the death; sometimes one crab would be so wily as to nip smartly in and close up his defences. Either way the bucketful was heaved overboard before hauling the dredges. It was a cruel kind of marine cock-fight but the fishermen had no other distractions, no transistor radios to blare at them all day, no pool coupons to fill in. The atmosphere in the fo'c'sle was thick and heavy with shag, tarry wool and fishing odours. The conversation was basic but I learnt a lot about human life and seamanship from those excursions.

The Herne Bay Sailing Club, which occupied a two-roomed wooden hut on stilts with a big veranda as starting platform, stood at the base of the low mud cliffs to the east of the town. Two types of boats were raced. The larger was a half-decked, eighteen-foot, carvel-built, centre-board boat rather similar to the East Coast One Design class but heavier and slower, which had to stay on moorings a hundred yards or so off the beach and thus dry out at every low tide. The coast there is unprotected from any northerly wind and although the prevailing wind from the south-west is off the shore, a north-westerly summer blow or a north-easterly gale can put up a nasty breaking sea which would pound the boats at the state of tide when they were just touching bottom and frequently filled and sank them. It was Bill the boatman's job to empty them at low water, even at dead of night if necessary. Occasionally they broke adrift and came ashore on to the shingle beach between the wooden groins, so they had to be strong to avoid being smashed up. These were known as the class-boats.

Smaller was a fourteen-foot double-ended centre-board dinghy, the Dublin Bay Water Wagtail. How these got to Herne Bay from Dublin originally I do not know, but there were in my time two of the original boats built in Ireland and some three or four boats built in Whitstable as copies, but much heavier and more crudely finished. The Water Wags had a single unstayed mast stepped right forward in the sharp bow and a balanced lug mainsail. They were lively boats which heeled over easily and shipped a lot of water, and the bailer was an important piece of equipment.

I graduated from the canoe to crewing in the class-boats. My first sail frightened the life out of me. The canoe had fitted round me like a coffin and it had remained more or less upright, but the eighteen footer seemed huge and I was chucked about. What is more, it heeled over to a degree that would certainly have meant a capsize for *Moggy*, and despite the narrow side decking and coaming, water came into the cockpit. This first trip was not a race. It was blowing quite freshly from the south-west with vicious little puffs funnelling down between the houses along the sea-front. (How well I came to know the William Street puff in the next few years and how well I have since come to know the East Cowes puff.) The two young men who had taken me out were seasoned and to me impressively unafraid, but after a while I asked timidly if I could go ashore as I wanted to 'be excused'. They put me into the dinghy on the mooring and set off again while I rowed ashore, went to the loo, and then rowed back to the mooring to await their return. Giving way to my fright in this way seemed completely to have cured me, though I have been frightened many times since in boats small and large, particularly when not at the helm myself. I decided in that brief pause that the pleasure was going to outweigh the terror and discomfort, and persuaded the owners to give me a regular place in their crew. Though not particularly large and muscular, I was agile and quick to learn the seaman's trick of making the elements do the work for one, rather than fighting against them.

After a year of this, by a miraculous chance, the oldest of the Water Wags became available – a beautiful boat made of the thinnest of mahogany planks on oak frames with elm garboards. She had been built in Dublin before the 1914 war and was over twenty years old; she leaked like a sieve due to her light construction and sailed like a witch. The only ugly thing about her was her name, which for no reason that I ever learnt was *Oakey*. *Moggy* was sold for a pittance and *Oakey* purchased, with my father's help, for the huge sum of twenty-two pounds.

Bliss followed. *Oakey* and I took to each other and we became almost inseparable. I attended to her every need and she in turn went wonderfully. Launched directly from the shingle beach (no launching trolleys), she would set off like a rocket over the steep incoming waves of a fresh northerly. We raced in everything except a really severe gale. Wet she was, and even reefed she would bend perceptibly. Water spurted through the seams, up out of the centre-board housing and in over the lee gunwhale, but on she drove and for me the excitement was intense. We did well in light weather too, and by the time I was fourteen we were virtually unbeatable in the neighbourhood.

My crews, who in a Water Wag had little to do other than bail, balance the boat and occasionally raise or lower the centre-board, were for several seasons drawn from school and other friends. But in my sixteenth year a very special girl appeared over my horizon. She lived at the other end of the town and, though not a Catholic, attended a local convent. Her father was a fairly senior civil servant on the victualling side of the Navy. Her mother had red

42

hair and was a 'character', known to all as Sammut, a garbled abbreviation of their surname; she didn't like her Christian name of Gertrude and I don't blame her, but since Gertrude is said to mean Spear-maiden it suited her character. The daughter, an only child, was precocious, intelligent and at the age of fourteen a tom-boy, so that she was speedily persuaded to come sailing and became a fearless and efficient as well as a highly attractive crew.

She of course became much more besides. She developed her sexuality, and mine too, very rapidly, and although when racing and in proximity to other vessels she was the essence of decorum, in a one-piece bathing suit (no bikinis or wet-suits) with a sweater or oilskin over it in heavy or cold weather, she did not hesitate when we were alone to allow the breezes to play more easily over her budding charms. Her first name was a particularly beautiful Greek one; I will for propriety's sake not reveal it but call her in this narrative Calisto.

We behaved pretty scandalously for those days but we were in-separable, not so much young lovers as two friends of opposite sexes keen to learn all the joys that might lie ahead of us. We did not smoke, knew nothing of drugs or the pill or other forms of contraception. My parents did not know what was going on; Calisto's did and did not seem to mind. Indeed Calisto's mother, who was after all only about twice my age, decided to take my sex education in hand – literally – one evening in the bathing hut and this led to further education one afternoon in her marital bed and then several more lessons to complete the course. She it was who introduced me to prophylactics – her husband kept a large supply in a tin of talcum powder on the top shelf of his wardrobe. I don't know how carefully he kept count.

He himself was somewhat eccentric. He frequently wandered about his house nude, and was known even to open the front door to a caller in that state. He also dabbled in witchcraft and claimed to have discovered the recipe for an ointment which would enable him to fly on a broomstick. The ointment contained a number of noxious items not in regular supply and it took him a long time to arrive at what he regarded as a sufficiently potent version of it. On the appropriate night at midnight a small number of chosen friends, which included me as a house pet but of course not my parents, were gathered together on the first-floor balcony at the back of his house. In the unkempt grass of the garden below he appeared stark naked, daubed all over with a brown greasy substance which even from our elevation gave off a formidably nasty smell, bestrode his broomstick, shouted an incantation in a high nasal voice, and remained obstinately earthbound.

Once I went to R.A.D.A. I rapidly drifted away from Herne Bay, and though I kept up with Calisto I never really saw her parents again. She went to an art school in Canterbury and studied dressmaking; she also became a professional life-model and obviously enjoyed her work. She visited me at Margate Rep and told me all her exploits. She made her own clothes – ancient Greek chiton-type garments with ribbons crossing under the breasts. One of these garments and sandals became her summer uniform: no bra, of course, and often nothing else either. Calisto became more and more catholic in her tastes after she moved to London, and on one of my early leaves in the war she enthralled me with the variety of her stories as well as providing pleasure not available afloat. We drifted apart, however, and though I did meet her once or twice again the old closeness had evaporated. She eventually married a rich and clever man much older than herself, had children and even became a marriage guidance counsellor. She had certainly done the field work!

My wish for adventure led me early in my sailing days to my first escape from drowning. I decided to make a cruise in *Oakey* from Herne Bay past Whitstable through the Swale behind the Isle of Sheppey and then as far up the Medway as time would permit. These were pre-Calisto days and I found another boy to go with me. He was neither as strong nor as experienced as I was. We took a tent, a small one just big enough for the two of us to lie down either side of the pole, a ground sheet, some blankets, a small meta-fuelled stove in a biscuit tin, a change of clothes, heavy linseed-oil impregnated oilskin jacket and trousers and plimsolls for going ashore in (bare feet in the boat), and, as principal basic ration, two round red Dutch cheeses.

It was the beginning of the summer holidays and our first day's sail in perfect weather took us gently out round the end of Herne Bay pier past Swalecliffe and Tankerton and the hazard of Whitstable Street, a shingly bank that lies to the east of Whitstable Harbour, and on past Seasalter to camp on the south-eastern point of Sheppey near the old ferry house. It was quite desolate, just marshes and sheep and totally tranquil on a lovely evening. We were tired, and cocoa and cheese made our supper. The surface under the ground sheet was far from hard and our mothers would have been horrified by the dampness of it all, but we slept and woke refreshed, feeling already that we had sailed half-way round the world. We had a coastal chart but no tide tables or detailed information. The next day we pushed on but found the tide against us and ourselves running out of water to sail in, so we turned in to Conyer creek on the mainland and tied up near a Thames barge at the little wooden quay. I don't remember what the barge had to load or unload but it could have been one of those great stacks of hay that one so often at that time of year saw sailing sedately up or down the Thames creeks on both sides of the estuary. I do remember that we walked up to the village shop in Teynham and sent postcards home and I also remember that as we strolled back to our tent in the balmy calm of the evening we met two local girls, apple-cheeked and giggly of course. We strolled on with them, drinking Cherry Cider (a harmless fizzy drink of those days) from the bottles we had bought in the village. Then we turned and strolled back until they thought they should not be seen with us so near home. A fumbled kiss in the hedge and a light slap for too much audacity brought that rural idyll to an end, but engraved in my mind is my girl's answer to my question of what her father did: 'Oh, 'e droives the shit-cart.'

The next day we woke to a fresh easterly wind, and finding the tide flooding up the Swale behind us, swept up to and under the Kingsferry swing bridge through Long Reach, made a right-angle turn to beat across to Queensborough past the stinking glue factory and shot out into the wide Medway. Turning to port we ran out into the deep-water channel with its enormous, to us, mooring buoys for Sheerness dockyard and equally large navigational buoys. Here the tide had just turned and I met a sea such as I had had no previous experience of – a strong spring tide against a fresh wind in a wide river. Running before the wind under a single sail in this condition was exhilarating but dangerous and hard work. Perhaps inevitably we broached, the dinghy capsized, and we were in the water somehere between Burntwick Island and the Isle of Grain and at least half a mile from shore. The Water Wag had no buoyancy bags or tanks; on the other hand there was not enough weight of metal in the centre-plate to sink it. All our gear was lashed to the thwarts and frames in boxes and canvas bags and helped with buoyancy to some extent until eventually it would have become too wet and sodden to hold any air. It was possible to right a capsized Wag by getting the mainsail off, pushing it into the boat and then standing on the centre-board, but loaded as we were this was very difficult. There was no shipping anywhere near us when we went over, and though the sun shone and the waves were all blue-green and white, things were distinctly worrying.

No one in our circle ever wore a life-jacket or even possessed one. Remembering the old injunction to 'cling to the wreckage', given to me by all my old advisers like Bill the boatman and the oyster smack men, none of whom had ever learnt to swim, I tied one end of the mainsheet round my waist, passed the other under my chum's shoulders, and then tied us both to the boat which was behaving like a half-tide rock and being continuously burst over by every short breaking sea. My friend was understandably more frightened than I was. (I have always found that command, or rather responsibility, diminishes fear, whereas dependence increases it.) He was under the sail when we went over and scrambling out from under it had put him in a state of near panic, but we succeeded in getting the sail down and its gaff and boom tied to the centre-board case cleats. The boat came upright but was completely waterlogged. My companion was getting very weak. Fortunately the rudder and tiller were attached by lanyards and did not float away.

All this took a little time, how much I cannot say, but when I had done all I could to secure ourselves and the gear and began to look around for some solution to our problem, I saw quite far away a steam pinnace heading in our direction. It was the Customs launch which, proceeding on its ordinary business between Chatham and Sheerness, had been too far away to see our capsize, but whose coxswain had spotted our mast with the little orange and blue burgee of the Herne Bay Sailing Club suddenly emerging from the white-capped waves in the roughest part of the channel. They came alongside, took my crew on board and chucked me a bucket with which I was able to gain enough freeboard by bailing to make *Oakey* seaworthy again. Slowly at first as I bailed, and then faster because they were being made late for some important appointment elsewhere, they towed us to a wooden pier on the desolate shore of the Isle of Grain on the northern side of the estuary. There they left us – and it was still only ten o'clock in the morning.

We were pretty shaken. All our gear was sodden with salt water, although fortunately oil pollution was not rife in those waters half a century ago. The day was fine, nobody came near us and we dried our things in the sun. We had lost nothing except the biscuit tin with the stove in it, but the matches and other stores were dry so we lit a driftwood fire, made ourselves cocoa and toasted cheese, and then, as the light faded, went damply to sleep in our tent. In the morning we regretfully but also with some relief decided that discretion was the better part of valour, abandoned our plans for a longer voyage and turned for home.

The day was fine with only a light south-westerly and we were able to dodge across the frightening Medway and sail calmly down Long Reach and the Swale to our first camping site by the old ferry house on Sheppey. From there it was an easy sail home. Our parents were surprised to see us. They had only just received our confident postcards from Teynham, and news of a mishap would not have reached them for some time. It seems extraordinary in these days of air-sea rescue and radio telephones, but the Customs men who came to our rescue did not even ask our names or where we had come from. Indeed they said very little, as though to pick two near-drowning schoolboys out of the Medway and put them and their boat ashore was an everyday kindness, like rescuing a spider trapped in the bath.

By the time my teens were behind me I was keen to go ocean racing but our flat tidal waters did not house any suitable boats. Somewhere I read that the Royal Ocean Racing Club had a crewing list which one could apply to join and this I duly did, no doubt making the most of my long years of sailing experience and the least of the fact that all that experience had been within the confines of the Thames Estuary.

After an introduction to the owners in the club house in Pall Mall Place beside the St James's Theatre and a few visits to Pin Mill on the Orwell, I found myself as part of the crew of *Phryna*, a twenty-ton, thirty-five-foot sloop, newly built and jointly owned by Robert Bevan and Harold Paton, both young and enthusiastic men of around thirty and at that time both unmarried. Bobbie Bevan (known as the Master) was the son of the well-known painter of horses and kindred subjects and was to go on through a dis-tinguished career in Naval Intelligence to become the head of one of the most successful post-war advertising agencies. Harold (known as the Skipper) was a barrister and eventually after a war-time Naval career in which he won the D.S.C. became a judge on the western circuit. I lost touch with him eventually, though I kept up my friendship with Bobbie until his death.

Phryna was a modern vessel, one of the new breed of yachts built more to be raced than sailed as cruisers, though by present-day standards she was heavy, comfortable and slow. She had a sister ship that was French-owned, called *Pompier*. We thought it odd to call a boat 'Fireman'. *Phryna* was to have been called *Phryne* but at the last moment when the name had been painted the owners found that that name had already been taken in Lloyd's Register of Yachts. The simplest solution was to change the final 'e', despite the classical inaccuracy.

We had a few weekends of sailing in the estuary and conviviality at the Butt and Oyster and then some not very successful warming-up races, but the first race in which *Phryna* did well was the Harwich–Heligoland race of 1938 in which she came fourth. Then off she went for the Baltic series of that year, a memorable series never, I think, since repeated as such a concentrated event. Quite a large international fleet set off from Dover. I could not go with her as I was working for the B.B.C. at the time but I did give a graphic description of the start as 'our yachting correspondent' over the B.B.C. National Programme, based entirely on my knowledge of the form of the entrants gathered from the previous summer's sailing. They raced up the North Sea to Kristiansand in Norway and from there to Copenhagen. I took the Harwich–Esberg ferry, crossed Denmark by train and was there to meet them as they sailed into Copenhagen and moored alongside the quay, the Langeline, by the old Royal Danish Yacht Club, a fine circular wooden building later destroyed in the war. Then followed two or three days of junketing. We were within walking distance of all the delights of Copenhagen, amongst the more innocuous of which were the Tivoli gardens with side shows and stands where you could smash as much crockery as you could hit with the Danish equivalent of 'eight balls for sixpence'.

We had as cook an ebullient Irish publican from a London hostelry (The Star in Belgrave Mews West), who was not much of a sailor and not much of a cook, but was rarely seasick. He was a never-ending source of rich, if only too rare, anecdotes. Copenhagen went to his head somewhat and he had to be rescued on two occasions. One was when he started to push a bedstead out of an upstairs window as he considered he had been cheated over what he had been led to believe the bed would provide in addition to rest; the other when he went shopping for provisions in the open market and, being unable to speak Danish, was found roaring at the good lady proprietor of a vegetable stall in his heavy brogue: 'Spuds, murphies, taters, can't you understand plain English, you silly auld bitch!'

The most important race of the series was to come – from Copenhagen out through the waters where Nelson fought his famous 'blind-eye' battle, round the island of Bornholm in the Baltic, to finish at Warnemunde, a small German resort but important service base. For this race the fleet was enlarged by yachts from two of the three German services, the Kriegsmarine and the Luftwaffe. A few German club yachts took part, but our impression was that they had no strictly private amateur entries such as ours.

On the day of the race we returned to the yacht in the early hours. From the English, French and Dutch yachts along the quay voices raised in song could be heard and lights showed in skylights and portholes; only on the German boats was all silent. The start was to be an early one, nights were short, and soon there was a general stirring. Before the startled eyes of the awakening German crews the scantily clad guests from *Firebird*, the appropriately named large Nicholson-designed yacht belonging to Ralph Hawkes (of Boosey & Hawkes, Stravinsky's publishers) began to stream ashore. 'Thick and fast they came at last, and more and more and more', for the good Ralph had excelled himself in hospitality.

It was a grey and chilly morning with a light southerly wind. We got a good start in our class and were beating down the narrow deep-water channel when we were overtaken by *Silber Kondor*, a big German Luftwaffe yacht. It was about 7.30 a.m. We, unshaven and hung-over, were just enjoying our special treat – a can of Guinness. (We had the only canned Guinness in the fleet, indeed probably the only canned Guinness outside the Guinness laboratories; one of our crew was a director and the cans were experimental. The lacquer used for the inside could not resist the powerful medicinal qualities latent in the brew for more than a few weeks and, our bilges having been filled with cans in Dover, we felt obliged to drink up before it went to waste.) The huge German yacht came majestically past us, her cockpit crammed with her after-guard in long overcoats and uniform caps, her crew lying upon her decks in uniform of course, leaping to their feet in response to the orders barked at them. The yacht tacked with all the appropriate noises of rattling blocks and slatting canvas, the crew lay down again and the officers stared with studied disgust – or was it envy? – at our languid, *louche*-looking handful who, as the helmsman said 'Ready about', as often as not replied 'Hang on while I chock my can off,' then 'OK, lee-oh.' Yet round we went, quicker and in a tighter turn than the big boat who had only her superior size to put her ahead of us. She did win her class but we finished ahead of her on corrected time over-all and at one time round Bornholm got ahead of her again as she found herself embayed in the light wind and strong current.

And so we got to Warnemunde and tied up in the canal-like harbour between pleached limes lined by cafés and beer-gardens, a uniformed brass band playing while we drank our *steins* of beer. We ordered fresh lemons and sucked them ostentatiously in the hope of disrupting the concert but this time-honoured ruse failed miserably.

Greeted on arrival by various uniformed officials, the welcoming committee, the Customs, the frontier police, we were not prepared for the unavoidable 'Heil Hitler' at the opening and close of every encounter. We found the right response, however. We were formally dressed when ashore, in the then ubiquitous cheese-cutter yachting cap with badge, reefer jacket with black club buttons, and blue or white trousers. It presented therefore no difficulty for us to meet every 'Heil Hitler' with a correct British Naval salute, rigid fingers in the same plane as the peak of the cap, and the words 'Rule Britannia'. Never did we get the slightest hint that our hosts found this anything but the normal response though we had difficulty in keeping our faces straight.

Nazi panoply was in full blazon. The dinner to celebrate the end of the regatta was held in a huge conference hall near by. Besides the visiting yachtsmen of many nationalities there was a large turn-out of Germans. Indeed we, the foreigners, were outnumbered by more than two to one. There were no women present; if they were represented in any of the crews, which I doubt, they certainly had not been invited to the dinner. We mingled in an ante-room for drinks beforehand, or rather stood about in little clumps grabbing as many drinks, *Sekt* or *Sekt mit Orangensaft* (Buck's fizz, although the *Sekt*, despite being fizzy, could not easily be mistaken for champagne) as we could. Then we trooped into the dining room in which was a high table with long tables at right angles and a seating plan which provided for every foreigner to be between two Germans. A formal banquet followed with meticulous service and excellent food including venison, a rarity to us, and more and more to drink. Then came the formal speeches and prize-giving and finally a long harangue from the host-in-chief, none other than Grand-Admiral Raeder himself, in which he told us of the great seagoing traditions of Germany, her superiority in men, ships and seamanship, her wonderful aircraft and the discipline and devotion that under the great Führer made them undoubtedly the master race. The final toast was to the Führer himself. Politeness alone brought us to our feet. What we said under our breath was our own business, but it was a shock when just as we were about to resume our seats all the Germans present shot out their right arms in the Nazi salute and screamed (there is no other word for it) *'Sieg Heil! Sieg Heil! Sieg Heil!'* In my case the shock was relieved by the fact that my neighbour, no doubt overcome with patriotic fervour, misaimed his salute and sent a nearly full bottle of Piesporter Goldtröpfchen Beerenauslese flying into the midriff of his mess-dressed compatriot opposite.

All was not yet over. The Germans were commanded to take a foreign guest between them to the terrace outside. Ranged on the terrace above a torch-lit courtyard we were treated to a formidable piece of marching and countermarching by an army band (for all I know the Waffen S.S.) with flying eagle standards and more torches, playing stirring military music and selections from Wagner. We were suitably awed as well as nearly deafened. Then the band broke into a slow march to a Mozart wind piece which died away and we all applauded, thinking we could go to where nature had been calling us for some time. Not yet. With dramatic suddenness the German national anthem erupted and the standard-bearers broke into the goose step and left the courtyard to us and silence. One of my colleagues at this point turned to his German companion and said politely: 'You know of course that the correct name for that step is the *passo romano* – it was invented in ancient Rome by Nero.' He was hastily hustled off.

On one of our races to Dinard we left the boat and all went up to Paris for a night out. Les Pyramides was part of the outing – I have a key ring to prove it – and Le Bœuf sur le Toit; at a less respectable venue I well remember being fascinated by the beautiful blonde Roberta with whom I danced only to find that, in the happy style of cheek to cheek or body to body dancing then prevalent, the thrust of my groin was surprisingly met by a counter thrust of formidable proportions. *Eheu fugaces!*

After Dinard we went on to the Ile de Bréhat for the start of a race to Brixham. The *île* gave us a marvellous welcome. The weather was perfect, and we rowed ashore from the anchorage and walked through fields full of flowers to the little village; it would have reminded me of one of those marvellously pastoral and evocative French films, except that it was before I had seen any of them. We were hot: coats came off, ties slipped, collars were unbuttoned. A village band from the mainland sweatingly entertained us. The local champagne cider was in constant supply, many of the bottles popping in the heat before the corks could be removed; there were biscuits and sour double cream, fruit and festivity, then into the little cinema, the biggest hall the island had to offer, where the mayor, of ample size and great humidity but little humility, delivered a splendid speech in his braces and a tricolour sash. We cheered to the echo and then walked arm-in-arm through the flowery meadows to the anchorage again. It was an idyll, or so it seems to me in retrospect.

The evening developed into a thunderstorm and the race began with tempers aboard – and ashore, judging by the conduct of the starting procedure which was somewhat edgy. There followed a nasty night and a hard beat to windward to Brixham, but we did finish fourth which was pretty good for us.

In the early spring of 1939 I got the chance to sail round the world. While I was with the Sevenoaks Rep I saw an advertisement in *The Times* for unpaid volunteers, sharing out-of-pocket expenses though with no fee or indeed contribution expected, to help to sail an ex-Bristol Channel pilot cutter round the world starting from Dundee. On an impulse I applied, met the owner – an extremely nice bearded Ulsterman named Jack Christian – in London and agreed to join him and the yacht *Raider* in Dundee at the end of March when my Sevenoaks engagement ended. I ordered myself a new shore-going reefer jacket with Royal Ocean Racing Club buttons (I had become a fully qualified member of the R.O.R.C. at the end of the 1938 season), got a set of heavy-duty oilskins from Gassons of Rye and duly presented myself on board. *Raider* was a fine vessel but virtually unmodernized. She had her original spars and gear, sails and cordage were in good condition, she was steered by a long tiller and had a heavy boom-gallows construction over the poop. The interior was much as it had been designed some forty or fifty years before when she had been built at Pill near Bristol to take the pilots out to the ships in the often stormy waters of the Bristol Channel between Lundy and Wales, with comfortable solid bunks, a good cabin, a galley with a paraffin stove, a fo'c'sle, but no plumbing other than a bucket and a pump from the fresh-water tank.

No one else had yet enlisted for the voyage but we did have a paid-hand. His name was Donald. He was a local east-coast Scottish boy of some seventeen or eighteen and had often been to sea in local fishing boats, but his skills did not include communication or the finer points of sailing or cooking, except that he excelled in the making of porridge. From a sack of the coarsest rolled oats (seemingly unobtainable today even in the most ethnic of health food shops), water, salt and sugar according to taste he could produce the most sustaining and delicious early morning food.

Jack decided that we would sail round to the south coast by easy stages in the hope of picking up two or three more members on the way – six would have been the ideal crew. He was an excellent seaman and experienced, but alas not robust. He had some bronchial or chest affliction which I believe turned out to be tuberculosis. Despite this he served with distinction in M.T.B.s but did not survive the war.

I had by then achieved a fair standard of coastal navigation and a good grasp of the theory, if not the practice, of off-shore navigation. I had a sextant, could take sights, and knew how to use the tables even if I had no idea of how the tables themselves worked – rather like today's situation when many of those who can use computers have no idea how the computers actually produce the answers.

Somewhere off Great Yarmouth, running on a dark night before a fresh northerly with Donald at the tiller, we suffered a monumental gybe. The main boom, which weighed the best part of a ton, came walloping across and wrapped the four-fold main sheet round the boom-gallows. We were in a 'right old mess' in a narrow and busy shipping channel. Jack and I were soon on deck and the mess was straightened out. Skidding past several coasters we took off the mainsail and proceeded until first light under a single headsail which gave us enough steerage way. The immensely strong boom-gallows had been ripped out of the deck and was wobbling about. With difficulty we dismantled it, disentangled the main sheet and carried on to Burnham-on-Crouch. Jack decided that the tiller steering, while satisfactory for the skilled manoeuvres of the Bristol Channel, was not going to be so good on long ocean passages and that we must convert to wheel steering before setting off.

Eventually we reached Gosport and went to Camper and Nicholson's yard for repairs. The threat of impending war loomed over us, no recruits to our crew were forthcoming, and the yard made a balls of rigging the steering which resulted, when the wheel was put to port, in the yacht turning to the right instead of the left and vice versa. Head-scratching and more delay followed. Donald pushed off for home, called by an anxious mother, and I suddenly felt that London was the place to be. War seemed imminent. Jack left *Raider* in Portsmouth and went back to Ulster. So the round-the-world trip faded, Dundee to Portsmouth being its total scope.

The initial excitement of digging trenches in Hyde Park soon palled, work in the theatre was hard to get, and I gratefully accepted the offer of more sailing. I had enough in the bank, perhaps £100, to pay my necessary outgoings in fares to and from joining boats, drinks ashore and occasionally taking the skipper-owner out to dinner, so off I went.

For the Fastnet race of 1939 I went as cook in *Phryna*. I am fortunate in never being seasick. Most people in my experience are sufferers from this malaise to some degree. Some sailors, like Nelson, are overcome for the first twenty-four or forty-eight hours every time they go to sea. Others are sick whenever the motion becomes violent. For some it is a certain type of motion which upsets them, and there are a chronic few who become seasick before the ship has even left the quayside and remain so till she docks – they have no place in ocean racing. All of us, however, even the immune, get to a point in continual bad weather where we have to force ourselves to eat. The constant motion, the effort of balancing oneself and moving about the boat, not to mention the hard physical effort of deck work or steering in bad conditions, induces a weariness that makes it seem too much trouble to brew up soup or open a tin, and one is tempted merely to flop into one's bunk and get some sleep. But even sleeping is tiring in bad weather, for subconsciously one is always bracing muscles against the pitch and roll of the boat, and a long tack to windward in short seas with a big angle of heel to the vessel is trying to all.

The modern ocean racer, even on such a long race as the Fastnet – 605 miles taking on average five days – makes the most of convenience foods and has a menu prepared in advance with as much economy of space and weight as possible, designed for simple cooking. In pre-war days it was not generally so. Stores were taken aboard at the last minute, members of the crew all bringing some contribution of their own, usually in the form of a delicacy which was mouth-watering ashore but soon became nauseous afloat. A pressure cooker full of stew which only needed reheating on the primus stove for the first night's supper was usual, and this was fine if the weather was too, but if the weather was not, some of the stew found its way into the scuppers via its consumers and a great deal of the rest went over the side the next morning in order to get the smell of it out of the boat.

This race was typical in that respect and, though not one of the epic Fastnets was quite a rough one for most of the time. After the stew our next major fresh ration was a beautiful honey-cured ham, with its baked brown sugary criss-crossed exterior stuck with cloves and a thick layer of juicy fat over the rich succulent flesh round the bone. Cries of greed and joy greeted its arrival on board at Cowes and a special stowage hanging beside the mast below decks was found. Once it had been started, however, its aroma began to pervade the boat. To begin with I served it up in good thick slices with salad and pickles; then as the weather worsened I made the leaner parts of it into sandwiches which were welcomed on deck and easier to eat. But eating fell off and still the huge ham hung there. Finally, not long after rounding the Fastnet rock itself, in response to a general request from the crew, I cast it overboard. It was a terrible thing to do as there were still several succulent meals to be had from it, but it had definitely outstayed its welcome. We carried on with tinned bullybeef, chocolate, biscuits and oranges, with hot soup and coffee made in a white enamel jug, and the occasional gin, whisky or rum to give us heart.

We did neither well nor too badly. That race was won on corrected time by *Bloodhound*, which was to become a royal yacht in post-war years, and the first boat home was the huge *Nordwind* sailed by the German Navy. No such display of military or naval might as had been given at Warnemunde took place at Plymouth, just a huge disorderly booze-up in the Guildhall and after a couple of days of recovery and roistering and recovering anew from roistering, the big Fastnet fleet split up and went its homeward ways. A small number of boats, mainly French and British, including *Phryna*, set off on the first-ever R.O.R.C. race to La Rochelle. The weather had improved and we had a fast sail in ideal conditions out across the Bay of Biscay to that beautiful and historic port.

This trip remains in my mind as one of the idyllic ones; for me steering a boat just before dawn, with the occasional phosphorescent wave breaking over the bow and flooding over the foredeck as far as the mast then running after along the scuppers, in a warm wind of just the right strength, is one of the great pleasures in life. As the light comes up, to find sardines that have come aboard with the waves lying in the coiled ropes round the mast and on the foredeck and to fry them fresh for breakfast is to pile Pelion on Ossa. We did well, too, to finish second to *Bloodhound* and ahead of our principal rival, the French *Aile Noire*.

La Rochelle in those days was not the tourist trap and yachting marina that it has become but a proper working port, with bars and cafés and restaurants of a simple sort. Making our way homeward from a night on the tiles we arrived on the waterfront of the inner basin just as the bakery there was producing its first batch of delicious bread. The baker was a hospitable soul and invited us in to his floury, sweet-smelling room behind the ovens, with a picture of the destroyer in which he served in the First World War on the wall, and gave us *croissants* and glasses of *Pineau des Charentes* while we swopped stories. Then back to the boat with crisp new *baguettes* for the sober one or two who had gone earlier to bed.

The news was becoming increasingly ominous. Fearing that it would soon get even worse, a few members of the crew left for home by land while four of us set off to sail back, intending to stop here and there on the way for a night. The wind was fair, the news became steadily blacker, so we pressed on, stopping only to go ashore for bread and fresh food daily. Still, it was highly enjoyable sailing and eating since we had the time and the inclination to do justice to the *moules* and lobsters and fish and fruit that our daily shopping produced. We even provided some of our own fresh food by catching mackerel, but sadly the sardines never arrived again.

It was the end of August as we cleared the Le Four channel inside Ushant. Instead of turning up channel to make our east coast base at Pin Mill on the Orwell as we had intended, we ran straight across, and late in the evening of 2 September picked up a mooring in Dartmouth harbour.

At eleven the next morning we sat in the cabin of *Phryna* and listened to the declaration of war on the ship's radio. Two of the crew left at once for their homes. I had nowhere particular to go, so I stayed on with Harold Paton, who made arrangements with the boatyard at Galmpton a few miles up the river Dart to put *Phryna* on a mud-berth for the winter or the duration of the war, whichever should turn out to be the longer. We made friends in the Yacht Club, and as I had volunteered to stay a few days and help to clear the harbour of other yachts and pleasure craft, a kind local family with a particularly beautiful daughter offered me accommodation. This I accepted in the confident expectation that such a valuable member of the R.N.V.S.R. (the supplementary naval reserve composed of yachtsmen with some navigational experience, which I had joined in 1938) would be instantly needed. I sent the head-quarters, H.M.S. *President* on the Embankment in London, a telegram informing them of my whereabouts and waited with impatience for my call to duty.

There followed a fortnight of luxurious ease. The harbour work was soon over and life in my host's house extended from day to

sunny day of riding, sailing a dinghy and getting a really good
romance going with the beautiful daughter. Finally I concluded
that the Admiralty had made some ghastly mistake or that my telegram had never arrived, so I packed what little baggage I had, bade
a fond farewell to the daughter, and informed her parents that we
were 'unofficially' engaged, a statement they took in their stride in
a war-time mood. Then I set off back to London to win the war.

Looking back on the inter-war years they read to me as a very
definite period, which my memory can just grasp,from the victory
flames of the First World War armistice bonfire on Beacon Hill to
the declaration of the Second World War heard in a yacht's cabin
at Dartmouth. They covered first a rather isolated childhood under
parents and grandparents who were essentially Edwardian in taste
and outlook, then burgeoned out through processes of exploration
almost entirely self-conducted. Finally I arrived through adolescence in a Bohemian world of the theatre which in effect became my
university, and found myself at the age of twenty-two at a crucial
point in my life.

Curiously in these inter-war years I knew little of worlds outside
my own circle. I had been too young to feel the collapse of the
French railways and the break up of my French heritage and I was
almost unaware of the Jarrow March and the Great Depression in
seaside Kent. When I first met the Left wing in the theatre it was a
totally new experience. In my time as a builder's labourer and as
an engineering apprentice it was sex not socialism that dominated
such discussions as there were. My plan to fight in Spain was
conceived of a wish for adventure and not from idealistic conviction.

I began to doubt whether acting was the right profession and
wished that I had entered the Navy instead. Short-service com-
missions were being offered in the Fleet Air Arm. I did not want to
fly, just to go to sea, but as this seemed my only hope of joining the
Navy I applied. One of the conditions was that the parents of an
applicant should both hold British nationality. To my great surprise and to that of my father also we found that he was still technically French. He had never been naturalized but had continued
to live and work in Kent without let or hindrance; he had a vote, all
the privileges of British citizenship, yet had never officially become
one. As soon as he realized that this made me liable to do national
service in the French forces he applied for, and got, his British
naturalization. I toyed with the idea of doing national service with
the French Navy but was dissuaded, and being given the necessity

of deciding my own nationality one way or the other, I opted for Britain. I am at home in France even though I speak the language only indifferently, but I feel sure I made the right choice.

Realizing that war was almost inevitable I decided that I would have a better chance of getting into the sort of ship I wanted, something small, a motor-torpedo boat or a destroyer, if I relied on my membership of the R.N.V.S.R.

FOUR

On the ocean wave

As soon as I got to London I went to the flat in Sloane Street, dumped my bag, went down to the Embankment to H.M.S. *President* and offered myself for immediate service. I was dismayed to be told by a somewhat supercilious lieutenant-commander R.N. that I was not needed, and would not be for possibly several months. On an impulse I rang up Betty Smithers in Sevenoaks. The Smithers had been very kind to me during my time in the Sevenoaks Rep and I was not wrong in thinking that they might be able to suggest something. They knew someone who was trying to find farm volunteers. 'Could I drive a tractor?' Yes of course I could, I said, though in fact I never had. The next day I was on my way to a farm near West Malling in Kent.

I was billeted with the Downtons in an old, half-timbered house known as Hodges Place next to the village pub in Offham. Jack Downton was a civil engineer, Joan, his wife, was busy and important in local activities, a good darts player and well liked in the local. Their son John, about my age, was already in the regular R.A.F. as a pilot officer, their elder daughter in the A.T.S. and the younger daughter still at school. This daughter was just sixteen and very beautiful, especially in her gym-tunic, but my mind was fully engaged with the girl in Dartmouth.

I settled down to enjoy farming, but four days after starting, early on a fine, bright, October morning, I was driving the tractor when Mrs Downton appeared at the field gate waving a letter. I was to report to H.M.S. *King Alfred* at Hove forthwith. This I duly did, not in the least knowing what to expect and taking with me only the minimum of gear. From Hove station I was taken, together with several other equally excited but innocent yachtsmen who had arrived on the same train, to join my first Naval ship.

The *King Alfred* turned out to be a newly built, indeed still unfinished complex of swimming baths and conference hall on the parade overlooking the sea. We were quickly processed – medical examination, next-of-kin forms and the like – and billeted in one of a number of requisitioned small hotels and boarding houses across the road. So, on 13 October 1939, I became Probationary Temporary Sub-Lieutenant Caplat R.N.V.R. Training began, rudimentary stuff. Square-bashing, semaphore, the morse code and the habits and practices of the Navy were hammered into us by a series of tough chief petty officers and rather, to our eyes, elderly R.N. officers who had been dragged back for the purpose. Being officers, we were responsible for our own uniforms; in the meantime, having been measured by the man from Gieves, the Naval tailors, we had only uniform caps and white silk scarves to add to our normal clothing. The caps were necessary as a great deal of saluting went on. The scarves were merely a matter of vanity: we thought we looked rather dashing in them. I was able to put brass buttons on to my yachting reefer, too. The man from Gieves said it would take ten days or so for the proper uniform to arrive, but we expected to be about six weeks at *King Alfred*.

I must somehow have persuaded the authorities that I could be of immediate use afloat, because after five days (all the Naval training I was ever to have apart from the special training for submarines and much later the Staff Course at the Royal Naval College, Greenwich), without having mastered either semaphore or the morse code and still without my uniform from Gieves, I was despatched to join H.M.S. *Sunniva* at Thurso in the far north of Scotland.

The *Sunniva* was an elegant, yacht-like vessel that normally ran a regular service between Scotland and the Orkney and Shetland islands. She had a fine clipper bow on which a four-inch gun had been hastily placed and a beautiful counter stern which now bore four dustbin-like depth charges which were 'fired' by setting the fuse and rolling them over the side. I joined as a supernumerary watch-keeper, and stayed with her only for a week or two before being moved to become navigating officer of the *Northern Isles*.

This was one of the Northern class of big, relatively new deep-sea trawlers that had their peace-time base at Fleetwood. She had a high rounded bow more like a whale-catcher than the conventional trawler, with a rounded stern, a tall funnel and quite a large high bridge structure amidships which included the captain's small cabin behind the wheelhouse and the chartroom and radio and a 'monkey's island' at the top. The foremast had a crow's-nest high up over the four-inch gun which had been mounted on a circular platform standing over the fo'c'sle, and the statutory four dustbins were in cradles on the narrow after-deck either side of a steel shed which did duty as the ship's only bathroom. This had in it a circular iron basin like a very large copper. Into the basin, by arrangement with the engine room, could be pumped sea-water which was then heated by means of steam injected into it, a perilous proceeding and only possible in port as the ship's motion at sea in the North Atlantic meant that neither bath water nor bather could remain in the bath for long. Coal-fired like the *Sunniva*, the *Northern Isles* could remain at sea for as much as three weeks or more. When fishing, the weight of the catch had presumably helped the stability as the coal went down, whereas we on patrol just got lighter and lighter and the roll worse and worse. Icing up was another hazard which added greatly to the top-weight. Frozen spray could coat the gun and upper works and had to be cleared away with a steam hose from the engine room. One of our sister ships foundered in a big gale, I think for this reason. I never hear the words 'No icing' in the shipping forecast for these waters without feeling the relief with which the trawlermen would greet them.

We were part of the Northern Patrol. Our job was to police the gaps between the Orkneys and Shetlands, the Shetlands and the Faroes and the Faroes and Iceland; we would stop, and sometimes board, the neutral cargo ships making for any part of Europe and oblige them, at the point of the gun if necessary, to follow us into Kirkwall for a search for contraband. Our patrols normally lasted ten days or so. Sometimes we would find ships quite near and take in two or three in one patrol. Sometimes we went further afield and had to escort some slow old ship hundreds of miles at a mere eight knots. On more than one occasion we had to heave to for days in a howling gale, with the gun having to be kept clear of ice, keeping station on some wallowing merchantman visible only intermittently when we both rose to the top of the huge waves at the same time. This sort of thing lengthened our patrols greatly. We were also on the look-out for U-boats and had one or two scares, but at that time attacks were few and far between.

The crew was headed by four commissioned officers. The captain, a lieutenant R.N.R.,* had been the first officer of a British India Line ship in peace-time. The first lieutenant was a lieutenant R.N.V.R. with several years of Naval training behind him. The gunnery and signals officer was a sub-lieutenant R.N.R. and I was

* R.N.R. then denoted the Royal Naval Reserve made up of qualified Merchant Service personnel with partial Naval training. R.N.V.R., the Royal Naval Volunteer Reserve, was made up of volunteers from all walks of life who had undergone partial Naval training. R.N.V.S.R. was the supplementary reserve, to which I have already referred.

the junior watchkeeper and navigator, though with two R.N.R.s on board we were well covered in the latter respect.

The coxswain and the leading-hand were R.N., as were the signalman and radio operator, but the engine room complement, the cook and the fifteen or so deck-hands and boats' and guns' crews were all trawlermen and R.N.R.s, some Fleetwood men and some from the Western Isles.

The captain was undoubtedly an affable out-going man but had probably been happier as second-in-command in the Merchant Service than as the solitary figure which the captain of a ship-of-war, however small, must be in war-time. Often at anchor on a winter's night and alone in his cabin he would whistle down the voice pipe to the tiny wardroom in the stern and ask one of us up to see him. This meant to join him in a glass of whisky; it was possible to assess fairly accurately how many glasses had preceded the invitation. His habit, sitting and sipping alone gazing at the photograph of his recently acquired wife, was to moisten the finger and thumb of his non-drinking hand with his tongue and twiddle up a section of his hirsute face into a point. Often it would just be the three points of his moustache and beard, but on a bad night he could look like a sunburst.

His nerves were not good. Although an excellent seaman, when confronted with the threat either of the enemy or of a social occasion beyond his modest experience he was inclined to go to pieces. In the first case this took the form of indiscriminate dropping of depth charges on supposed U-boats which were in reality basking sharks or small whales; in the latter a story will illustrate to what involuntary excesses nervous anxiety can lead a well-meaning man.

The first Christmas of the war we were at anchor in Kirkwall bay on one of our two-day pauses between patrols. We had received a signal the previous evening to say that the Commander-in-Chief Western Approaches, of whose command we in Northern Patrol formed a part, would be visiting H.M. ships in harbour before lunch. The ship was duly smartened up and the admiral appeared with an aide but no other staff. After talking briefly to the ship's company he accepted the captain's invitation to take a glass of sherry with him and the officers in his cabin on the bridge. The admiral was a short man known to be of abstemious habits and strict principles, and when we were all crowded into the tiny space with glasses in our hands conversation flagged. The admiral looked round and saw the photograph of the smiling and buxom young

With my Scottish grandmother, 1919.

With my mother, 1924.

My father, c.1934.

In *Oakey* with 'Calisto,' 1935.

Tempest's wardroom, with Neel-Wall the gunnery officer, 1942. Note the photograph of *Phryna* on the bulkhead, the box of Ludo - 'uckers' to the navy - and the soda-water syphon.

With Beverley Cross in *Griffin III*, 1967.

woman on the bulkhead. 'Is that your wife?' he asked. 'Yessir,' said the captain, flushing from excitement, embarrassment and the fact that he had already got several twiddles in his whiskers. 'Been married long?' asked the admiral. The captain lost his head. 'Well, three nights effective, sir,' he replied. 'Oh, do you think married life is going to suit you?' Then disaster struck. Throwing caution to the winds he burst out, 'Oh, yessir, isn't it marvellous when you fart in bed and pull the sheet over her head.' 'Happy Christmas, gentlemen,' said the admiral, and departed.

It was at Kirkwall that I first came fully to realize the professional seaman's mastery of that four letter word beginning with 'f' that has so many uses, not to mention abuses. I had of course met it many times before in my life from fishermen, builder's labourers, stage hands and others but it was not then in the more or less general use it is today. One of the crew was a little bandy-legged stoker named Bloggs, or something like it, a splendid man at sea, indefatigable and cheerful in any weather and always ready to lend a hand, if sometimes a little too free with his advice. He was, however, a terrible nuisance ashore, always becoming sloshed out of his senses, getting into fights and being picked up by the Naval Police, and having to appear before the captain as a defaulter.

One typical night in midwinter I was the duty officer. The captain was in his cabin in the bridge, I was in the wardroom writing letters, the first lieutenant and the other sub were at the pictures ashore and not due back until the last boat. I heard the second and last ratings' liberty boat bump alongside just before six o'clock and the coxswain came down, stuck his head round the wardroom door and said, 'Everyone aboard, sir, except Stoker Bloggs.' 'What, again?' I said. 'I warned him. I expect he'll be coming off in the first officer's boat with some cock-and-bull story. When he does, wheel him straight down here and I'll deal with him.'

An hour later came another bump, which I knew must herald Bloggs as the two other officers were not yet due and everyone else was aboard. Footsteps sounded in the alleyway and the coxswain's head appeared again: 'Not only do you want to see Bloggs, sir, but he says he wants to see you.' With that little Bloggs popped under the coxswain's arm and into the room. Wild-eyed, smelling strongly of whisky and none too tidily dressed, his speech ran something like this: 'I'm f...ing sorry, sir, I ....ing am. I didn't mean to ....ing let you ....ing down ....ing straight I didn't. I only 'ad a few ....ing drinks, sir, and I ....ing watched the ....ing clock like a ....ing 'awk so I wouldn't miss the ....ing boat, sir. I heard the

....ing klaxon, sir, and I ran like .... all the way down the ....ing pier but the ....ing boat 'ad ....ing well ....ed off, sir. I was fair ....ing flabbergasted, sir, and wondered what to ....ing do, so I goes back up the ....ing pier sir to the ....ing officer of the ....ing day's ....ing office sir and knocks on the ....ing door. An officer appears, sir, with gold ....ing lace 'arf ....ing way up to 'is ....ing elbows. "I've missed the ....ing boat, sir," I say all ....ing polite like. "Spring smartly to attention when you speak to me," 'e says. ".... you, sir," I says, to 'im, sir, and ....s off. I thought I ought to tell you, sir, in case there's any ....ing trouble.' There was.

There was not much to amuse anyone ashore. Kirkwall offered a bar or two and a cinema. Lerwick was officially 'dry' though drinks could be freely purchased from the grocers by the case and drunkenness ashore seemed no less than elsewhere. No female company offered itself at any level, and Lerwick then was far from having the prosperity the oilfields have since brought it.

In the Faroe islands during the early days of the war, while they were still neutral, H.M. ships were supposed to stay outside territorial waters. Sometimes, however, in bad weather on a long patrol, with no escort duty assigned at that particular time, it was not unknown for a ship to slip into one or other of the little fishing settlements on the north-western side of the group. A tin or two of 'Ticklers' (Navy tobacco), a few cigarettes and the promise of a bottle or two of whisky to be brought ashore could produce an instant *ceilidh* or its Faroese equivalent, with a squeeze-box and dance in the local hall and some willing partners. In the morning, on a last call ashore to pick up stragglers or get some 'fresh' supplies (which consisted of little but fish), we would be met with blank stares, as though the preceding night of jollity had never been. Shades of the girls from Woolworth's in schoolboy days!

On return to Kirkwall after one patrol I found in my post a communication from my kind host in Dartmouth to say that, most unfortunately, his daughter had had a slight shock which resulted in her having totally lost her memory for that period when she and I had become so close. As there was little likelihood of our meeting again in the near future, we had perhaps better consider the incident closed, sad though he and his wife would be not to see more of me. Many things had happened since those last days of pre-war rapture in Dartmouth and I think I felt more relief than sorrow at this sudden affliction. I am happy to say it appears to have had no lasting effect on her, though we never actually met again.

After a short refit period in Aberdeen, which only gave opportunity for mild dalliance ashore, we sailed for Kirkwall for orders and straight out on patrol. After a few days I began to feel a certain discomfort in the urinary tract which, if not quite the sensation of passing fish-hooks and broken glass that certain old salts had described to me, was a bit worrying and caused me to ponder on whether you could get syphilis by immaculate conception. (Dorothy Parker's dog said he got his from a lamp post.) Finally I consulted the captain who, from his Merchant Navy experience on the west coast of India and elsewhere, I deemed to be vastly experienced in these matters. 'No doubt, my boy,' he said, 'you've got the clap, sticky fingers are enough. Or,' he went on darkly, 'you've been paying too much attention to yourself and are suffering from wanker's wear and tear.' I hotly denied either possibility, but at the end of the patrol in Kirkwall I reported sick. I was immediately whisked off to the hospital ship in Scapa Flow and missed the next patrol. First I was given tests, which happily were found to be negative, then I was put on a crash course of the new synthetic drug sulphonilamide (M. & B. 693) which made me feel lousy. Within a few days, no longer having a discharge or any pain, I was pronounced fit. I was not, however, eligible for sick-leave – perhaps it was thought I hadn't earned it – so while waiting for *Northern Isles* to return I worked in the operations room at Kirkwall, which experience was to stand me in good stead later. I rejoined *Isles* on her return a couple of weeks later – my shipmates, I liked to think, regarding me with a certain awe.

At last the news came that we were to have a major refit and go in company with our sister ship, the *Northern Sun*, to West Hartlepool for four or five weeks. The usual staggered leave would apply, which meant that I would have two weeks to spend in the south of England in early June.

On 31 May I travelled by train from West Hartlepool, with a suitcase and a kit-bag full of gear and the invaluable duty-free allowance of cigarettes. Arriving at Euston in the late evening I took a taxi directly to the Royal Ocean Racing Club. The door was locked, which was usual after dark, and I rang the bell. After a pause the door was opened by the steward's wife. She said that she was expecting me and had a bed ready but the steward himself was not there as he had been called up to man one of the great armada of small vessels that had been mobilized for Operation Dynamo, the evacuation of the army from Dunkirk. She also told me that a number of older members of the club had gone too. I knew that something pretty terrific was in progress in the Channel but little had been said about the completeness of the Army's withdrawal – they had just been 'pulling back to a defensive position' – and the true gravity of the situation had not yet struck home.

It was late, I was tired, and after a drink or two I went straight to bed. In the morning I was brought a cup of tea and asked if I minded having breakfast in the library rather than in the dining room, a floor above. I of course agreed, and was half-way through my one rasher of bacon and reconstituted egg when the telephone rang. I answered it, saying 'Royal Ocean Racing Club.' A male voice asked, 'Who is that speaking?' 'Sub-Lieutenant Caplat,' I replied. 'I'm speaking for Admiral Sir Lionel Preston, Admiralty. Have you anyone still there who could take a yacht or small vessel to sea – and what are you doing there anyway?' 'I've just come on leave from Northern Patrol, sir.' 'What's your job?' 'Navigating officer, sir.' 'Well, I've got a job for you. Go to Charing Cross Station, get a warrant from the office there and report directly to Admiral Taylor at Sheerness.' So I took my kit-bag with a certain amount of seagoing clothing (we were not very formal in trawlers) and did as I was bid.

It was about noon when I got to Sheerness and reported to Admiral Taylor's office, in fact to Lieutenant-Commander David Holland-Martin, Maintenance Officer for Operation Dynamo. 'So you're a navigator, Sub, are you?' 'Yes, sir.' 'Right! There are half a dozen Thames passenger launches in the basin; each has a sub in charge but they've all come straight from *King Alfred* and have no experience whatever. The launches have no navigational equipment but we've found a compass for one of them. We've a lot more boats than compasses here at the moment. I want you to take charge of that flotilla and sail at 1600 for Ramsgate, routing instructions for Dunkirk from there.'

I went down to look at my 'flotilla'. They were identical, about thirty feet long with a big saloon and an upper deck with bench seats on it. They had been brought down the Thames to Sheerness by their civilian crews and each made 'Naval' by the additions of a small blue ensign and a probationary temporary sub-lieutenant R.N.V.R. Now they were being fuelled and victualled. Victualling was generous in terms of emergency rations as it was already known that the troops were likely to be hungry. Their range was not great; refuelling at Ramsgate they could probably get to Dunkirk, do a little ferrying between the beach and larger vessels off-shore and then get back to Ramsgate with their own load of passengers. The weather was fine, as it miraculously stayed almost throughout the operation except for a few hours of an uncomfortable northerly that caused surf on the beaches. How these launches would have behaved had they been full or over-laden in a real Channel chop, I do not know.

Shortly after 1500 a paddle steamer arrived at Sheerness, having steamed all the way round from Portsmouth, and proceeded to coal as her bunkers were small and the journey of some two hundred miles had run them dangerously low. She was the *Freshwater*, normally used on the Portsmouth to Ryde, Isle of Wight, ferry service, a run of some seven miles in each direction.

Just before my flotilla was to sail and while I was trying to position the compass and wondering how accurate it would be, Lieutenant-Commander Holland-Martin appeared on the dockside and called me ashore. 'I've got another job for you. These boats can sail under the senior sub in a convoy and follow the others to Ramsgate but *Freshwater* needs an officer with recent experience. She's got her civilian crew, but they've sent her here with a lieutenant ex-R.N. in charge. He left the Navy some time ago and has only recently been recalled to do a mining disposal course at Whale Island [the Naval gunnery school at Portsmouth]. He's worried about having to drive *Freshwater* by himself. I want you to join him. By the time she's coaled, it will be too late for her to get to Dunkirk tonight. Things are so bad there now that we can only operate with any hope of getting away with it during the hours of darkness, so you'll get your sailing orders tomorrow and be going straight to Dunkirk and back to Ramsgate to unload.'

I lost my first and, when it comes to that, last command in the Navy and left the launches to chug off with a motley collection of other craft on the ebb tide to Ramsgate while I joined *Freshwater*. First we put a lot of things ashore to provide more space and lighten the ship as far as possible, because the plan was to put her bows right on to the beach and have her boarded by the soldiers wading out and climbing on the sponsons (the flat platforms at water level that surrounded the paddle wheels). Then we inspected the boats and made sure that they could be lowered and used. They were heavy wooden rowing lifeboats stuck into their chocks by paint, and their davits were not of the modern self-launching variety. I don't know when *Freshwater* was launched but I am pretty sure that this was not her first war.

My captain, Lieutenant Church, twenty-odd years my senior, was just as Holland-Martin had described him – long out of the Navy, a worried family man, unhappy at having to go on such a dangerous course as mining in the first place, worried at the responsibility of command, but brave and kind and, I felt, in some way relieved by my youthful enthusiasm for this unforeseen adventure. After a couple of pints in the NAAFI and a canteen meal, we turned in as best we could on the benches in the little bridge cabin while the crew dossed down in the saloon. Nobody left the dockyard and nobody went on the razzle. The atmosphere of Sheerness was too electric. Small vessels, and larger ones, were continuously arriving and what had happened to me, my flotilla and *Freshwater* and all those involved was being multiplied ceaselessly. Dynamo was an inspired name for the operation, though in fact it was taken from the cavern below Dover Castle in which Admiral Ramsey masterminded the operation. That cavern had been, in the First World War, the site of the dynamo for the auxiliary lighting of the castle.

On the morning of 2 June we anxiously awaited our sailing orders. The optimum time to reach Dunkirk was as soon as possible after dark. We realized, though we did not then know how strong the German air attack in daylight was, that we should spend as little as possible of the daylight hours within range of the Luftwaffe. Our speed of advance was a maximum of twelve knots but we had to conserve fuel because of our small bunkers, and the Channel tides were strong forces to be reckoned with. We were given a precise time of departure, as was every other craft leaving on a similar mission.

We left shortly before noon on a beautiful summer's day and chugged, as paddle steamers so prettily do, down the swept channel past my old friend the Girdler light-vessel, not yet made into the anti-aircraft fort on metal piles that it was soon to become, on past Herne Bay, Reculver, Margate and the North Foreland in the sleepy, balmy, summer dusk. Because of the amount of shipping and its inexperienced crews, more coastal navigation lights than normal were working and the whole picture remains vivid to me: the calm sea, the occasional flash from a shore light on an otherwise blacked-out coastline, and the rumble of gunfire audible over the rustle of the bow wave and the gentle thud of the paddle wheels.

On our way past the Girdler we took stock of our armament, which consisted of almost nothing. The captain had a service revolver and a few rounds of ammunition issued to him by Whale Island on his departure. We were otherwise defenceless against attack, but I thought that perhaps we could deter the enemy if we appeared to have machine-guns on the upper deck. With the help of some of the deck hands, a few broom handles, bits of canvas and the craft of improvization that several years in the theatre had taught me, we rigged up a number of not very convincing dummy guns at strategic places on the bridge and upper deck, with instructions that if enemy air attack appeared to be imminent, they were to be manned and threateningly manoeuvred. In fact that evening passage to the North Goodwin was totally without incident. We turned to port and headed for France. After it was dark and we were approaching the buoy off Gravelines – the turning mark for the inshore channel, which runs parallel with the shore and only about two miles off it – the flashes of distant shell and bomb bursts, of which we had seen the 'loom' since dusk, became a vivid firework display. As we turned into the swept channel shells began to fall around us, not too many and none too near. The firing was obviously unaimed and indiscriminate; there was no radar in those days so it was a matter of luck. Ours held.

Our orders were to carry on past the entrance to Dunkirk harbour, where destroyers and deeper draft vessels were constantly loading at the quay and ferrying day and night, always under bombardment and in the daylight hours under air attack. The range of our Spitfires and Hurricanes at that time was just sufficient to fight over the battle front round Dunkirk, but there were not nearly enough of them and reserves had to be kept at home for the defence of England itself. Having passed the harbour we were to go on to the beaches east of Dunkirk towards La Panne, find as many soldiers as we could, get them aboard and beetle off home, aiming to be well beyond the Gravelines buoy by full light.

We had no radio, nor any means of signalling, so we were on our own as far as any strategy was concerned. The shelling from behind the shore was constant and it was obvious that a good many shells were exploding on the beach itself where the tide was still rising with an hour or so to go. We were navigating by the seat of our pants, with no echo-sounder and no time for a lead line. We chose a spot about three miles to the east of Dunkirk harbour which appeared to have slightly fewer shells falling on it and nosed in to the shore, which there consists of a shallow, shelving, sandy beach backed by a wide area of sand dunes. About seventy-five yards from the beach the keel touched the sand and we went gently astern; the great thing about a paddle steamer is her ability to turn over her big paddle wheels very slowly so as just to inch forward or back. On the other hand, full power can provide a hefty shove and she is just as powerful and manoeuvrable going astern as ahead.

We had expected the beach to be crowded with soldiers but it was deserted. I suggested that, while the captain continued to manoeuvre *Freshwater* to keep her afloat but as close to the shore as possible, I should take a boat and go to look for 'the silly sods who didn't know their own luck'. I took two of the deck hands and we were on the sand in no time. The odd shells were coming over, and every minute or two one would land out to sea, on the beach not far away, or in the dunes in front of us. Leaving the men with the boat I set off up the beach and into the dunes. I hadn't gone far when I came across a bunch of Army officers, of what regiment I do not know, sitting in one of the hollows in the sand. There were some other-ranks with them too but sitting apart. They were busy eating their rations. They appeared to be surprised that a junior Naval officer should suddenly appear and interrupt their meal. When I told them that the *Freshwater* was handy the senior officer asked how many men we could take. 'Several hundred,' I answered, adding that there were only two lifeboats usable and it would take a long time unless they were prepared to wade or swim out. This they seemed reluctant to do, so while they were still debating I moved along the beach to the eastward and found more soldiers in the dunes. This time they were less disciplined, or perhaps just more ready to get out. Anyway, they followed me down to the water's edge. The two men in the boat rowed her along and the captain brought *Freshwater* right in until her bow was just aground. The tide now was almost at its peak. Some soldiers got into the boat, others hung on to the stern and waded out with others following. By the time the boat reached the forward edge of the starboard sponson those wading behind were up to their chins, but we had proved that, even if you were a non-swimmer, you could get to the paddler wet but safe. We then established the same procedure on the port side and before long had two steady streams of men coming aboard in an orderly fashion. Some brought their rifles, holding them over their heads, some did not. Scrambling on to the sponsons was not easy, but with the help of loops of rope and strong arms they managed well enough.

Moving the paddles only gently so as not to create a strong wash, *Freshwater* kept backing off as the tide began to fall. How long this went on I do not now recall, but the stream of men dried up and the tide continued to fall so that eventually with every space below decks packed we hauled off and headed back to pass Dunkirk, make for the Gravelines buoy and then turn to starboard and set course for Ramsgate. Such rations as we had were being dished out, and though shells were still falling intermittently and Dunkirk was burning I had a feeling that the mission was accomplished. But all was not yet done.

Other vessels from further along the beach and some from Dunkirk itself were now streaming in a steady procession for Gravelines. Dawn was beginning to break behind us. Near the buoy we saw a medium-sized French trawler, ahead and to port of us, suddenly go aground. She drew a lot more than we did and was already down to the scuppers in the water. No amount of revving up of the screw did anything to move her, either ahead or astern. The tide was falling fast now and when the light came up she was going to be a sitting duck for a German Stuka, so we went alongside her with two or three feet to spare under our keel.

What we expected was that there would be the crew of the trawler plus a number of refugees to be taken off. What we got was another matter. The hatches of the trawler were flung open and on to our deck streamed what appeared to be the better part of the French Army, more and more of them. I had not then seen Wagner's *Flying Dutchman*, but there is much the same effect in its first act when the Dutchman arrives and disgorges a vast chorus of sailors from a rather small stage ship. There was no room for them below decks with us. Both saloons and every space were already full of tired men, and the new arrivals swarmed all over the upper decks, the fo'c'sle, the stern and wherever they could find a place to perch. Off we went, behind on our schedule and with the paddles thrashing away rather deeper in the water than they were designed to do.

A little way further on and we spotted a Carley life-float adrift. Closing it we saw two men inside, so we went alongside and hauled aboard the bodies of a British Naval officer and a rating, both of whom had died of bullet wounds. The raft showed bullet holes too so it must have been machine-gunned. The Germans had a number of E-boats operating at night and we concluded that this must be evidence of some such engagement.

The Luftwaffe showed up once it was properly light: a two-engined plane circled high above us and then turned as if about to make a run in. There was no point in manning the broom handles now, for the decks were crammed. At that moment the first wave of Spitfires from Kent came screaming overhead on their way to Dunkirk and the German plane obviously thought better of it and made off. That was the end of that and we had no further trouble until mid-morning. As we thrashed our way onwards, the white cliffs of England hove into view out of the hazy sunshine. With cries of excitement the French army rushed over to the port side for a better look, the ship heeled violently, the port sponson went right under, the starboard paddle came half-way out of the water and we careered in a semicircle like a duck with a broken wing. Shouts from the French officers were not enough; they actually had to draw the stubby little automatic pistols they carried in their belts and order their men at gun-point to balance the ship.

And so we made Ramsgate. The berthing officer was a lieutenant-commander wearing his gold lace stripes on the sleeves of a smart blue pin-stripe jacket. Berthing was not easy. We had to wait our turn and finally got alongside another vessel already at the quay. The soldiers, French and British, swarmed ashore across the other vessel and joined hundreds, perhaps thousands, more. How those ashore ever managed to get the arrivals sorted out I can't imagine. Certainly we had no idea how many or whom we had had on board.

As soon as we had disembarked our soldiers and the two corpses we shoved off. There was no coal for us there, our stocks were low and we were ordered to return to Sheerness forthwith. It was now mid-afternoon on 3 June. We paddled quietly back to the Medway, the noise of the battle still coming over the water, and discussed how we should conduct the next trip.

At Sheerness once more, late that evening, we were told that we should take coal at first light but meanwhile get some sleep. Next morning we learnt that we would not be going over again, for Dunkirk was falling to the Germans. In fact the swastika was hoisted on the eastern mole of the harbour at 10.20 a.m. on 4 June.

I left *Freshwater* and Sheerness together that afternoon. Apart from a note, hand-written by Holland-Martin authorizing me to proceed on three days' leave, my only trophy was a pair of 1900A binoculars taken from round the neck of the dead officer in the Carley float. He had no further need of them but they gave me good service thereafter in the war and ocean racing, and still do. I thank him for them often.

I was to see *Freshwater* again, however. She went back to Portsmouth and resumed her ferry duties. In November 1941 I was doing my submarine training in H.M.S. *Dolphin*, at Fort Blockhouse on the mouth of Portsmouth harbour. My room, or 'cabin' as it was called, overlooked the approaches to the harbour but its windows were heavily blacked out. There were nightly German air raids, with mines being dropped into Spithead and the Solent.

One early morning while it was still pitch dark there was the sound of a heavy explosion out to sea and my cabin windows shook. I took no notice and went back to sleep but when, just after it was light, I opened the black-out and looked out, I saw about a mile away the foremast, the funnel and the top of the bridge of the poor old *Freshwater* sticking up out of the grey water. On her early morning run from Portsmouth to Ryde she had hit a newly laid mine. Thus ended her long life and short but gallant service career.

I returned to Herne Bay for a few days to see my parents and then went on to stay with the Downtons at West Malling. Here I saw the delectable Diana again, out of her gym tunic but not yet as far out of it as I was to see her later. I think I spent most of my time playing darts in the pub next door with her mother, and after two or three days back I went to West Hartlepool and the *Northern Isles*.

The Battle of the Atlantic was beginning to emerge as the crucial struggle for the survival of Britain. The Americans were not yet in the war and the Royal Navy was in desperate need of escort vessels. Churchill did his famous deal over bases in the West Indies whereby we became the owners of fifty First World War American destroyers. They had to be taken over very quickly, and the effort of finding crews for them was a terrific strain on the manning departments of the Navy. So it was that I was whisked out of the *Northern Isles*, given a few days' leave – needless to say spent at West Malling where the delectable Diana seemed even more so – and found myself aboard the R.M.S., now H.M.T.S., *Duchess of Richmond* bound from Liverpool to Halifax, Nova Scotia.

On board the *Duchess of Richmond* (one of four sister ships on the North American run known as the drunken duchesses because of their propensity for rolling along) were the entire crews for a flotilla of eight destroyers, each crew made up in much the same way. The commanding officer was an experienced man, in our case a lieutenant-commander R.N. who had commanded a submarine on the China station in the pre-war period but who had lost his promotion due to an unfortunate accident there which was no fault of his but for which, as C.O., he was held responsible.

The rest of the officers were a mixture drawn from all sources – some R.N.R., some R.N.V.R., some junior R.N. None had any experience of the type of ship we were to take over. The non-commissioned officers and senior ratings were as mixed a bag. That was the end of it as far as know-how was concerned. Perhaps fifteen or twenty men in each crew knew more or less what they were in for, the remaining one hundred were as green as grass, and most of them rapidly assumed that colour as the *Duchess* put to sea.

The voyage across, in convoy, was uneventful as far as we, the passengers, were informed, though I believe there were several alerts because of U-boats. Our time on board was spent trying to put the beginnings of a shape into our own ship's company.

When we arrived in Halifax we were taken to our quarters to await the arrival of our flotilla, the second of six to be handed over by the Americans. 'A' flotilla had just left for St John's, Newfoundland, on the first leg of its journey to England, and 'B' flotilla was due the next day. The ratings all went to billets in the grandstands of the local racecourse, the officers to shared rooms in the principal hotel. The town and port of Halifax still showed signs of the explosion of an ammunition ship in the First World War which had killed many people and left the place a minor Hiroshima.

Not only that, but Halifax was 'dry'. There were no drinking facilities whatever, except via the bootleggers. These, however, were plentiful. One only had to walk out of the hotel, hail a taxi and say you wished to make a purchase and you were driven round to a back street in the suburbs. The taxi would stop and the driver, having collected 'the necessary', would then disappear down a side alley or round a corner, so that one never knew which particular house, garage or shed he had visited, and reappear with a parcel and drive one back to the hotel. A request for soda, ice or any other soft thirst quencher to be delivered to one's room was immediately complied with in the shape of a trolley fully supplied with all the necessities of a bar except the alcoholic drinks. Wine of a sort could be had, but the principal trade was in Canadian rye whiskey, not of too bad quality nor of a really exorbitant price.

Our new ships were the famous 'four-stackers', which were mass-produced for the U.S. Navy towards the end of the First World War and then mothballed in Florida. Some of them had hardly seen service, some were well worn, and some had had to have their plates redoubled along the waterline because of corrosion. With two engine rooms, hence the four funnels, they were said to be capable of doing thirty knots (this was not the only exaggeration on the part of their sales force). Very 'narrow-gutted', they could, as we were to find out, roll through a really frightening number of degrees. Those who have seen the film *The Caine Mutiny*, or read the book, will know what they were like, as Captain Queeg's command was just such a vessel.

The two or three days after the destroyers arrived in Halifax

74

were spent in 'familiarizing' ourselves with the ship, while the American crew was aboard and she still flew the stars and stripes. This included a short trip or two to sea where the weather was quiet though somewhat foggy. We found the American habits strange: 'dry' ships, of course, but lavish provision of towels and bed linen whereas in British ships we officers had to provide our own, and rationed at that. Many strange 'pipes' or orders came over the Tannoy system, the one that struck me most being, 'Away gasoline gig and postman's bicycle'. The Americans assured us that the ships were not only fast and manoeuvrable but excellent sea-boats snd that some of them had recently comfortably survived a tornado in the Gulf of Florida.

Take-over day approached. We were to march ceremoniously down from the racecourse to the quay, all eight ships' companies properly fallen in and dressed, to the accompaniment of military bands of the Canadian Navy and Marines. Then there would be a formal transfer, the stars and stripes would be hauled down as the white ensign rose to take its place, and the destroyers would become H.M. ships-of-war.

The night before led to a great run on the bootleggers' wares and the following morning, having packed our gear into lorries for transference to the quay we, the officers, were embussed, with splitting hangovers (speaking for myself and friends, that is) to join our ships' companies at the racecourse. Judging from their appearance they had managed to have quite a good time too. The fact that the majority of them had come straight into naval training as conscripts from the back streets of Glasgow indicated that they had not been perfect material for precision drilling in the first place, and they had had little of it on board the *Duchess of Richmond*. They did not exactly fulfil Whale Island standards. To make matters worse it was a hot and stuffy morning and the midges were out in force.

We found ourselves marching directly behind one of the bands which had a tremendous brass section including two of the biggest sousaphones I have ever seen. The combination of the heat, the hangover, and the relentless pounding rhythm of the band over that two and a half mile march just about finished me. The ceremony was duly completed, however, and the U.S.S. *McLanahan* became H.M.S. *Bradford*. The American crew had hardly left the ship before the local Saccone & Speed's van drew up at the gangway with the wardroom wine stores, at which the American officers came smartly back on board for a friendly visit.

That evening was spent in stowing our gear and getting straight. The ratings found large stocks of comforts unknown to them before, in the shape of candy bars and Coca-Cola fountains, the officers found wonderful towels and linen sheets which became their personal property, and the medical officer, who also happened to be the wardroom wine caterer, found, on checking the medical supplies, several demijohns of pure alcohol not normally supplied to H.M. ships.

The next day we went for a trial trip with a few key Americans on board and then, having landed them, set off as a flotilla for Londonderry, Northern Ireland, via St John's, Newfoundland. The stop at St John's for fuelling was vitally necessary as the bunkerage of these ships could only just provide us with the fuel to get to Londonderry at a steady speed of twelve knots.

We were not considered to be in danger between Halifax and St John's and so sailed under normal steaming lights, though we were at pains to perfect our black-out drill for later use. From St John's onwards we would be in the war zone. Apart from rough conditions, which showed us how the ships could roll, how vulnerable most of the crew were to seasickness and how badly some of the American gear was stowed, the trip was uneventful. The worst damage was done in the radio room where a number of pieces of equipment fell to the deck and were rendered useless, but we were going to have to keep radio silence after St John's anyway so the fact that we could not get them repaired seemed then not to matter greatly.

Oiling took only a few hours and around noon on a really horrid day of driving rain we sailed for England. The weather was worsening all the time, and by dusk we were ploughing on at our twelve knots into a north-easterly gale that was still rising. All eight ships were blacked out, and when it got dark the only thing to be seen apart from the white crests of the waves was the shielded stern light of the next ahead on whom we were keeping station. The first night out was nerve-racking stuff for the captain and the watch-keepers on the bridge. For the crew it was like going to hell – stuffy mess-decks with everything battened down, and the appalling motion of the ship. Their supper that night was not to be with them long and a number of them made their wet, and unauthorized, way to the starboard leeward side to make use of the rail to puke over.

In these ships the steering mechanism consisted of a large wheel in the bridge wheelhouse which was connected by wires that ran, partly open, partly in tubes, along the scuppers on the starboard side to the steering motor in the rudder flat right aft. This in turn provided the power to turn the rudder. Constant minor corrections of course were necessary for the helmsman to follow the stern light ahead, and if he went too far off, the officer of the watch would give him a correction to bring him back into position. The captain had called for just such a correction when the coxswain who was steering at the time, a most experienced fellow, said: 'I've lost steerage sir. The wheel's jammed with ten degrees of port helm on.'

Round we went in a big semicircle. The captain ordered 'Stop both' in case we crashed into one of those astern of us, and we lay wallowing. Then the coxswain said, 'I have steerage now sir, but it's very stiff.' What had happened was that the combined weight of the seasick crew members standing on the open steering wires on the starboard side had caused them to become immovable. In addition a discarded balaclava helmet had been drawn into one of the tubed sections, continuing to render it stiff after the weight of the feet came off. By the time all this was sorted out and we resumed our course and speed, we had lost touch with the rest of the flotilla. So crucial was the speed restriction that the captain decided he should not increase speed in the hope that we might catch up. The chances were that, come the daylight and in such poor visibility, even a few miles' separation would find us out of touch with each other. We had no radar, of course, and though we could hear our flotilla leader and, later, Canadian search aircraft asking us to break silence and come on the air, we found we could not transmit after the damage caused to the radio equipment by the rough weather. We held our own course instructions and these we adhered to, but then trouble struck in one of the engine rooms and we were obliged to reduce speed even further.

The rest of the voyage was uncomfortable but relatively uneventful. We plodded on for several days. Those of us who were well enough to eat lived almost entirely on the coxswain's ability, as a West Countryman born and bred, to produce 'tiddy-oggies', or Cornish pasties, in sufficient numbers. Gradually things returned to normal and as we got nearer to Europe we began to receive information about supposed U-boat positions which we endeavoured to avoid, apparently successfully.

Finally, some three and a half days behind schedule, we approached the entrance to Lough Foyle leading to Londonderry. It was just coming up to dawn, we exchanged the right signals with the shore, pulled into the entrance and waited for the pilot to come off and take us across the wide lough and up the river to Derry. The western side is Republican Irish and though the city of

77

Londonderry itself was, and is, in Ulster, we were close to neutral territory and the pilot we had to embark was a citizen of the Republic.

The captain, knowing that we were going to be based in Londonderry, no doubt not trusting the pilot too much, and perhaps even in the knowledge that the captain of one of H.M. ships could, if he dispensed with professional pilotage, claim a small fee for himself, said to me: 'Pilot [the Navy's name for the navigating officer], you take the port wing of the bridge and I'll take the starboard. Make a careful note of the exact distance we pass from all marks of the channel and our speed.'

The Irish pilot was rowed out to us in a small boat. He scrambled up the ladder and lurched on to the bridge, wedged himself into the small space in front of the wheel, let out a great belch of whiskey-laden breath and said: 'Course south-west a half south, full speed ahead if you please, sorr.' 'Full speed!' said the astonished captain. 'Well, twenty-foive knots then.' The captain looked at me, held five fingers down and I rang the engine room telegraph for revs for twenty knots. Away we screamed across the calm waters of the lough in the half light before dawn, faster than *Bradford* had gone since she had been given her new name.

The pilot burst into song, much to the captain's horror, and then, even worse, lit his pipe which was particularly evil-smelling. I could see, even if the pilot could not, that the captain was not well pleased but he wanted to get the fellow's local knowledge without too much trouble. At the end of the ten-mile dash we approached the narrow mouth of the river itself. 'Twenty knots if you please.' At a nod from the captain I rang down for fifteen. 'Eighteen,' the pilot commanded as we entered the river, and down we went to twelve. Turning to the captain the pilot said: 'That was great. Oi've never been so fast yet.' Gradually we reduced speed as we hurtled up the river on the last of the flood tide until we came to the bend before Londonderry itself. We were then doing a mere eight knots, though the pilot thought it was ten.

We were in the middle of the narrow fairway when suddenly round the bend came a file of four motor mine-sweepers on their way for the morning sweep of the main channel in the lough. 'Hard-a-starboard!' yelled the pilot, and hard-a-starboard went the cox-swain, up on to the mud and shingle bank went *Bradford* with a horrible crunching noise; almost at once, 'Hard-a-port!' yelled the pilot and captain together and we bounced off the bank back into the channel, narrowly missing the stern of the last mine-sweeper.

Three weddings: My own, 1943.

Left: Simone's, 1965, and right: Dominique's, 1974.

Inset top left: With John Christie, 1951.

John Christie addressing the company in Glyndebourne before the Edinburgh Festival, 1951. In orchestra pit: Fritz Busch and members of the Royal Philharmonic. Front row left to right: Peter Ebert, Owen Brannigan, M.C., Alfred Poell, Lisa Della Casa, Carl Ebert, Genevieve Warner, Dorothy MacNeil, Marko Rothmüller. In audience are: John Pritchard, Anthony Besch, Jani Strasser, April Cantelo, Harold Williams, John Piper, Rosemary Vercoe.

We were bucking like a bronco – it was clear that both our propellers were badly bent. We edged into the quay in a series of hiccuping leaps. The pilot turned to the captain and said: 'Jaysus Christ, that's the third ....ing toime Oi've done that.'

We now found ourselves in a peculiar situation. To start with the ship had been posted as 'Missing, presumed lost' since nothing had been heard or seen of us since we parted company with the flotilla off St John's. Fortunately our next-of-kin had not yet been informed. Our two screws were, in the words of the diver who went down to inspect them, 'folded up like cauliflowers'. Although we had generous spares from the Americans, these included neither the right bits for the radio nor spare propellers. It was not normal practice anyway for destroyers to carry spare propellers, in the way a car carries a spare wheel.

We were just thinking that *Bradford* would have to pay off and that we should all be home for Christmas when news came that there would be one replacement propeller arriving at Cardiff soon and several more at Devonport. We were to await a tug that would tow us down the Irish Sea to pick up the one in Cardiff and then proceed under our own steam with one screw to get the second one in Plymouth. Having already been in Londonderry a fortnight we were impatient to be gone, but we had to wait even longer for the tug, and it was not until just after Christmas that she arrived.

Londonderry wasn't any fun. The locals did not like us much and I was actually spat on by an old crone while walking very respectably, in uniform, with a Wren cipher officer down a side street one Sunday afternoon. There was little to do except lick the crew into some sort of shape with endless drills, have new British radio equipment fitted and watch later flotillas of our sister ships arrive, usually battered, and sail again for convoy escort duty. Because of their fuel problems, these destroyers could only go a certain part of the way out with the convoys from Liverpool and the Clyde and then turn and pick up an inward-bound convoy. The corvettes had much greater endurance.

No Christmas leave for us. The tug arrived on Boxing Day and we set off immediately. She was a fine seagoing tug and the master made it obvious that he thought his services were being wasted on towing an old destroyer that had been foolish enough to damage itself. However, he took us away from the quay very expertly, turned us, and on a short tow-rope took us slowly and carefully out to the open sea. Once we were outside he lengthened the tow to several cables and went off at a good steady fifteen knots down the

Irish Sea. Having started off, the tug ceased to communicate with us at all. She answered neither on the radio nor by Aldis lamp. Our captain was enraged but there was nothing he could do. We were powerless to move ourselves so we just had to go where the tug-master took us, even though that involved crossing a mined area off the northern tip of Wales. Finally after some thirty hours, in the pitch dark of a nasty rainy January night off Cardiff, he suddenly stopped towing and turned back towards us. He hailed us and told us to cast off the tow and drop anchor. We had no choice but to obey and he steamed off, leaving us helpless and not too sure of our position, until a local tug came at first light and took us into the docks.

We went to a dry dock where the one available new propeller was fitted. A day or two later we left for Plymouth under our own steam again – but only just. At Devonport we dry-docked once more and were given another screw, then we went to store and oil. Amongst the stores issued were some big brand-new coir fenders, handsome things of plaited rope more suitable for going alongside oil tankers in bumpy anchorages than the rather effete objects the *McLanahan* had sported. The oiler was out in the Sound and it was a dark and dirty night. My job going alongside was to be in charge of securing the after part of the ship. Out went our new fenders and we manoeuvred alongside. All this had to be carried out with the minimum of lights, but once we were safely tied up with breast ropes and springs I duly reported to the bridge. On returning a few minutes later to check the wire spring I found to my horror that the big new fender was lying on our deck. There was a fearful grinding of metal as our ship's side rose and fell against the filthy plates of the oiler. I demanded of the little Glaswegian seaman who had been left in charge of the fender what the bloody hell he had pulled it in for. 'Well, sir,' he explained. 'That ship next door was squeezing it.'

From Plymouth we were sent to Scapa Flow for anti-submarine exercises. These I found fascinating. My job was to keep the navigational plot. Asdics were new then and by no means perfect; radar was not yet fitted. My captain, being an ex-submariner, was good at guessing the target's intentions, and after a few days of this I asked him if he could get me permission to go in the target for a day so that I could assess for myself the feel of being hunted rather than hunting. This he was able to do. I found it all wonderfully exciting. I did not suffer from claustrophobia for I have always felt happier in small and intimate ships. The atmosphere of quiet and informal efficiency particularly appealed to me.

On escort duty in the Western Approaches life was hard. *Bradford* suffered from constant engine trouble which, together with her short fuel range, made her not the most efficient fighting machine afloat. Our doctor-cum-wardroom-wine-caterer succumbed to chronic seasickness. I took over the wardroom wine and thus discovered the secret of the success of the doctor's stewardship in terms of low mess bills and strong drinks: he had been lacing our Plymouth gin with the American supply of neat alcohol from the sick bay.

FIVE

Under the ocean wave

Bradford's unreliability became too much and we were ordered to Chatham for repairs and a refit. When we got there after a tricky passage by night up the channel and through the Straits of Dover, we found that it was not a refit we were in for. We were going to be paid off; the ship was going to be taken out of commission and all the crew dispersed. What was intended for the *Bradford* was not stated. One of the 'four-stackers', the *Campbeltown* from 'C' flotilla, was turned into a monster torpedo, packed with explosives and launched at the lock gates at St Nazaire.

The captain, as was the custom of the times, went up to the Admiralty to give his opinion of his officers and senior ratings and, as far as possible, to see that they got the next appointment for which they were most suitable. We sat around the wardroom that evening awaiting his return, our bags packed, due to leave the ship next morning for an unspecified number of days' leave before re-appointment. The Captain returned on board and over a drink gave us all our fate.

To me he said: 'You liked going out in the submarine at Scapa. Well, you've been accepted for submarines now that they've decided to let in the R.N.V.R. You'll get your call up to the first available training course. Good luck!' And so I found myself a 'volunteer' for submarines.

My immediate and instinctive move was to Offham and the Downtons, not far from Chatham and a lot jollier than the parental home in the dilapidated castle of Tantallon. Here I sat anxiously awaiting my summons but also hoping it would not come too soon. Diana was ravishing, her parents understanding, and apart from the frequent noise of patrols taking off from West Malling fighter station near by, a good many air-raid alerts and the appalling smell of Diana's mother attempting to follow the advice of the Minister of Supply, Lord Woolton, life seemed well worth living. Joan Downton was set on trying to make up for the scarcity of bacon by producing 'macon'; the process consisted of hanging a raw leg of local mutton up the open chimney of the old house and smoking it by burning oak or apple wood on the hearth. The trouble was that the Hodges Place chimney was a much better conductor downwards than upwards, consequently producing the loud roar of aircraft engines and the even louder smell of rotting mutton.

Life was particularly good since Diana's parents allowed us to become officially engaged, although she was still only seventeen. Third time lucky indeed for me. Diana, who never likes to look forward too far, was of the private opinion that once I went into submarines she would never see me again. Our engagement was celebrated by a ration-busting lunch for two (paid for by Diana's father, of course) at Le Coq d'Or in Grafton Street, under the benign eye of Barducci, the head waiter, whom Jack Downton had helped to get out of internment at the beginning of the war.

Despite this idyllic situation I was itching to be at sea again and, as at the start of the war, I could not understand why their Lordships of the Admiralty seemed so reluctant to make immediate use of my enormous potential. Finally the call came: I was to report to H.M.S. *Dolphin*, Gosport (Portsmouth), on 23 June for enrolment, medicals, and so on before proceeding to Officers Training Class No. 47 at Blyth, Northumberland. I passed my tests and found myself in an encampment of huts beside the railway sidings in a desolate little coal port on the coast of Northumberland. Work was hard, for there was a great deal to be learnt in six weeks. There were few if any shore delights and my time was spent in the classroom, in an old L class submarine on daily exercises – sometimes rudely interrupted by enemy aircraft – or on the telephone to Offham where the reversed-charge telephone calls during that period nearly beggared Diana's father.

The class itself consisted of nineteen lieutenants and sub-lieutenants of whom four were R.N.V.R. There were two foreigners, a Frenchman and a Norwegian. Of the R.N. contingent three were volunteers, and the rest drafted. On 'passing out' the Frenchman came top, second was Sub-Lieutenant Godfrey Place, R.N., a draftee who went on to win his V.C. in Midget submarines and became a rear-admiral. I was fourth. I returned to *Dolphin* as a 'spare' officer before being appointed to H.32.

During the few days I was in Fort Blockhouse Diana and her father came down to Portsmouth so that she could enrol in the Wrens. Diana had been taught to drive by her father, whose driving was excellent except at such times as he was tired and emotional, which were not infrequent. It was her first long drive and she arrived shaking all over. However, a night in the Queen's Hotel at Southsea made all well and the next day she went to enrol, only to be told that she could not be called up until her eighteenth birthday in just over a month's time.

H. 32 was a very small submarine, one of a class that had been built in America by the Electric Boat Company towards the end of the First World War. She was a contemporary of the *Bradford* though she had always been a British vessel. Life aboard was cramped and primitive. Mainly used for training, she had done some war-time patrols in the Biscay area and had formed a weak link in the 'Iron Ring' that had been set up to try to keep the German battle cruisers *Scharnhorst* and *Gneisnau* bottled up in Brest; her few elderly torpedoes, her slow speed, low endurance and inability to dive safely below thirty-five feet hardly made her a potent weapon. So cramped were the quarters that the one lavatory (or 'heads', as it was called in the Navy) was in the middle of the control-room area on the starboard side. When the boat went to 'action stations' I found myself seated on the heads with the top half of the stable-type door open and a protruding ledge on the bottom half forming the plotting table and accommodating the 'is-was', an early instrument for working out enemy and our own courses and speeds and finding the correct angle for firing torpedoes. (The 'is-was' was superseded by a more sophisticated instrument known as the 'fruit-machine'. The familiar name of the modern computer attack system is presumably top-secret information.)

I joined H. 32 at Rothesay and we sailed for *Dolphin* at Gosport. Much of the way we were on the surface under escort but somewhere off the Scillies we were left to make our own way, under water by day, on the surface by night, up channel to Portsmouth. At that time fast German motor torpedo boats (E-boats) were operating in the Channel with considerable success. At night convoys were protected by similar vessels and during the day, when dive-bomb air attack by shore-based fighters was the principal threat, by towing barrage balloons on cables sixty or so feet above them.

We made slow progress dived, running on the power from the electric batteries. These had to be charged each night by the diesel engines, which in turn could only operate on the surface since they required a lot of air. The only source of entry for this was down the conning tower. Schnorkels, tubes operated like periscopes which could be raised above the surface to bring air into a dived submarine, were not yet in use. The submarine was anything but quiet when running diesels and could easily be detected by the underwater listening gear with which E-boats were fitted. These basic facts were true of most of the submarines in which I served, which by modern technological standards were as Noah's Ark to the *QE2*.

The first night up channel we surfaced as soon as it was dark enough. It was mid-October, calm but cold, with clouds obscuring the rising moon. We set watch in the little bridge on the conning tower, started the diesels to drive us at a modest eight or ten knots and to charge the batteries, and set out along the course eastwards that our routing instructions had given us. We kept a sharp look out for E-boats but hoped that our small dark grey hull carrying no lights would remain undetected. The captain was on the bridge or just below in the control room all the time we were on the surface at night, snatching what sleep he could during the dived daytime hours.

There were three of us on the bridge, a leading seaman lookout, myself as officer of the watch, and the captain, all of us scanning a different sector of the horizon through our binoculars. Suddenly the leading seaman said, 'Object green three-five, sir'. 'I'll take it,' said the captain. 'Keep the other sectors covered.' He looked for a few seconds and then said 'Dive, dive, dive,' down the tube to the control room and pressed the klaxon. The seaman was first down the hatch. I had just time to snatch a glimpse of the 'object'. It looked like the bow of a grey painted vessel head-on and perhaps half a mile away, stationary, no bow wave, picked up by a glint of moon through the clouds. Down I went with the captain treading on my hands on the ladder and shutting the conning tower lid as we dived.

'Twenty-five feet,' ordered the captain, and then, 'Up periscope.' He had a quick look, snapped up the handles. 'Down periscope.' 'There's something there all right. Any H.E.?' [hydrophone effect]. The hydrophone operator asked, 'What bearing, sir?' 'Green three-eight.' After a short pause: 'No contact.' 'He must be stopped and listening, silent routine, group down, steer o-one-o, thirty-five feet.' This would take us away at an oblique angle towards the English shore at our maximum permitted safe diving depth with everyone in the boat moving as seldom and as quietly as possible, spanners and valve keys muffled with rubber to prevent metal to metal noises, but at a miserable speed of two knots. After a while the operator reported: 'H.E. on the starboard beam, faint.' (It was remarkable that given the information that an object was on a certain bearing operators could almost always detect a faint noise where none had existed before.) 'Twenty-five feet,' then, 'Up periscope.' 'He's still there,' said the captain. 'Thirty-five feet, keep quiet.'

Shortly after this the chief engineer tiptoed into the control room. 'Starboard shaft is overheating, sir. I'll have to stop the starboard motor and see what the trouble is.' 'OK,' said the captain. 'Stop starboard, and be as quick as you can.' The port motor alone was left to drive us and our already minimal speed was still further decreased. Slowly our depth increased, for we had not enough momentum for the hydroplanes, our 'wings' as it were, to keep us up against gravity. The captain did not want to 'group up' the batteries on the port motor to give us increased revs as the batteries had had hardly any charge that night. We were not well off for compressed air to empty the ballast tanks and in any case higher revs or a discharge of air-driven water would cause noise which any listening device could pick up instantly. Down we sank slowly past forty feet, past fifty, sixty and at sixty-five the old thin riveted hull started to groan under the pressure and little leaks appeared. These would soon involve starting the pumps, which would be another drain on our slender power resources, and also noisy. The chief came to report: 'I'm sorry, sir, I'll have to strip the shaft.' The captain made his decision, as all captains must. 'Group up port motor, twenty-five feet, steer three-two-five.' Quite slowly – nothing happened very fast with H. 32 – we came up to periscope depth. 'Up periscope.' The captain looked astern. 'He's still there but further away. We'll have to try to get away on the surface. We'll never make it dived. Surface, prepare to man the gun.' The gun was a machine-gun of some sort which had to be manhandled up the conning tower hatch and fixed to its mounting at the after end of the bridge; not a quick operation, nor a very effective weapon once achieved.

We broke surface and the bridge was manned in the reverse order of descent. The captain looked out on the bearing of the enemy, now right aft, and the seaman and I shared the rest of the sweep. A short pause from the captain and then in a quiet voice: 'Look at that, Caplat.' I looked and what I saw now brightly illuminated by a near full moon shining through a gap in the clouds was one of our barrage balloons, broadside on and quietly resting on the water, no doubt having broken adrift from a cargo ship and held to the water by the weight of its cable. 'Well,' we said, 'it's all experience,' and went on our way, undisturbed to Fort Blockhouse.

H. 32 was being taken out of service and a few days later I was posted to a new submarine, known only by her job number J3268, nearing completion at Cammell Laird's yard at Birkenhead. The Navy talks, certainly talked then, of 'building' ships. Some of the officers and key ratings were appointed to a vessel while it was still in the hands of the shipwrights and while the choice and layout of its internal fittings, such as chart tables, lockers, bunk curtains and other more technical niceties, could still be influenced by those who would be using them. It was rather like the new production of a well-known play or opera – the structure exists but the new production team can mould it in different ways; thereafter that particular production stands, and a new cast has to fit into it just as a change of crew has to accept the details of a ship as they find them with only minor alterations possible. In times of peace this practice would lead to each ship having its own character. In war, however, mass-production sometimes takes over. Britain never built enough submarines to go in for mass-production, but the Germans did and the U-boats of the wolf-packs were stripped out, relatively simple but efficient, and as alike and impersonal as peas in a pod.

H.M. Submarine *Tempest* as she was commissioned was one of the newest class of large boats introduced shortly before the war. One, the *Thetis*, became famous by failing to surface on her trials in Liverpool Bay. Despite valiant efforts by those on board and the rescuers, the majority of her large complement of naval crew and dockyard specialists were lost. She was eventually raised, refitted and served in the war under the name of *Thunderbolt*. Of 1090 tons displacement, with the largest torpedo armament of any submarine then in service and a four-inch gun on a platform just forward of the conning tower, *Tempest* was commodious and comfortable. The later 'A's and more recently the 'O's are cramped by comparison, partly because of all the technical marvels that have been added and the demands these make on space and manning.

My captain was lieutenant-commander W. A. K. N. Cavaye R.N., a man of considerable experience and, by the standards of the rapidly developing submarine service, 'old' – that is to say he was over thirty. His name was Charles Cavaye and his nickname for some unknown reason was 'Crow'. In our wardroom he was referred to, in his absence only, as 'the old crow'.

Birkenhead was a noisy, dirty place, affected by nightly air raids on Liverpool, some of them fierce. We lodged in the scruffy Royal Rock Hotel at Rockferry. It was all hard work and living off fish and chips and beer in the locality of the shipyard. Work went on night and day and more crew turned up; stores were put aboard, but as yet no torpedoes or ammunition.

After a hectic few weeks we set off, flying the red ensign because *Tempest* had not yet been 'accepted' from the builders and with a number of dockyard people on board, to do our acceptance trials at Dunoon in the Firth of Clyde. Then, the boat being ours, we had a couple of weeks of intensive exercises, gun drill on the torpedo range, a deep dive to twice our normal maximum depth which was a great deal deeper than poor old H. 32 could have managed, and a rather novel trial, the purpose of which we were yet to appreciate, of steaming down and then up the Irish Sea with our ballast tanks nearly full of water so that we were 'trimmed-down', that is to say we had only just got positive buoyancy and the bow wave was round the gun platform rather than in the proper place. This was a wet experience for those on the bridge. Finally, on Saturday 1 January 1942, we sailed for Gibraltar and the Med.

On passing Ailsa Craig I ceremoniously if not over-seriously threw my razor overboard and decided to grow a beard, not to be shaved off until I returned home.

We had an uneventful trip to Gibraltar. The only personal fright, which turned into an unforgettable memory, was being 'attacked' on the surface by night off the Portuguese coast by a large school of dolphins making a phosphorescent firework display of mammoth proportions.

Gibraltar was in a highly nervous state and nightly panics occurred over the presence, sometimes real and sometimes not, in the outer anchorage of one-man underwater devices working from Algeciras. We were berthed alongside the depot ship *Maidstone* in the inner harbour. One night there was an alert because a one-man submarine or mine-laying submersible device was thought to have got into the harbour itself. At that moment there was a cocktail party going on in the *Maidstone*'s wardroom for the officers of the submarines and their escort vessels then in harbour. The alert was of the most serious kind, which meant that we had to shove off with whatever part of the crew was duty watch on board and proceed out of the danger area until recalled. It was dark. There was a great deal of jostling. Practically every craft in the harbour was in motion and little depth charges designed to bring the intrepid raiders to the surface were being lavishly dropped, making a clanging din in the hull of a submarine even on the surface. The cocktail party had had its effect and some of the manoeuvres were hair-raising and might well have caused more damage than the enemy. Two hours or so later we returned alongside *Maidstone*, soberer and wiser men. As far as I know that alert was a false one, but two armed trawlers were blown up in berths quite close to us soon after.

From Gibraltar *Tempest* was sent to Malta with her ballast tanks full of aviation spirit, and laden with spare parts ultimately destined for the submarines in Alexandria. Now we realized the import of the Irish Sea trials. On the surface we were permanently in the trimmed-down state with most of the casing under water; when dived the fuel in the ballast tanks was lighter than water and therefore gave us excess buoyancy and attendant problems of depth keeping. We had no trouble from the enemy until diving through the minefields between Sicily and Malta. There we experienced that classic submarine drama of hearing the scraping of mine mooring-wires along the hull and praying that they would not get snagged and so bring the mine down to touch us. This happened twice, and I am grateful that it did not happen a third time.

Surfacing to make our way by night in to Malta we were treated to a view of Valetta under bombardment from the air and had to wait outside for things to cool down before entering harbour. Our short stay was less than peaceful. We could only be alongside on the surface at night; every morning we had to have a duty crew on board and lie dived on the bottom of the creek to avoid air reconnaissance. Every night there were air raids from Sicily.

Once we had discharged the fuel and had gone to the submarine base at Fort St Angelo in Lazaretto Creek, we expected to be sent on to Alexandria to make it our new base. However, it was not to be. The two battleships *Queen Elizabeth* and *Warspite*, which had been damaged by Italian two-man submersibles in Alexandria, were to be moved out of the Med to the U.S.A. for repair. A massive plan for this move was made and every available ship in the fleet was deployed to help ensure their safe conduct.

At short notice we were ordered on the night of 10 February to take up a patrol line in the mouth of the Gulf of Taranto. Our object was to blockade that important port and prevent the Italian fleet from coming out and interfering with the necessarily slow westward movement of the limping battleships. The following night we had a fire in the forward torpedo compartment; a rating had left his wet oilskin to dry on one of the electric heaters which were used to combat the condensation. The fire was quickly put out but not before it had damaged the Asdic gear beyond repair. From then on the only means of detecting the enemy when we were dived was by the obsolescent hydrophones.

Our patrol line ran roughly north and south about twenty-five miles off Cape Alice in very deep water. Two U class boats *Una* and *Upright* were deployed on parallel lines some ten miles either side of us.

On 12 February, in the morning, while going north dived on our line we sighted a medium-sized tanker on our port side, unescorted and heading south. We immediately prepared to attack but in good time recognized it from a signal we had received about a tanker on some international protected mission which was to be given safe passage from Taranto to Genoa. The captain broke off the attack and we went deep. Not long afterwards we heard two explosions and after an appropriate pause came up to periscope depth to see the tanker obviously damaged and in a bad way, though not sinking.

Realizing that the situation was capable of misunderstanding, to say the least, 'Crow' decided to withdraw to the south, stay dived until nightfall, then to approach again cautiously on the surface in the hope that a useful target or targets might have come out from Taranto to rescue or take revenge for the tanker.

After dark we surfaced and started charging while moving steadily northwards again. The night was moonlit with a good deal of quick-moving cloud in a fresh north-westerly wind, and shortly after 2200 we came in sight of a glow of light round the wounded tanker and closed cautiously to investigate. I had just come on to the bridge to join the captain and relieve the sub-lieutenant as officer of the watch when suddenly out of a dark patch under a cloud we saw the bow wave of a ship approaching at high speed. We dived at once and thought we were safely down when the first pattern of depth charges exploded uncomfortably close.

We knew we had been seen and were to be hunted. What we did not know at that date was that enemy vessels in the Mediterranean had Asdics. Whether their first sighting of us on the surface was visual or by other means I do not know, but once they had found us they certainly managed to stay 'locked on'.

The first pattern of depth charges came almost at once while we were still on our way down to the depth of 150 feet which the captain had ordered. It was disastrously close. All the lights went out and many instruments throughout the boat were shattered, the hydrophones were put out of action, the fore-planes damaged and one of the propeller shafts was out of true and instead of turning noiselessly was making a loud knocking sound. The explosion had forced us down almost out of control to 350 feet, which was near our maximum permitted depth, but the coxswain and second coxswain, by superhuman efforts with their hydroplane wheels, managed to level the boat and slowly brought her back to 150 feet. The emergency lighting from such lamps as remained unbroken was barely adequate.

We soon realized that we were being hunted by a destroyer or frigate. The stalking went on relentlessly. We went into full silent routine, doubled and redoubled on our tracks, but their 'pingers' always found us. However, they did not drop any more depth charges for several hours. We could not sit motionless on the bottom because of the depth (over 2,000 fathoms), and we obviously became an easier and easier target as the knocking of the propeller shaft became more insistent.

Just when we thought that perhaps after all our hunter had lost his quarry, he came right over us and dropped another pattern as accurate as the first. From then on the depth-charging was remorseless, and though he never scored a direct hit we had a pattern within yards of us every ten or fifteen minutes for the next three hours.

All gauges first became unreliable and eventually gave up. The gyro-compass went off the board fairly early on, the magnetic compasses pointed in all directions, and the interior of the boat began to disintegrate from repeated shock treatment. Through all this the crew behaved impeccably.

My navigational plot became impossible to keep so I filled in the lulls between attacks by lying in my bunk, which was in the alleyway near the control room, reading H. G. Wells's *Joan and Peter*, a novel which to this day I have never finished. We altered course after every pattern, but from an unknown to an equally unknowable course. We did not dare to use much speed so our position must have been almost stationary in relation to the land; currents were negligible.

Finally, the main battery gave in. There were by now numerous valve leaks and the battery cases had cracked; their rubber sheaths were also presumably ruptured because chlorine began first to seep and then to pour into the boat. 'Crow' Cavaye gave what was, and is still in my opinion, the only order he could have given. Since escape for the boat itself was patently impossible and bottoming to let the enemy tire of the hunt out of the question, he decided to surface and engage the enemy with the gun. We prepared to surface, uncertain of our depth, whether we had enough compressed air left to get us up, which way we were facing, and what was waiting for us above.

As it turned out we were not as deep as we thought and we surfaced quickly. The gun was manned but the frigate was confidently placed on our quarter and the gun on the forward casing, with the bridge behind it, could not be brought to bear much abaft the beam.

It was about 11 a.m. on the morning of Friday 13 February, the weather was cold and rough, the attacking vessel started to close from astern with the apparent intention of ramming or boarding, and opened fire with machine-guns. The captain gave the order to abandon ship. The crew, wearing Davis Escape equipment which they had donned below to combat the chlorine from the batteries, came on deck and jumped from the after casing in orderly fashion. The frigate broke off its immediate attack but stood by. When only the officers and the signalman and coxswain were left on board the confidential books were ditched in their weighted bag, the foreplanes put 'hard-a-dive', the motors grouped up, the fore and after hatches opened and the ballast tanks flooded with the intention of driving the boat down head-first. The standard demolition charge situated in the forward torpedo compartment was reported as fused to detonate some minutes later, and then the submarine was abandoned by all, the captain last.

She did not sink as quickly as expected. In fact the fore-planes were damaged and jammed 'hard-a-rise' and the boat steamed off over the swimmers' horizon, sinking by the stern but held up by the fore-planes and her motion through the water. The demolition charge did not go off either, for what reason I do not know.

The Italians raced off in pursuit, and I believe, from what they told me later, succeeded in boarding. They tried to take *Tempest* in tow but she sank despite their efforts. Our crew were left strung out in a line over several hundred yards, perhaps as much as half a mile. The water was as cold as the Mediterranean can be in winter and the crew exhausted after some eight hours of bombardment, decreasing oxygen and finally the chlorine. The escape equipment, designed to bring one up to the surface from a submarine or the sea-bed, was not an ideal lifebelt when on the surface, and in many cases the crew had over-inflated the breathing bags so that they burst and they and the oxygen cylinders became dead weights round the men's necks.

I saw several about me drown, including the captain and the sub-lieutenant. I managed to keep buoyant by presenting my back to the breaking waves and half-floating, half-swimming. After a while one of the stokers and I took the leading signalman – who, as far as I know, was the only man not wearing escape equipment –

between us and we three abreast, with arms interlaced, backed the waves and concentrated on keeping afloat. Strangely, although there was no evident hope of rescue and we were at least twenty-five miles off the beach, I had no doubt that I would survive.

After a considerable time, perhaps two or three hours, the frigate hove intermittently into view over the tops of the waves. She approached closer, stopped, lowered a whaler and started to pick up survivors. The signalman swam to the whaler. The whaler's crew made that curious Italian gesture for 'come on' (a downward flick of the fingers with the palm towards the person signalled) which looks to us like 'stay away', and the stoker and I trod water. The whaler picked up some more people and the frigate came close to us with a scrambling net over the side. The last thing I remember for a time was grasping the net.

The next was coming to in the forward mess deck of the frigate. All twenty-three of the survivors of the crew of sixty-two were in bunks with blankets, warm drinks, brandy and biscuits. Part of the Italian crew, though as I recollect no officers, hovered about in a friendly way. Some of the Italians spoke English and began to ask questions of our survivors, who were rather over-excited by their experiences. The Italians did not at that point know anyone's rank or rating since we had all been dressed in submarine sweaters or shirts and trousers without badges of rank. A quick reminder to the effect that nothing was to be given away other than 'name, number, rank or rating' was enough.

An Italian asked one of our crew, a cheerful cockney stoker, what the name of our submarine was. He correctly said: 'I'm not going to tell you, but what's the name of this f...ing ship then?' The Italian gave it as *Circe*, pronounced with both 'c's as 'ch'. 'Blimey, fancy being sunk by the f...ing Churchill!' The *Tempest* crew and the Italians who understood laughed quite naturally, but by then two small men in a different uniform had come, unnoticed, into the mess deck. 'Churchill *schweinhund*!' exclaimed one of them and spat loudly and liquidly. They both clicked heels and retired. It was then we realized that German Asdics and operators, as well as depth charges, had been supplied to the Italian Navy.

The Italian torpedo boat *Circe* sank four British submarines: the *Grampus* in 1940, the *Union* in 1941, and, with the help of her German equipment, *Tempest* and ten days later *P. 38* in 1942.

We were landed at the Naval base at Taranto and admitted to the Naval hospital where we were well treated. Each of the three officers, the first lieutenant, the chief engineer and myself, had a room to himself in a small block that was adequately but discreetly guarded. We ate in a dining room furnished in mess style, waited on by Italian mess waiters in white jackets, served with good food and regular though not excessive – we were after all supposed to be invalids – amounts of wine. We were allowed daily visits to the ratings, who were equally well treated in accordance with their rank. We were kitted out by the local equivalent of the Gieves representative in facsimile Royal Naval uniforms and caps of superior cloth and workmanship but rather un-English cut, for which our accounts in the pay credited to us under the Geneva Convention rules were duly debited!

We were interrogated separately in a half-hearted way by an Italian of commander's rank speaking near-perfect English. He began by saying that he did not expect me to reveal secrets. He then went on to lighter matters and, knowing that I was R.N.S.V.R., asked me about my pre-war yachting and ocean racing experience. He asked if I had been on the last Fastnet race and then enquired if I knew Uffa Fox. I said I had an acquaintance with him and had actually last seen him at the end of the Fastnet in a state of some inebriation, stark naked and waving a golf-club, chasing the secretary of the Royal Western Yacht Club up the stairs. As I recall it that was the end of my interrogation.

After some three weeks of comparatively blissful hospital life we were told: 'For you the war has ended, you are lucky. You will go to a pleasant camp in a villa by a lake where you will be able to swim and play tennis.' We were then transferred to the less than tender care of the Italian army at a hell-camp near Bari and a whole new experience began.

SIX

In the bag

My parents received a telegram from the Admiralty to say that I was 'missing presumed lost'. My father, so my mother said, was stamping up and down their bedroom saying that he didn't believe it when the telephone rang. The caller was Diana's mother. Though not a habitual listener to that station she had by some chance tuned in to the Vatican radio and had heard them read out a list of the survivors from *Tempest*. It was this news that she gave my parents just minutes after the arrival of the telegram.

We three officers were now to go to one camp, the twenty petty officers and ratings to another. We were assured that we should be well treated and that there would be regular deliveries of Red Cross parcels, containing soap, butter, tinned meat and other luxuries which the Italians themselves were not getting.

Dressed in our new uniforms of excellent doe-skin cloth we three, under armed guard and in the charge of an Italian officer, were driven in two taxis to the station and put into a first-class carriage with a sentry on each door. Civilian passengers passing down the corridor asked our escort our nationality. On hearing that we were *inglesi*, and not *tedeschi*, several of them offered us cigarettes and wished us *buona fortuna*. Why they thought that Germans might have been travelling under guard I never found out, but they clearly did not like their allies.

Not knowing our destination we imagined that we were being taken to a camp in the north of Italy, but after a journey of only a couple of hours we were decanted at Bari on the Adriatic coast in the south-east of the peninsula. I have been to Bari a good many times since but the impression of that first afternoon remains the same – the heat, the dust and the diminutive stature of the local populace. I am not tall, yet I felt the sort of sensation Gulliver must have had amongst the Lilliputians. Our polite escort took us to the guardroom in a waiting room at the station and formally handed us over to the military police, the *carabinieri*. That was the end of the politeness.

The kitting out in Taranto had included not only a uniform suit and cap but a greatcoat and an adequate supply of shirts, socks and underpants. Each of us also had a suitcase. The *carabinieri* officer spoke no English and I had only basic Italian, having spent two or three weeks on holiday in Italy, mostly in Capri, when I was twenty-one. He made himself quite clear, however. We were to be marched under escort to our camp some two or three kilometres away; no, there was no transport provided, we must carry our own luggage; *but*, if we had the wherewithal to pay, we could go in one of the horse-drawn cabs – *carozze* – which stood outside the station; our guards would be glad of the ride too. Yes, he would accept the lira notes with which we had been provided in the hospital. We had just about enough between us to pay the exorbitant sum demanded. We did not want to arrive at our 'beautiful villa camp beside a lake' looking tired and disreputable. What is more a torrential rain storm was turning the dust into gluey mud and our shoes had been well polished by the hospital orderlies. So in we climbed, the three of us jammed together, two armed guards inside with us and the senior guard on top with the driver under a huge green umbrella. The poor wretched horse which, despite its bells and tassels, didn't look capable of pulling anything was flogged into unwilling motion by the driver and off we went.

As we proceeded, the surroundings became more and more un-promising. The suburbs were insalubrious to put it mildly and we looked in vain for a lake. Eventually down a narrow, unpaved, rutted and muddy lane, we stopped before an untidy but vicious barbed-wire fence, more of a mad entanglement than anything else, in which was a gate and a guardhouse. Campo 75 consisted of three or four wooden army huts, some smaller buildings and an area of trodden earth become slimy mud in the downpour.

We disembarked, were handed over once again – this time to some singularly scruffy and disgruntled-looking soldiery – and herded to one of the huts. The door was opened and we were bundled inside. The hut was full of iron beds of the most primitive kind, with only a few inches to spare between each; there was a long trestle table down the middle surrounded by benches, and no other furniture. Most of the beds were occupied by British Army officers, wearing what was left of battledress. A few of them were Sikhs in turbans. There was a general air of despair. The inmates looked with amazement at the three smartly dressed Naval officers with suitcases who had suddenly arrived in their midst. We found three beds and began to take stock.

The 'ablutions', we were told, were in a nearby building. When it was not raining most of the prisoners lay or sat against the outside walls of the hut. There were four roll-calls a day when we had to fall in and be counted outside, and our beds were inspected twice nightly. Rations were miserable, there were no Red Cross parcels, no comforts, no recreation, no books, and though there was a constant trickle of arrival and departure no one seemed to know how long they would be there or where they were destined to go. The commandant was a sadistic bully, many men were lousy, the bedding was never changed.

All in all the Sikhs seemed to manage best. They had several advantages, in that they didn't miss smoking or drinking, they didn't seem to mind a diet which consisted of two identical meals a day brought in and dumped on the tables to be doled out with meticulous fairness by the prisoners themselves, and shortage of loo paper didn't bother them because they were in the habit of using water and one hand, the other hand only being used for eating. Their nightly intoning of their holy offices and the elaborate ceremony of unwinding and rewinding their turbans from day to night wear without at any time leaving the head uncovered, as well as the tying up of their beards and moustaches in white linen bandages before sleeping, caused a certain amount of irritation to their less ritualistic neighbours, but there is no doubt that their morale was as high as their standards – in sharp contrast to the British officer of the Indian Army who occupied the next bed to mine. He had never been without a batman before and was incapable of, or just plain unwilling to try, doing anything for himself. He hadn't washed, he said, since he had been taken in the desert several weeks ago and didn't intend to until he got to a decent bath with real soap; when he pulled back his blanket in the morning his bed was so full of leaping fleas that it looked like the top of a glass of Eno's fruit salts in full effervescence.

The meals consisted of a bowl of thin soup with either a lump or two of nearly raw cauliflower floating in it or four or five inch-long pieces of large-diameter pasta made from some flour that gave them the appearance and taste of coarse brown cardboard. A small army-issue roll of 100 grams of coarse gritty bread, an orange or mandarin, and a mug of coffee substitute – made, we were told, of acorns and sweetened with some sort of saccharine – completed the feast. Hunger led to my eating the citrus fruits whole, skin, pith and pips as well as the juicy part. I developed such a taste for the zest that I now enjoy the peel more than the middle, and particularly like the bitter taste of the pips. We also got five cigarettes a day: called *Milits*, they came in little blue-paper packets rather like old-fashioned Woodbines. They were standard issue to the Italian Army, hence their name, but we were all convinced they were made of dried millet. They became currency, exchangeable for oranges or used for gambling.

This diet quickly sapped one's strength. We three arrived fresh and well, whereas most of the soldiers were already weak and dispirited before they got there. Two of them did make a break for it, however. Early one morning they found a way through the wire but were quickly picked up and brought back into camp. The *comandante* made us all fall in and had the two men marched before him by a posse of the miserable Italian soldiery with fixed bayonets. The order was given for the guard to load their rifles. One poor wight undid the ammunition pouch on his equipment to get the clip of bullets but unfortunately for him produced a packet of *Milits* by mistake. The *comandante* let out several hysterical screams and the man was despatched to the guardroom. Whether it was this incident that further exasperated the *colonnello*, I don't know. He next ordered the two escapers at the point of the now loaded rifles to demonstrate exactly where and how they had got through the wire. I discovered from some of their friends afterwards that they did not want to indicate the hole they had found in case some others could use it. Instead they approached the wire in one corner and started to climb through it as best they could. They became totally stuck and the enraged *comandante* ordered his troops to fire. Obviously shocked and unwilling, they hesitated, only to be screamed at again. Then they fired and killed our two fellow-prisoners before our eyes. We were herded back to our huts and locked in for the rest of the day. The two men were accounted for as having been killed trying to escape – as would anyone else who tried it, said the *comandante*, through an interpreter at the next roll-call. He got his deserts, however. I believe he was one of very few to be tried, convicted and executed after the fall of Italy.

After two or three weeks I suffered a recurrence of the tonsillitis which was apt to hit me whenever I became overtired or run-down. This occurred always at awkward times, particularly when I was acting. The fashion in my youth was against tonsillectomy and I did not have mine removed until I was in my early forties. Since then I have never even had a sore throat and wish that I had been spared the agonizing attacks from an earlier age. This latest attack struck just as word came that I and a few others, including my two shipmates, were to be moved to a 'permanent' camp, Bari being considered only suitable for transit.

No horse-cab this time; we were marched to the station, made to wait what seemed hours in great discomfort, and bundled into a train with wooden benches and the doors and windows tightly locked. By now I was feeling really ill. I had a high fever and could not speak or eat. It was late March and very hot. At Rome we changed trains and guards and were allowed under escort to go to the loo. I remember, through the haze of my fever, the shock I got when the woman attendant in that station lavatory issued me with three sheets of bumf and sat on her stool and watched me through the door kept open by my guard. From Rome we went to Arezzo and had another dreadful wait in a filthy, hot and airless waiting-room for the army lorry to come to take us to our new camp. By the time I got there I really thought I was going to die, and indeed might well have done so because I had developed a full quinsy and could barely breathe. I was rushed to the sick bay and an Italian doctor thrust a wooden spatula down my throat, causing me great pain but doing little else. There were two doctor prisoners there, however, and they nursed me and dosed me through the next day. The following night I had a fit of retching and disgorged a disgusting lump of infected material. This apparently did the trick and I soon recovered.

I found myself in Campo 38 in a house on the top of a fairy-tale hill at Poppi in Tuscany. The house was the summer residence of an order of nuns, from Florence I believe, who were remaining in their winter quarters. It was plainly furnished but clean and spacious and we were only four or six to a largish room. My fellow prisoners this time, apart from the few who had come with me from Bari, were all New Zealanders. Some fifty or so as memory serves, they were all of the same unit and had come from New Zealand to fight in the North African desert. None of them except one who had been a professional tennis player had ever been in Europe, still less England which they nevertheless constantly referred to as home.

They were avid for information; every evening groups of them gathered around to hear the most simple facts about the 'sophisticated' life of London. One of them told me that his greatest dream was to go out to dinner and a theatre. 'But surely,' I said, 'you can do that in Auckland?' 'No,' he replied. 'First there's very little theatre there and never seems to be any when I get to town, and second we don't have dinner in the evening, we only have high tea.'

99

If this camp was not the 'villa by the lake etc.' that we had been promised, it was quite civilized. Red Cross parcels appeared, not one per man per week which was the aim but, with reasonable regularity, one between four per week. Containing Klim powdered milk, sugar, cheese, tomato purée, soups, Ovaltine, cocoa, tea and a variety of 'goodies' including hotel-sized tablets of real soap, they provided us with necessary vitamins and a great deal of interest. The division into four parts was here, and in my next camp, a ritual conducted with strict impartiality. Anything once opened had to be consumed fairly rapidly; there were no refrigerators and not much in the way of storage space except the cardboard boxes themselves. To divide a tin of butter into four involved the following procedure: 1. Open the tin with the key provided on the side (a crucial operation needing concentration and skill since we had no alternative tool if, as often happened, the key broke). 2. Turn the butter out on to a plate belonging to one of the four – we took it in turns to provide the plate as this offered the bonus of a slight residue. 3. Cut the cards (we not only managed to get a few packs from the Italians but we made our own out of Red Cross cardboard boxes and packaging) to decide who should divide the lump of butter into four as far as possible equal parts. 4. Cut the cards again or draw straw lots to decide the order of precedence for selecting whichever of the four portions looked fractionally bigger. 5. Draw again to decide who got the empty tin, itself a valuable commodity. Variations on this basic procedure were followed for everything in the parcel; even the cardboard box itself was either carefully divided or drawn for.

At Poppi there was another attempt at escape. Standing as the house did on a hill, it was surrounded first by a wall and previously well-cultivated kitchen garden, then by a steeply terraced vineyard. As it was early spring, the vineyard was being turned over by pairs of big white oxen drawing a primitive single-furrow plough and controlled by a beefy lady uttering strange cries. The wall had barbed wire on it and there was a sentry box at each corner with searchlights that swept around at irregular intervals. Three of the New Zealanders managed to conceal themselves in the garden before we were locked in for the night, having planted dummies in their beds to deceive those counting heads on pillows, but the morning roll-call was three short and the alarm was given by ringing the chapel bell loud and long. The three had succeeded in climbing the wall and negotiating the wire, but it had taken them a long time and at daylight they had gone to ground in the vineyard.

They were ill-prepared for escape, having only the battle dresses that were normal prison wear, and no faked papers or maps, nor much in the way of rations. The peasants who might have helped, and on whom the escapers were banking, could and would do nothing once the alarm had been given. Hiding under a terrace wall the three were faced by two snorting oxen, a plough and a large lady, and decided to call it a day. Back in camp they were put in a separate room and were only allowed to be visited by their own senior officer with an interpreter present. They were not otherwise ill-treated, however, and were transferred to one of the high-security camps which were rapidly becoming full of similarly adventurous and determined fellows.

In mid-May, after I had been there just a month, the authorities decided that they had not meant to send a few miscellaneous Englishmen to join the Kiwis and we were moved once more. Though news was hard to come by we were getting the message that things were going less well for the Axis in Africa and we lived in constant dread that we should be moved further and further north, eventually perhaps to camps in Germany. Consequently I was surprised to find myself once again at Arezzo station and heading south, no change of train in Rome or Naples, on through Battipaglia and then, just as dawn was breaking, turned out at the little station of Padula. It was wonderful country again, bleached and barren after the green hills of Tuscany but with a marvellous clean and classical light, the little hill villages dotted around a central plain. A march of a kilometre or so with baggage on a cart behind and I found myself at the imposing gate of a vast and beautiful building, the Certosa di Padula. This important Carthusian monastery had become *Campo Concentramento di Prigonieri di Guerra Numero Trenta Cinque*.

The cloisters, said to be the biggest in the world being some quarter of a mile round, had opening off them on ground level a number of separate residences for its original senior and wealthy inmates; we called them 'quarters'. Each of these consisted of an entrance hall, two large rooms and a long passage leading to a loo. Each quarter also had a small walled garden entered by a flight of stairs from a terrace outside the living-rooms and further enclosed by the wall of the next quarter on one side and the passage and loo on the other, with a high wall at the end which was part of the main wall of the building. Beyond this wall were the fields of the monastery, themselves surrounded at a greater distance by the boundary wall of the whole estate. The level of the ground in the garden was considerably higher than the surrounding fields so that what was a three-metre wall from inside was at least another couple of metres higher on the outside. The gardens were irrigated by a system of pipes and channels in the outer wall fed with water from a spring in the hills behind the village.

The monks who originally occupied these quarters were obviously prepared for clandestine visitors as there was a small door and a flight of steps from each garden to the greater world outside. When it was turned into a prison the doors were bricked up, the garden walls provided with barbed-wire tops, and sentry boxes with searchlights provided at frequent intervals round the perimeter, which was marked by more barbed wire.

Above the cloistered walk was an ambulatory, a covered walk for bad weather with big windows opening on to the central courtyard. The main staircase reaching this from one corner of the cloister was a fine marble spiral one with open windows giving a view of the countryside; below this a barbed-wire enclosure the size of a football field was provided for exercise. No windows either on the ground floor or in the ambulatory looked on to the outside world. The only ones that did were tiny squares cut in the loos from which, by gripping the sill and hauling oneself up from the non-existent seat, one could look out of the unglazed barred window. Straight ahead was a field of maize standing some ten metres away from the wall; inset into the edge of the maize was a continuous barbed-wire fence and one of the sentry boxes. Somehow, whenever I looked out, it always seemed to be occupied by the same little soldier busy masturbating before the sergeant came round again.

The ambulatory was made into four dormitories which we called 'wings'. There were some five hundred officers in the camp, a mixed bag from all the services with the Army in the majority and the Navy and R.A.F. about equally represented. There were also some fifty other ranks who acted as mess orderlies and worked in the kitchen. These were volunteers, as I understood it, who had decided that they would rather work in the officers' camp than do the less menial but more boring work that was meted out to them in the men's camps. They also got a bit of extra money and some of them no doubt felt that their chances of escape might be better.

Discipline amongst ourselves was good. The camp was well run by a committee of the three senior officers of each service, under the overall command of the senior British officer, Brigadier Mountain. The more junior officers were billeted in the four 'wings', each under the charge of a 'wing-commander', and the more senior in the 'quarters' with some ten or twelve officers to each. I apparently just qualified for a quarter and was pleased to be there.

Meals were taken in two or three sittings in the big refectory, a fine room which we also used as a theatre. It opened directly off the cloister on the south side. Beside it the old kitchens with their huge wood-fired coppers and stores were brought back into use for us; the walls were tiled in a virulent yellow-and-green checked pattern which was said to be efficacious in keeping out unwanted flies and wasps. Next to the kitchens were rooms fitted up for mass showers, with twenty nozzles in the ceiling controlled by a guard who could be sadistic in the sudden change from hot to cold or vice versa.

Food was less good and plentiful than in Poppi but still a lot better than Bari. The all-important Red Cross parcels arrived in big loads but spasmodically and we imposed our own rationing system, which sometimes meant divisions into portions even more scrupulously meted out than in Poppi. A small proportion of the parcels were 'medical', designed for the weak and feeble with things like calves-feet jelly, beef tea and vitamins such as Bemax. These were handed over to the doctors amongst us to administer as needed. The only mishandling, if that is the word, of these that I recall came about when a certain prisoner, thought to be short of Vitamin B was put on a crash course of Bemax. The unfortunate result was acute discomfort and inflammation of the penis brought about by having a permanent and relentless erection in contact with rough prison blankets. A reduction of the dosage brought relief in more ways than one.

When I got there the only theatrical entertainment being organized was a camp concert – 'camp' in both senses – in which such inmates as could remember any of the words strove to emulate the music-hall entertainers of the day, particularly of course the Crazy Gang and Max Miller. Dressing up as best they could with Klim tin lids as brassières, they cavorted about in clumsy imitation of the Tiller Girls.

Some of us thought we ought to go for more sophisticated theatrical enterprises. The first improvement I made was to direct a mixed bill of scenes from Shakespeare, all chosen for male parts only, in which I performed Richard in *Richard III* and Bottom in the play scene from *A Midsummer Night's Dream*. Two distantly related Johnstons – Johnny of the Indian Army and Gordon of the 60th Rifles, the first as author and lyricist, the second as composer –

set to work on a musical comedy entitled *Be Brazen* which I was to direct. The opening chorus began: 'At seventeen Clover Street, Right next door to Dover Street . . .' which will give some idea of the style and location of the piece. In the event it was a huge success. A small charge was made for tickets, and by the last performance the black-market price was twelve times its face value; there was even talk of putting the show on in London for charity when we got back.

Our ideas were ambitious and involved the purchase with camp funds, which were a levy on everyone's pay, of large quantities of dress materials, electrical flex, bulbs, bulb holders and plugs, all of which we were allowed to have for the purpose of improving the stage and lighting effects in the refectory. The camp itself was supplied with a rudimentary sort of electric lighting coming from a generator in the village above and failing every time there was one of the not infrequent thunderstorms. It was direct current run on two wires loosely attached to the walls and with switches that worked, when they did, in the opposite way from normal. The searchlights on the perimeter were run from army generators and were not susceptible to failure from local causes.

Escape was never far from the minds of some of us, and it was decided to make a tunnel from the garden of our quarter no. 5 out into the maize field at the back of the sentry box. We were already gardening hard in the little enclosure with seed bought through the extremely pro-British interpreter. (He had worked as a waiter in England and dreamt of retiring there, after 'we' had won the war, to open a restaurant to which naturally all his distinguished friends, ex-prisoners-of-war, would flock.)

The escape scheme involved making a tray about three feet by two, six or eight inches deep, out of wood purloined from the kitchens and elsewhere. This was filled with soil and buried just below the surface of the garden, up against the side wall and some distance back from the end wall. Under it a manhole was excavated, shored up with anything that could be found, and from this a tunnel, just big enough for a man to wriggle along on his stomach, was begun at an angle calculated to take it below the foundations of the end wall, after which it would level out and go under the barbed wire into the maize field. The tray was kept planted with tomatoes and was lifted out immediately after roll-call, when a man went down. Roll-calls were at fixed times and it was possible to get the man out, put the tray back, cover the traces and have everyone on parade before his absence would be noted. There was, however, the danger of a spot check between roll-calls, and for this reason there were always two or three prisoners busily at work in the garden ready to take immediate action should one of the Italians enter the quarter.

As an extra activity we kept rabbits on the terrace from which access to the garden was gained. Discussion of their ailments and breeding capacity with any visiting Italian was calculated to give the gardeners enough time to get the tray in position and cover up. Only once did this actually happen; the discussion revolved round the fact that the enormous rabbit we thought to be the buck had just produced a litter and the buck was therefore the diminutive frightened object at the other end of the cage – a situation which led to much joking to the Italian taste. The gardeners hastily clapped the tray over the miner in his narrow, unventilated and unlit burrow. The jokes went on and on, the visiting Italians at last departed with aching sides, no doubt to regale colleagues with the success of their racy remarks with the normally po-faced English. When the immolated miner was at last recovered he had to have artificial respiration to get him on parade in time for the next roll-call.

Digging in this tunnel was slow, mostly done just in front of the digger's face with a tablespoon; the tin he thus laboriously filled was passed back between his legs to a gardener by the manhole, who then scattered the earth as casually as possible. By the time the outside wall was reached it was clear that the tunnel was too small and not deep enough. Although a primitive pair of bellows had been constructed to pump air down to the worker through a tube made of old tins, it had become impossible to stay at the face for more than a few minutes at a time.

Somehow the game was given away. How they thought of it we never knew but one day an Italian search party appeared and a spot roll-call was made. They entered our quarter with spades and quickly discovered the lid and what was beneath. We were given a minor punishment in the temporary removal of some privileges and extra roll-calls, and thereafter the gardens were gone over daily with long steel probes. No one had escaped, the Italians' honour and reputation had not been put in jeopardy and no higher authority had to be called in, so the matter was soon glossed over.

Roll-calls involved falling in, in squads of not more than fifty, under the arcades of the cloister. The nominal roll was called by a British officer, then two soldiers counted each group, one watching while the other walked backwards and forwards between the lines of prisoners, solemnly counting off each one. The soldiers counting carried their rifles with fixed bayonets slung on their backs, the tip of the short blade being just above their head which was in turn generally rather less high than ours. A favourite trick was to write some schoolboy-like derogatory remark on a piece of paper and impale it on the bayonet point as the soldier went by without any of them realizing where it came from. The Italians were understandably annoyed and stamped out the practice by keeping the squad concerned on parade for another hour or two.

Amongst the Red Cross comforts and the occasional personal parcel from home were a number of hand-knitted garments, such as mittens, scarves and sweaters; these were sometimes of a size or shape that was not entirely to the liking of the recipients. Our Senior Naval Officer was adept at knitting and started a class to teach others. Wooden knitting needles were available and wool was obtained from unravelling worn-out garments. One day, to the fury of the camp commandant, the Naval knitting class went to roll-call each with a ball of wool in one breast pocket of his battle-dress and needles sticking out of the other. A good part of our roll-call time was spent 'at ease' and we all started to knit, putting the gear away whenever we were called to attention. Will Scarlett, our teacher, was summoned before the *comandante* but was able to argue that there was nothing in the Geneva Convention to prevent officers knitting while at ease and, with less truth, that it was common practice in the Royal Navy. No disrespect was implied, he said, indeed perhaps the *comandante* himself would care for a little slip-over or even a tie? After that no more was said, though the practice diminished as winter came and fingers were too cold.

Another appeal to the rules of the Geneva Convention arose over our retention of beards. The Italians decided to issue each prisoner with an identity card which included his photograph. The principal reason for this was obviously so that, if we did get out, we could be identified. To this end they demanded that all prisoners should be clean-shaven before being photographed. We refused, the Army and R.A.F. claiming that moustaches were permitted to them and the Navy that beards and moustaches, provided no part of the face was shaved, were acceptable adornments. So we kept our whiskers, knowing full well that their removal was the quickest and most effective way of assuming a disguise. Our projects for the theatre were a considerable help to the escape industry. The escapologists and the escape committee decided to make a more efficient attempt at another tunnel. Quarter no. 6 was chosen, as were a couple of dozen of those keenest on escaping. The idea was brilliantly simple. The loos at the end of the passages and against the outside walls were originally nothing more than six-inch holes in the floor which gave access to a large windowless and doorless basement beneath. The far end of the cellar directly under the hole had in early times been dug out in a deep pit into which anything dropping from the hole above would be absorbed in cool and earth-bound darkness; no doubt noisome and insalubrious enough in its day. When the near-ruined *certosa*, long since out of use for its original purpose, had been adapted as a prison camp, flushing cisterns worked on the old irrigation system for the gardens had been established over the holes, two 'foot-prints' supplied beside them and a waste-pipe run direct from the holes via a U-bend to a new but rudimentary drainage system at a shallow level all round the walls outside the perimeter. All this had been found out by our continuous exploration trips, and digs and soundings were made in order to learn exactly how the complex building worked. Night-time trips over the roofs had shown what lay beyond the area we inhabited, and careful soundings of walls and floor were equally revealing. One of the latter led us into the big cellars under the quarters.

Once again a tray was made, this time in the tiled floor of the loo passage, and cleverly camouflaged and insulated so that it sounded no different from the rest of the floor if struck. Dropping through this trap door by means of a rope ladder made of carefully hoarded string, one could reach the ample space below. Down in the corner, under the hole which now had its own connection through the wall to the new drainage system, ideal conditions existed for quick and silent digging.

The old 'long-drop' pit was found to be full of two hundred year-old monkish ordure which had matured into an odourless fibrous mass like dried peat. It could be cut into neat blocks with a knife and removed to the back of the cellar. This led down, making a four foot square wall, to below the level of the wall's massive foundations. Tunnelling under these was easy; there was no need for pit props until the hard clay ground of the field was reached. A four foot square tunnel was big enough to kneel in and wield a makeshift pickaxe. A little railway was set up on wooden rails made of battens acquired for the theatre, on which a truck carrying several bucketfuls of spoil at a time could be hauled back and forth. Electric lighting, 'borrowed' from the theatre, and the size of the tunnel together with the air space of the cellar, made ventilation less of a problem than in the earlier tunnel, but a more sophisticated pump was made and operated. Noise was of little consequence due to the thickness of the walls until near the end some yards into the field of maize, which itself would not be cut for some time yet. The spoil, what seemed like (and probably was) tons of it, was easily accommodated in the enclosed cellar. As many as six men could work at a time, two taking it in turns at the face, one working the railway, one dumping the spoil and two on watch outside. It was even found possible to cope with roll-calls occurring at short notice, so good was the drill.

Meanwhile the escape industry was growing. Cooking facilities for dealing with Red Cross parcel food were initially non-existent but some became expert at making stoves or *stufas* – at first simple braziers and then sophisticated contrivances made out of empty tins that were capable of boiling a tin of water in three minutes on the fuel provided by one end of a cardboard Red Cross parcel box. Even ovens were made. The expert craftsman was 'Fingers' Lewis, a small dark bearded Welshman from the Fleet Air Arm who was a wizard with a tin, a pair of scissors and a small hammer. His biggest effort was almost an Aga in size and efficiency. The Italians did not seem to mind this; the *stufas* were used quite openly, and only when some unappreciative souls started to break up beautiful old walnut doors and panelling in the effort to keep warm in winter did the Italians get cross. In these *stufas* iron rations of cocoa mixed with powdered biscuit and raisins were baked hard and hidden away for issue to escapers when needed.

Documents and passes were painstakingly forged, each letter being cut in cork and stamped by hand. Needles were magnetized and turned into compasses; maps were made by piecing together information gleaned from many sources or simply from memory. Clothes were altered and adapted most ingeniously.

Finally the tunnel was ready, and lots were drawn to decide the order in which the first dozen should go. It had been calculated that, with a bit of luck, twelve people could have dummies substituted in their beds to deceive the night-time checks. The twelve would be hidden in the cellar when the quarter was locked after lights out, and ten others would occupy the quarter itself. The chosen twelve would get out of the tunnel, leaving those in the quarter to make everything appear normal. If, by some miracle, the cover-up plans were successful, a further, larger party would go the second night, after which concealment would be impossible. All this worked perfectly and the twelve were despatched soon after dark.

My task was to follow the twelfth man down the tunnel, see him out, help him from inside to conceal the exit as far as possible and return to the quarter. That was as far as I ever got towards a successful escape. I did just get my head out into the field before putting strutting and boards up for the last man to cover over as best he could.

Alas, at the midnight round of the dormitories one of the dummies was discovered. The Italians went mad and turned the place inside out. At first they thought that so large a number could not possibly have left, and searched the buildings high and low; then, realizing that most of the missing men came from quarter no. 6, they broke into the cellar through the side wall and all was discovered. They did not enter the tunnel themselves, they merely took a hose and flooded it, then cemented the floor over and did the same in all the other cellars.

We never saw the escapers again but were told that they were all recaptured, mostly near by, though three did get to the coast near Bari. We always imagined that it would be possible to get to the coast somewhere, steal a fishing boat and try to reach Malta or Jugoslavia or even North Africa. In fact all the boats were closely guarded and as far as I know this plan never succeeded. The very few escapers to get out of Italy before the Allies invaded the country spoke reasonable Italian, managed to get on to trains going north and then, either bluffed their way with forged documents over the frontier to Switzerland, or jumped off the train and did the last part on foot. Once Italy began to crack under the invasion, the prisoners from Padula were loaded on to trains and taken into Austria; quite a few managed to elude the guards, however, and were sheltered by Italian civilians, until at last the advancing Allied forces retrieved them.

Those of our escapers caught near by were returned to the camp for a few days' interrogation before being sent to a higher security prison in the north – the notorious Campo Cinque, a sort of Italian Colditz near Genoa. They told our senior officer when he was allowed to see them that their interrogation had been relatively mild, the main question being whether they had had any contact with Italian civilians. The interrogators were apparently of the opinion that as it was clearly impossible to get out of Italy, the only reason to leave so comfortable a prison for the rigours of life in the countryside was a sexual one. They were convinced that the fugitives must have made a bee-line for the first woman they could get to.

Apart from a tightening up of regulations, the withholding of parcels, locking up of all theatrical equipment when not in use and a change of *comandante*, little altered in our way of life as a result of this episode.

Emboldened by the success of female impersonation in *Be Brazen* – indeed the leading 'lady' and some of the chorus girls became camp celebrities overnight – I suggested that, since Shakespeare had done his plays without women, we could now tackle a complete play. We were able to get books through the Red Cross and there was no great difficulty in coming by the classics. I kicked off with my old favourite, *Twelfth Night*. I decided to set it in Ruritania, which meant that by a judicious admixture of the uniforms of three services plus some fanciful additions in the form of epaulettes, sashes and headgear, quite a lot could be achieved.

My two dressmakers, hefty antipodeans who had worked in a fashion house in peace-time, did wonders for the women's dresses. I was lucky too in my cast. George Millar, the writer whose book *Horned Pigeon* has his own account of life in Padula, was blessed with a roseate complexion on a fair and delicate skin and extremely shapely legs, and made a wonderful Olivia. At least he did so up to the penultimate rehearsal; with my agreement he used this activity as a cover for the fact that he was about to escape. We had an understudy ready and the show went on as planned. Father Hugh Bishop, later to become Superior of the Mirfield Brethren and later still to take the bold step of 'coming out of the closet', was a dignified and mellifluous Orsino. I had a wonderful Feste in Gordon Johnston, who also set the songs to music for the production. My Aguecheek was 'Olly' somebody – the name is gone from me but the memory of his high-class inanity lingers on – and my Toby Belch was Neville Lloyd, a great motor-racing authority, now alas no longer with us. All in all *Twelfth Night* was a triumph, and all the innuendoes in Malvolio's speeches went over with an impact surely unknown since Shakespeare's own time.

We had such a mixed bag of inmates that there was always some new interest, and when things were comparatively quiet the guards, or more particularly the interpreters could be persuaded to bring in the occasional newspaper. The Red Cross provided a gramophone and classical records. Study groups were set up on all kinds of subjects and lectures given.

After the tunnel incident, the quarters were temporarily closed and the inmates dispersed to the dormitories, adding considerably to the existing congestion. I became 'wing-commander' for the one

Tea in the canteen, Glyndebourne, 1950. Left to right: M.C.,
Sena Jurinac, John Christie, Audrey Christie, Erich Kunz.

The family arrive for the Edinburgh Festival, 1953.
Left to right: M.C., Marc, Dominique, Diana, Simone.

Paris press conference, 1958. Carl Ebert speaking, flanked
by M.C. and Vittorio Gui. Oliver Messel extreme right.
Seated below: Elda Gui, Fernanda Cadoni, Ilva Ligabue,
Monica Sinclair, Sari Barabas, Graziella Sciutti.

Elegy for Young Lovers, 1961. Left to right: W. H. Auden
(Librettist), Carlos Alexander (Principal baritone),
Hans Werner Henze (Composer), M.C., Günther Rennert
(Producer), Chester Kallman (Joint librettist).

into which most of the theatrically minded made their way. Our end of it in particular became known as Greenwich Village. In those days this carried no other connotation than 'Bohemian'. Indeed at no time as a prisoner-of-war did I come upon any overt homosexuality. There was little privacy to permit any 'acts', however consenting the adults might have been, and, though there were some close friendships struck, sex as such was not an important topic – perhaps the diet was too low.

The prisoners' 'shop' varied very much in what it could supply in return for camp money. We got a small ration of terrible red wine most of the time; sometimes it was stopped as a punishment, sometimes it just ran out. Occasionally there were deliveries of a particularly sweet and sticky Marsala; once one of the interpreters whose 'uncle' made condensed milk, negotiated for us the black-market purchase of four huge wooden barrels of a turgid yellowish goo such as M. Nestlé never knew. The barrels were driven into the courtyard on a bullock cart. Three were successfully unloaded and rolled into the canteen; the fourth fell off, exploded and mingled with the dust in a huge puddle. Eager prisoners rushed out with any receptacle they could find and scooped up as much as they could. Flies and wasps arrived in myriads – we were never short of either – mosquitoes too, and ants in armies. It took several thunderstorms to wash the mess away. Just before Christmas the shop astonishingly received an enormous black-market consignment of talcum powder, which a lot of people found a welcome luxury since there was more in our surroundings to chafe than to soothe.

Wine was hoarded for Christmas, and delicacies from Red Cross parcels. Some people managed to ferment strange liquors from raisins or other dried or tinned fruit, and the Italians on Christmas night wisely suspended the usual ten o'clock curfew until after midnight and kept themselves out of the interior of the camp. Festivities began, and eventually most of the inmates were well away. There was a fancy dress parade and the whole thing culminated in a procession, singing and dancing its way round the wings. Suddenly somebody said, 'Let's have a white Christmas,' and emptied his large box of talcum powder over his neighbours. Soon the idea spread and the whole place was covered in it. This resulted in a fearful mess that took a lot of cleaning up.

Apart from Christmas the winter was cold and dreary and the heating was not much use; it consisted of just a few *La Bohème*-type wood-burning stoves with pipes out of the ill-fitting windows.

After the tunnel incident, thoughts of escape went in different directions and the escape committee had many proposals put before them. Most of these were turned down as being impractical or 'not in the public interest'; there was after all a big lobby in the camp that preferred to be on good terms with our captors, believing escape to be a near impossibility for anyone and a total impossibility for them personally.

One of the keenest would-be escapers was George Millar. George was a great individualist. Not for him the mass escape, though he was concerned in both tunnels. During the hard days and longer nights of the winter he carried out a series of exploratory trips over the roofs of the big kitchen, the refectory and the old library. This latter was out of bounds to us though some did get into it over the roofs. It was full of great leather-bound tomes rotting away behind wire-mesh doors in huge walnut bookshelves.

George established a lot of interesting facts which he kept to himself until his plan was complete enough to put to the select few of the escape committee for approval. Behind the kitchens there was a small courtyard surrounded by the old stables and domestic outbuildings which were now in use as barrack accommodation for the soldiers and guards. George found a perilous route over the rotten roofs which would allow him to get into this courtyard. The big gates in an arch in the wall which led to the road outside stood open by day with a guard on duty. The main iron gates from the outer courtyard to our cloister (over which was a Latin inscription to the effect that all who entered here renounced the world for ever) were heavily guarded and lit at night. There was no way through them for a prisoner unless he were under escort. George's idea was simple and daring. He and his three companions were to disguise themselves as Italian soldiers and, by way of the roofs and a route they had explored, to get into the guards' part of the building. Then they would just walk out of the front gate, choosing the late afternoon hour when the day and night shifts were changing and it was normal for soldiers to go casually out of the gate on their way to the village without having to show papers. The four would then make their way on foot to one of the air-strips that had been set up in the area to counter the expected Allied invasion, seize an aircraft and fly to North Africa. George was the brains and he had chosen a pilot, a radio operator and a strong and ruthless hit-man to go with him.

The uniforms were concocted from old Italian uniforms issued to prisoners with defacing grey patches on the sleeves which were ingeniously covered with black cloth to make them look like mourning patches such as were commonly worn. All went according to plan, and they were nearly through the gate when someone spotted that they were wearing the wrong boots – English boots.

After their recapture they were taken into the punishment cell near the main entrance and stripped. A message came through that they would not be returning to this camp and their personal belongings were to be taken through to them. George was a 'Greenwich Village' inhabitant and I as his wing-commander was deputed to gather up the gear he had left behind together with that of his companions and hand it over to the authorities in return for a proper receipt. I found myself in the ante-room of the punishment cell and could see through a crack in the door that the four were standing naked, with the *comandante* raving at them and hitting them between shouts with a heavy metal-bound ruler. I was given a receipt by a sergeant and hurriedly bundled away. I did not meet George again until years afterwards on a yacht in the Beaulieu River.

After *Twelfth Night* I tried my hand at producing a thriller, *I Killed the Count*, which helped to pass the time, and by early April 1943 we had got as far as the dress rehearsal of another musical comedy. This was to be bigger and better than *Be Brazen* and was put together by the same team. Unfortunately I have forgotten its name and much about it. I do remember, however, that Gordon dubbed me 'Doves-with-Everything' Caplat because of my wish for elaborate staging. (I had to wait for *Die Entführung aus dem Serail* in my last year at Glyndebourne actually to get doves on the stage in any numbers.) It was after the evening meal and before the ten o'clock curfew, when the unpleasant interpreter who had been a coal merchant in Cardiff burst in to the theatre-cum-refectory and told me that the *comandante* wanted to see me immediately. 'Go away,' I said. 'I'll come when the rehearsal is over, not before.' 'You must come now. It is very important!' 'No,' I said again, and he sat there fuming while we finished. Excitedly he led me to the office and there I was told that I and three other naval prisoners were to be repatriated and that we must be ready to leave at four o'clock next morning. Dazed, I reported back to my own senior officer.

No reason was given for our selection; it seemed to be an arbitrary decision. We were not the most senior, nor the least, we were not ill. Nobody could offer an explanation except for the fear at the back of all our minds that sooner or later we would be moved to

Germany and that this might be the first of a series of ruses to get us to 'go quietly'.

In the next few hours we were kitted up by the escape committee; that is to say we were given tissue-paper maps to aid us if we were able to get off a train or otherwise elude our guards, compasses hidden in boot heels, and some of the precious cakes made with cocoa, Ovaltine and butter from the parcels. There was no time to get any false documents even if we had known what we might need.

At 4 a.m. we presented ourselves at the main gates. Outside in the courtyard was an army truck, a surprise as it was normal for prisoners arriving or departing to be marched to the station. An officer and four guards came with us and treated us with unusual politeness. On the train we were put into a first-class compartment and to our surprise again the train set off not to the north but in an easterly direction. Incredulous though we had been when we started, we began to think we might have been told the truth. At Potenza, that Crewe of the *Mezzogiorno*, we had to change trains. We learnt that we were off to Bari, where a hospital ship awaited to waft us home. Now we became very keen not to lose our guards. Far from wishing to get away we were concerned not to be left behind.

Bari of the hideous memories of a year ago was still a transit camp, but it had been cleaned up and improved facilities greeted us everywhere. We found ourselves part of a rapidly growing collection of naval personnel – officers and men drawn from camps all over Italy, all equally bemused by their sudden change in fortune. The ship, we were told, was in the harbour. We would go on board that evening. Meanwhile a scratch meal and wine was offered and the inevitable documentation hurried through. We also had to be searched before going on board. Now began a series of visits to the loo, not only from excitement but also to dispose of our escape gear before the search. Maps were eaten or flushed away, compass needles disposed of, iron rations consumed; only a little hoard of Red Cross cakes of soap, the highest barter currency available to us at the time, was retained. We need not have worried. The search was cursory, we were embussed and taken to the docks, and there was the hospital ship *Gradisca*.

Gleaming white with red crosses painted on her funnel and on her sides, old but elegant, she awaited us. Ushered on board by stewards, we sorted ourselves out. Five of us were submariners and succeeded in getting a cabin together. The ship was crowded but there was a festive feeling in the air. We would sail at about 2100 and dinner would be served. We were back in the gracious atmosphere of the naval hospital at Taranto but with one even more astonishing difference – there were women on board. These were voluntary nurses, not the lower orders of staff but in the upper echelon of the Italian Red Cross. All of them were ladies of distinction, some titled, most spoke excellent and charming English, and some of them knew England well and found friends among our mutual acquaintances. It was like a mad dream, the transition was so great and so fast.

In the morning though we, the submariners, began to get nervous. It was obvious that we were steaming east, unescorted, not zigzagging. Rumour correctly had it that we were heading for Mersin in neutral Turkey, but we realized two things. First, we could see the high land of Crete to port, so we were out in the open Mediterranean; secondly, we knew that the British were justly suspicious of the uses to which the Germans had put Italian hospital ships in ferrying their troops to and from Africa. We thought of our colleagues at sea and prayed that we would have a safe passage and not get torpedoed by one of our own boats. I remembered how *Tempest* had so nearly attacked a ship given safe conduct.

We pooled our Red Cross soap packets and with them bought copious supplies of wine from the stewards. We got as high as decency allowed, so that our conversation with the ladies of quality at mealtimes was balanced on a razor's edge, but we survived.

Two days later in the early morning the *Gradisca* anchored in the bay of Mersin. She must have looked more like a large private yacht or a cruise ship than anything normally seen in war-time. On the other side of the bay, perhaps half a mile away, was anchored a British India Line passenger vessel – sleazy, old, but, and this certainly cheered our hearts, flying a tattered red ensign.

The Turkish Red Crescent appeared in a launch bringing us, unbelievably, a consignment of Turkish Delight and Turkish cigarettes. After some delay the Turkish Navy appeared, in barges manned by piratical-looking crews with bare and horny-toed feet. We were ferried to the old ship with the red ensign, the S.S. *Talma*.

In April 1941 three Italian destroyers had scuttled themselves in Saudi Arabian territorial waters and the crews were interned on an island off Jedda. The large numbers caused considerable embarrassment to the Saudi Arabian government. The German advance on Alexandria was in progress and the presence of eight hundred hostile naval personnel on British lines of communication was a cause for anxiety. The neutral Turks enquired whether Britain would agree to the Italians being transported under safe conduct on a British ship to a Turkish port. H.M.G. quickly concurred. The Italians were taken from Jedda in the *Talma* and the day before she arrived in Mersin an Italian bomber dropped a stick of bombs on her. Luckily all missed, but the Italians on board, who had been pleased to see one of their own aircraft, were somewhat downcast by the event. Had any of the men on either side been sick or wounded and repatriated under the Geneva Convention they would not have been allowed to return to active service.

Once on the *Talma* things changed again. She was as tatty below as on deck and there were no ladies to welcome us, but the old first-class saloon bar was just as it had been for years throughout her service on the Indian coast – a mock Tudor room with a mock log fire in an ingle-nook hung with horse brasses. What is more we were immediately greeted with large scotches and soda with ice. We hadn't had anything like that for a long time. Later we learnt that our mess bills began again on the instant.

We were each allowed to send one short telegram home. I don't remember what I put in mine and nobody appears to have kept it, but I know the address I sent it to – Hodges Place, Offham, Kent.

SEVEN

In war-torn Britain

On 23 March *Talma* tied up in Port Said. A telegram was waiting for me. It said: 'Congratulations wedding bells and champagne await you stop Jack Downton.' There was also one from Diana that said 'Ready when you are', or words to that effect. How impatient those made me for the future, though I had no idea quite how long it would take me to get home again.

We were soon on our way by train to Alexandria. Here we were 'de-briefed'. The answers I gave were I hope of some use to someone, though they seemed pretty pointless to me. The party of repatriates was split up and a small number of officers, of whom David Abdy and I were two, were put in a rest-home, a luxurious villa in the Rue Belgique, run by the equivalent of our Italian nurses on the hospital ship only this time they were Greeks who had come to Egypt as refugees.

A Turkish bath and a clean up, including, at long last, the shaving of my beard begun so long ago on sailing from the Clyde, put literally a new complexion on things. For several days we did nothing but swan around in luxury.

At that time the 'Queens', the liners *Queen Mary* and *Queen Elizabeth*, were running a trooping service by way of the Cape of Good Hope. Relying on their speed for safety they went fast and unaccompanied. It was suggested that all of us from Italy should travel back that way. The submariners amongst us demurred. We said we would feel most unsafe and would probably arrive home in a worse state than our present one. It was also going to take eleven weeks to get back.

The First Submarine Flotilla at Alexandria had been moved some time before up the coast to Beirut, the depot ship *Medway* having been sunk on the way. The Senior Officer Submarines in Alexandria agreed that the five of us, instead of being sent home via the Cape, should travel to the base at Beirut and take our chance on being repatriated from there by air as and when opportunity occurred. David Abdy, being the senior of us, would obviously be the first to go.

David was keen to take something home for his wife that would be a real luxury. He accordingly consulted the Greek ladies. 'Of course,' they said, 'we know just the thing. A friend of ours, a princess, has a little shop here in Alexandria where she sells the most beautiful hand-made and embroidered silk lingerie. It is all made in a convent and is of the most exquisite beauty.' Abdy asked me to go with him on the shopping expedition. I reckoned that Diana would have her own trousseau and could not anyway have afforded to contribute to it, but I was naturally interested in what might be on offer.

All was as the ladies described. The princess was charming, and lovely nightdresses, négligés, slips and other loose and slinky garments were produced from tissue-paper-lined boxes and perfumed wardrobes. Everything relied for its erotic appeal on its clinging line and silken smoothness – no see-through black vulgarities here. David made a careful choice and was preparing to sign a handsome cheque when he thought again. 'Have you,' he said, blushing slightly, 'got any knickers?' 'Knickers?' asked the princess, pronouncing the word with some difficulty. 'Well,' said David, taking his courage in both hands, 'I mean what we call French knickers, not bloomers or even cami-knickers.' The Greek princess looked totally puzzled so David in desperation drew a diagram. The princess looked embarrassed and then laughed. 'No,' she said, 'I know such things exist but neither I nor any of my friends ever wear them.'

The trip by train across the bridge over the Suez Canal and on up through Palestine to Beirut into Syria past Tyre and Sidon was constantly interesting, through citrus groves and past familiar biblical place-names. The new state of Palestine, not yet called Israel, was a simple place in those days and my impression was of dozens of beefy girls in shorts and shirts all engaged in manual labour.

Beirut when we got there was still as elegant as the French had made it, with fine streets as well as a sleazy area, but undamaged, a sort of Nice of the near East. A shore base for the submarine flotilla, under the command of Captain Ruck-Keene, had been established in what had been a large French Cavalry barracks on the southern side of the city, next to a strange little orange-coloured desert with palm trees that became the commercial airport of post-war years. All this and much more has since been smashed up and some of the worst things have happened just where our base was.

I was there for two weeks, waiting to be sent home. Nothing was required of me except to relax and enjoy the amenities. After dinner in the mess – a very good dinner by war-time standards – would follow a few more drinks in the bar: cheap drinks, local arrack and copies of European liqueurs made by Wolfschmidt in Palestine. Crème de menthe, also known as sticky green, starboard light or tart's tickle, was popular. Then, by our own regular transport, came a trip into Beirut itself. There were a few night haunts where one could talk and drink with pretty young Syrian girls; their services were available for a bit more than chat but seldom taken.

A few incidents stick out from this strange limbo. A midshipman, having bought a bottle of tart's tickle from the bar (it was not obtainable 'ashore') and surreptitiously hidden it inside his jacket, slipping on the stone staircase of the barracks and, miraculously without injury from the broken glass, getting up and opening his jacket to reveal the crushed bottle with all its contents flowing over his shirt and down into the top of his trousers. Arriving with a party of six or seven others in a jeep outside one of the bordellos and being greeted with the polite information from a male head at an upper window: '*Non, fermé, tutti bint sono occupato.*' Sitting with a smaller party in one of these establishments while the 'girls' plied needle and thread to sew on missing or loose buttons to our garments. Leaving in an open jeep – the standard 'liberty-boat' run came round at about midnight – which was somewhat overcrowded so that the last on board, a Canadian, couldn't quite make it and grasped the knotted rope which was anchored to the floor of the jeep just as the driver roared off. Not daring to let go, he was towed, running, all the way back to base, arriving utterly whacked and having ruined his best shoes by the marathon sprint.

Captain Ruck-Keene ('Ruckers') thought we ought to be engaged in healthier pastimes. Every so often he would come into the bar after dinner, look round, pick four or five of us and say, 'You and you and you will report outside my house in battledress at o-three-thirty, we're going skiing,' which he pronounced in the old-fashioned manner as 'sheing'. So no trip ashore that night for his victims; instead a few hours in bed and then, while it was still dark, piling into two or three cars and driving for an hour or more up into the mountains of Lebanon behind the city. Skis with skins were put on and a long climb of another hour or so made up the mountain in the beautiful dawn light. Wolves were said to be a danger but we only saw one or two loping away in the distance near the tree-line. Once at the top it was 'off-skins' and a much quicker *piste* down back to the cars before the sun got hot enough to melt the snow surface. I had done a bit of this sort of thing in my film-making on the Matterhorn so I didn't get on too badly. Less experienced conscripts than I came off worse; sprains and bruises there were in plenty but I only remember seeing one brother-officer in plaster as a result. Back in the cars, the next stop was at a roadside café for breakfast of coffee and croissants, then straight down to the beach for a swim. Those with daily work to do could still get back in time to do a stint before lunch. We few, the leisured classes, could stay on the beach as long as we liked.

My turn for repatriation came at last. I was ordered to take the train, to Cairo this time, and told that I would fly from there when room permitted on a regular shuttle service to Algiers, which was now the base for the Eighth Submarine Flotilla in the western Mediterranean, for onward routing home as opportunity offered.

I knew that Diana had an uncle in army intelligence in Cairo. He was a legendary figure in his own family and to a lot of other people as well and, never having met him, I thought that as I would be bound to have a few days' enforced stop-over in Cairo, it would be politic to 'make my number' with him.

Eric Dunstan was a famous name: ex-Westminster choirboy, the 'golden-voiced announcer' of 2LO, the pre-BBC radio station in Savoy Hill, a commentator for voice-over on British Movietone News, one-time secretary to Gordon Selfridge, and a friend of the Prince of Wales, even accompanying him on the famous cruise down the Dalmatian coast.

He was not generally thought to be of 'the marrying kind'. One of his female relations said that he was the only man she had ever met who sat down at his dressing-table. He had been briefly married to a wealthy, beautiful and well-connected American who had been killed in a terrible accident on their honeymoon. Their car, stopped on a mountain road in California while Eric and the driver were picking flowers, had slipped backwards over a cliff taking her and her maid with it. He was a great gardener and had a most beautiful house converted from an old olive-oil mill near Grasse in France, then of course in other hands. I knew all this but I was still not prepared for what I was to find.

He welcomed me in the most generous way. He was tall with aquiline good looks and wonderful blonde-gone-silver hair. His flat in a smart part of Cairo and his uniform were both immaculate and he was looked after by his personal servant of some years, John Knight. The flat was always full of people, and every social celebrity who passed through Cairo came to visit him. His next move incidentally was to be head of E.N.S.A. in India where again his connections were invaluable. He was a snob certainly, but kindness itself behind his catty wit and he gave the boy, as he called me, who was going home to marry his niece a wonderful few days, showing me everything, even the pyramids, as well as the high life of Shepherds Hotel. John Knight was a card, famous for his rudeness to guests, especially to anyone he considered to be a hanger-on to Eric. He accepted me at once as 'family', however, and I still have two naïve seascapes which he painted and gave me towards the end of his life.

After a few days I was told to report the next morning to the American Air Force field at Heliopolis. Eric had me sent there in an Army limousine and I duly weighed in. I found that I was to be the only Naval person of a very mixed lot of passengers in an old Dakota. These planes did yeoman service all over the world for many years and I imagine that there may be some still flying somewhere. Twin-engined and aluminium-bodied, their inside had an arrangement of metal benches running down both sides. These resembled a long line of shallow wash-basins in which one sat facing inboard, the small square windows behind one's shoulder. By screwing oneself round one could just see out but the view was restricted by the wings, and the position excruciatingly uncomfortable. Most of my fellow-passengers were only going as far as our first overnight stop, Tripoli, which had recently been vacated by the retreating German and Italian armies. The flight was uneventful if uncomfortable. I don't recollect the rest of the crew but certainly the only officer, the captain and pilot, was unforgettable – a Texan who looked and sounded like the model for all movie cowpunchers, tall, long-legged, slim-hipped to the point of appearing to have no buttocks at all, and with the drawly insouciant manner of speech to go with it.

He and I were the only 'guests' for the officers' stop-over arrangements in Tripoli; that is to say we each had one of the two-tier cots in an otherwise unfurnished room in a battered building on the airfield itself. The cots had metal frames strung with any old bits of wire in a sagging meshwork and one blanket each, no pillow. It was hot and sultry, there was no need for a blanket over one but every need for something to mitigate the cutting effect of the wire underneath. After a scratch meal in the canteen there was nothing to do but go back and finish an uncomfortable day with what was clearly going to be an even more uncomfortable night. My friend managed to 'win' half a bottle of whisky from somewhere, so after several nightcaps and a good deal of mutual line-shooting we retired.

After breakfast, which was I remember quite good – coffee and fried eggs – we set off again. I had asked Hank, or whatever his name was, what time he reckoned we would get to Algiers. 'It's a long haul,' he said. 'The battle for Tunis is still going on in the desert and my orders are to fly west till we reach a point due south of Algiers, then go straight for it up and over the Atlas mountains. Our official E.T.A. is mid-afternoon but I reckon we'll be there by noon. I've got a girlfriend there and she's very good in the afternoons.' 'How will you make up time?' I asked. A laconic 'You'll see,' was all the reply he gave.

This time I was invited to 'come up front' with him as there would be something to see. After we had left Tripoli airfield he dutifully went into a slow climb heading west. A few miles later, however, he headed the Dakota in a north-westerly direction and began to lose height; soon we were just skimming over the empty desert, so low that it seemed to me that if we met a man on a camel he had better fling himself to the ground. Hank explained that, as an unarmed transport plane, we would be much safer down here, since any combat planes would be higher and probably would not notice us.

A few more miles and the desert was not quite so empty. There was evidence in burnt-out tanks and trucks that it had been fought over – and not so long ago, either. Then we saw a column of smoke from a tank still burning, and suddenly there were puffs of gunfire and more smoke and the splash of explosions. Hank pressed on and we swept right over the tank battle. They were well spaced out and it was only a minute or two before we were over and gone. Someone fired some tracer at us but missed; whether it came from one of our side or the enemy I did not know. Luckily for us there wasn't any low-flying air cover about and we must have been a totally unexpected sight for anyone on the ground who had the time to notice us.

Hank changed course again to the west and we began flying over the apparently peaceful foothills towards the towering mountain range ahead. He climbed, but not much. I was convinced that we must strike the mountain side when suddenly a narrow winding valley appeared. Into it we went and out on the other side. 'We're in Algeria now and my date looks OK,' said Hank. There were other mountains which he negotiated in a more conventional manner and then I saw the sea ahead and Algiers spread out on its edge. We landed safely a few minutes before noon. I never saw Hank again but I hope he had a good afternoon and managed his short-cut as safely on his next trip.

Somewhat shaken I reported to the depot ship. They couldn't tell me when there would be a chance of a seat on a plane for home, since that depended on a host of conditions and priorities. Anyway, they said, it was not too nice a trip. There were a lot of enemy planes about over Biscay and the approaches. That evening there was a major air raid on Algiers, with every ship in the crowded harbour banging away and bombs all over the place.

Next morning in the mess at breakfast I met an acquaintance from earlier days who was now one of the officers of a U class submarine. I learnt from him that they were on their way home via Gibraltar having finished their tour of duty. I went along and asked Commander (S) whether he thought they could possibly take me too. It would be much slower than flying, but not if I had to wait indefinitely in noisy and dangerous Algiers. Anyway, I had had enough flying for the moment and much preferred the quiet progress of a nice safe submarine, particularly one that wasn't looking for trouble. They had a spare bunk in the wardroom and the thought of another watch-keeper to lessen the length and frequency of watches seemed to be welcome so I was on. We sailed almost at once. The boat was the *Unbending* returning from a successful tour of duty. We reached Gibraltar easily and spent a day or two there, leaving behind all but the minimum of torpedoes and ammunition and in consequence being allowed to ship a few personal goodies. My loot was a whole case of La Ina sherry, then unobtainable at home at any price but still available and cheap in duty-free Gib.

Our orders were to steer clear of danger zones near the coast and in the Bay of Biscay, and although we heard some sounds of distant depth-charging (not pleasant to anyone's ears and particularly mine) we met our superannuated S class destroyer escort at the appointed time off the Scillies and set course behind her on the surface for the Needles channel and Portsmouth.

The weather was threatening and just before dark, when we were somewhere in Lyme Bay, it began to blow extremely hard. The heavily breaking seas and rain made it difficult to see the shaded stern light of the ancient vessel we were following. Finally we lost contact. Neither we nor she had radar and we could not break wireless silence. The captain decided to press on so that we could get to the Needles at day-break and avoid having to dive as we should have had to do if daylight had caught us unescorted in mid-Channel.

As dawn broke I was on the bridge with the captain and a couple of look-outs. There was a huge sea from what turned out to be one of the worst south-westerly spring equinoctial gales in living memory; the submarine was almost surfing down the face of the waves coming up from astern. We were outside the Portland race but the sea was wild and confused. Some waves broke over the bridge from astern, and the 'bird-bath' was already rigged in the control room below. When operating under diesels, submarines of that time had to keep the conning tower open as it was the only source of the enormous amounts of air the engines consumed. If the hatch were to shut before the engines had been turned off and the electric motors started, the diesels would suck all the air out of the inside of the boat and lower the atmospheric pressure to a point where ear-drums would be ruptured at least. The bird-bath was a device consisting of a large canvas tub with sides several feet high which was rigged round the foot of the conning tower ladder when in bad weather and on the surface. Any water that came down – and sometimes there were some very impressive amounts – was collected in the bird-bath and pumped out.

A further complication was that there was now a roaring spring tide coming out of the Needles narrows against the wind which created a really awesome sea; yet another was that the Needles channel is quite shallow and we could not dive to get out of the effect of the surface waves. With England, home and beauty so near, the captain determined to have a go at it and get it over as quickly as possible. The two look-outs were sent down and some rope passed up with which the captain and I lashed each other to the periscope standard. I got the job because I knew the Needles channel well from sailing days. Then came the ultimate step of putting the hatch lid down on its clips. This meant that it was only open a crack, provided by jamming in it the massive clips which normally held it shut when dived. The rush of air through the narrow slit caused a shriek audible even above all the other noises of wind and water. At full speed the submarine charged ahead into the breakers. Wave after wave came over us; each time the bow of the boat and the casing disappeared under the water; then, taking a deep breath and holding on, so did we. The boat could not sink, and although our time submersed on the bridge seemed never-ending we soon broke surface to breathe again before the next one. Ten minutes or so later we came into the comparative calm of land-locked water and carried on our way to Gosport.

Formalities were quickly done and before evening everyone was away on leave. I had an interview with the Commander (S). 'I hope you enjoy your repatriation leave,' he said. 'Where are you going?' 'Back to Kent to get married, sir.' 'Married eh? Well, good luck! Anything I can do to help?' 'There is one thing, sir. I've got a case of La Ina in the boat, which I thought might go down well at the occasion. How can I get it ashore quickly, Customs and all that? If I have to leave it, it may take months to come through.' 'What train are you catching?' 'The fifteen-forty-five from Portsmouth Town station, sir.' 'Right, leave it to me. I'll get your case to you. Wait by the station entrance at fifteen-thirty.'

I stood by the entrance, exactly at three-thirty. A uniformed motor-cycle messenger from the staff of the C.-in-C. roared up with a black tarpaulin-covered shape behind the saddle. 'Lieutenant Caplat, sir?' 'Yes.' He whipped off the cover, undid two straps and consigned to me a heavy object wrapped in official brown paper and tied with cord and wax seals. I signed an indecipherable receipt and he went off.

Diana got leave at once. She was one of the signal Wrens on C.-in-C. Portsmouth's staff and had been spending most of her time at Leydene or deep in the tunnels under the old Napoleonic Fort Southwick on the hill behind. She was given compassionate leave for the time leading up to the wedding in view of my being a returned P.O.W. and we busied ourselves in the preparations, in getting me kitted up again and in enjoying being together. Diana confesses that when she knew I was almost home she asked her mother if she must go through with it, as it was so long since she had seen me. Our correspondence while I was away had not been exactly voluminous nor had her thoughts been solely on me. Her mother said she must, and that was that. Diana also confesses that she steeled herself with the thought that our marriage was unlikely to last more than three years, either through the hazards of war or our growing away from each other. Unfortunately for her perhaps she was wrong. We had our ruby wedding anniversary last year.

Despite the nightly alarms and frequent raids, despite the rationing, life passed all too quickly. The weather was idyllic. Diana's grandmother died, full of years as the saying is, and thereby presented Diana and me with our first married home: a convenient small modern house set by itself in the midst of a Kentish cherry orchard in the same village of Offham.

The wedding and the honeymoon had to be arranged, all made very difficult by rationing and restrictions, such as the one on the number of consecutive nights one could stay in any London hotel.

I had no friends or colleagues handy whom I could ask to be best man. My parents were little help in far off Herne Bay (no car and not good travellers anyway, as well as having to look after my aged grandmother). In fact I was rather in the position of an unattached stranger in a friendly foreign land. But the nearby R.A.F. fighter base at West Malling sprang to my aid, perhaps even more willingly because they had a chance to show a lone member of the senior service how things ought to be done.

Liam Griffin, an ebullient Irishman in the best tradition of Irish doctors, was the Station medical officer. He had become a frequent visitor to Hodges Place and happily agreed to be my best man. On the evening of 28 May I moved up to the Fighter Station, was given a stag party in the mess (the commanding officer who presumably condoned all this was the famous 'Cats-eyes' Cunningham, the great night-fighter ace), and put to bed in the sick bay. The morning of my wedding dawned bright and clear, which was more than I did. I was awakened with early-morning tea delivered by a pretty W.R.A.F. nurse. After breakfast there was a car waiting to take me to a mystery destination. I was driven across the airfield to a Mosquito which was already warmed up on the tarmac. The pilot, whom I dimly remembered from the night before, greeted me and said that as it was such a nice day they thought I would like a little trip aloft. The Mosquito, a dual-engined two seater plane much in favour at the time, took off and we sailed into the empyrean. It was a dual-control trainer and I was encouraged to have a go. It seemed to be quite easy to fly straight and level and to do a few banks and turns. Just as I was feeling confident, my host said: 'I think we ought to turn back. We're well over the Channel and we aren't armed.' I looked down and, sure enough, on this beautiful clear late May morning I could see the whole coast of Kent from the North Foreland to Dungeness and the French coast on the other side, evoking thoughts of Dunkirk and similar weather on a similar date only two years before, but seeming an age ago.

We turned back just in time to see a squadron of our fighters take off and head for France on a routine sweep. Then my pilot said: 'Let's go and have a look at Offham. Can you identify your bride's house?' 'Yes easily, next to the pub, there it is.' It was especially easy to identify because already trestle tables with white cloths had been set up on the lawn. (No marquees were available or necessary.) Suddenly the pilot put the plane into a steep dive and we 'roared up', as the saying went, Hodges Place, coming to within a few feet of the chimneys and then screaming away again in a rapid

Early rehearsal for *La Calisto*, 1970. Left to right:
Peter Hall (Producer), John Bury (Designer), M.C.,
June Dandridge (Production Manager). In pit:
Raymond Leppard (Conductor).

Planning meeting, *The Visit of the Old Lady*, 1972.
Left to right: Michael Annals (Designer), John Cox
(Producer), John Pritchard (Conductor), M.C.,
Gottfried Von Einem (Composer), George Christie.

At the Rosehill Theatre, 1952. Left to right:
M.C., Miki Sekers, David Webster.

With David Hockney in his studio, 1974.

climb. I think we did it twice. I understand that the manoeuvre nearly wrecked the whole reception. Helpers busy arranging flowers and doing all the hundred and one things that people do at such times took terrible fright and it was some time before some of the more elderly could be persuaded that it was 'one of ours' and they might therefore come out from under the tables.

Back at the airfield I was invited to spruce myself up and join my best man for a horse's-neck in the bar before lunch. He made a quick assessment of my health and decided that the flight and fresh air had restored me from the depredations of the night before. Lunch was carefully selected to give me as much medical help as possible for the ordeal ahead and as a last honour from the Station I was taken to have coffee and South African brandy with the W.R.A.F. officers in their separate drawing room.

Then, with my groomsman beside me, I was driven in an R.A.F. car to the nearby church in the village of West Malling. The church seemed full and there was a photographer already at work in the churchyard. In somewhat of a daze I made my way, directed by Liam, into the front pew on the starboard side. As we settled ourselves my aged grandmother in the pew behind said in a loud and disapproving voice: 'What a strong smell of incense in this church.' As a Congregationalist and a teetotaller she had to be excused for not recognizing the aroma arising from the two uniformed figures in front of her.

The organ played, my bride appeared beside me, looking staggeringly beautiful and not as obviously doubtful of the step she was taking as by her own account she must have been. To the stirring strains of Grieg's *Sigurd Jorsalfar* march, specially chosen by my mother-in-law to pay tribute to her triumph in getting us wed, we left the church. Outside the door a guard of honour of the R.A.F. Regiment lined the path, the bells rang out (the ban on church-bell ringing for anything other than warning of invasion had recently been lifted) and a squadron of Belgian Spitfires based on West Malling, having just taken off on their regular patrol, flew low over the church and wagged their wings. The official photographer fell backwards over a gravestone and passed out.

The reception in the garden rolled on in a haze of sherry and champagne conjured up from somewhere, speeches and photographs; the two pages, sons of the best man, peed publicly in the lily pond and off we went by train to London and the Dorchester Hotel for three nights of real luxury. Our double room and bathroom cost us the huge sum of two pounds ten shillings per night including breakfast, our bill for the three nights with luncheon one day and dinner on two evenings coming to fifteen pounds eight shillings and eightpence.

While I was a P.O.W. I had promised one of my fellow-prisoners that when I got back I would look up his wife and give her personal news of him. I telephoned her and she said she would come round to the Dorchester and meet us in the bar. Our surprise was considerable when in walked, accompanied by a Polish airman and a miniature poodle, the most complete stage tart imaginable. She listened to my news with little apparent interest and tottered off. I forbore to write to her husband.

After three more days at the Mount Royal in Oxford Street, we went for the rest of our fortnight to Boscastle in Cornwall, where we stayed in an old hotel at the bottom of the steep street and hired bicycles for daily excursions. The snag was that these had no brakes and the only way of stopping on hills was to run into the bank. Diana was much better at this than I.

Also honeymooning in the hotel were a Canadian Army officer and his English bride. We became friendly; he had a supply of cigars which were rare and which in those days I much enjoyed. He also had a supply of rum. One evening after dinner the ladies retired and we sat in the twilight smoking, drinking neat rum and shooting our own particular lines. This took longer than we intended or the girls expected and it was rather late when we went unsteadily to bed. Our room was on the top floor, where the staircase, rising round a large well that was the hall, culminated in a circular gallery off which the rooms opened. Diana was not best pleased with me. I undressed rapidly and then something she said seemed to call for retaliation. I seized the lavatory brush from the bathroom and, playfully but meaningfully, approached her. She jumped out of bed and in her nightie dashed out of the door on to the gallery, thinking that in my state of nudity I would be unlikely to follow. Such was not the case, however, and whooping 'tally ho' or something of the sort I gave chase. Round the gallery several times we went, and the noise of Diana's laughter – mixed with the odd yelp when the brush got home – together with my whoops aroused our fellow guests. Though the lights were dim they could not but see what was going on. Diana dragged me back into our room and slammed the door. There were some very odd looks given us next morning at breakfast. More of the effects of rum on me hereafter.

Soon after our return I received my next appointment. I was to join another T class submarine, this time building at Chatham. It was extremely kind of whoever was responsible for my appointment because it meant that I could continue to live at Offham in the house in the cherry orchard and, borrowing my mother-in-law's old but well-loved Hillman Minx, commute daily to the dockyard.

Diana's marriage leave had another few weeks to run and she had no wish to return to the Wrens. The only way to avoid this was to make sure that she was pregnant as soon as possible. Though this was by no means an unpleasant task it did involve considerable inroads on time and energy and up to the last moment we thought we had not made it. First we sent a telegram to say she could not return owing to indisposition, but a few days later we were able to despatch the doctor's confirmation of her condition and she hung up her Naval cap for good.

The new submarine, Job No. D2286, was a sister ship of *Tempest* to be named *Tradewind*. The principal improvement was that she had radar but not yet a schnorkel. Her captain was Lieutenant-Commander Lynch Maydon, R.N., a tall, charming man with an equally tall wife, Joan. He had already, as captain of *Umbra*, sunk the Italian cruiser *Trento* and severely damaged a battleship in the Ionian Sea. After the war he became an M.P. but unfortunately died young or we should have heard much more of him.

Tradewind was commissioned on 1 July and we went, under escort, to Holy Loch on the Firth of Clyde where the *Forth* was the depot ship. This was to be our base for the next few months while we exercised and prepared to sail for Gibraltar and eventually for the Far East. I was the torpedo-officer this time. The first lieutenant was a senior and experienced officer. The idea was, I was told, that after our arrival at Gibraltar he was to go back to Fort Blockhouse to do his 'perisher', as the course for commanding officers was called, and I would take over as first lieutenant.

The first dive of a new submarine is always a nerve-racking business which for me the memory of the *Thetis* disaster did nothing to relieve. It is of necessity made before the final acceptance of the boat from the builders and therefore with a large number of men on board, not only the boat's crew but all the necessary dockyard technicians and specialists too. *Tradewind*'s first dive was made in the Gare Loch which is suitably deep. Our dive did not go without incident. It was taken very slowly of course, everything being checked at every stage. We were down to periscope depth when suddenly the bow tipped steeply down, there was the noise of gushing water, the roar of compressed air being let into ballast tanks in a hurry and we soon levelled out at a somewhat greater depth than had been intended. All was now quiet except for the sound of spurting water from several valves and fittings that required no more than further tightening down. After a consultation between all the pundits as to the cause of the sudden misbehaviour the dive continued uneventfully. What worried me privately was the sudden flash of panic I had felt and the sense of unease that the sound of water entering the hull had given me, but I kept this to myself and did not mention it even to Diana. Until this moment I had had no qualms at going back into submarines, no sense of claustrophobia and no feelings of anything but pleasure at being back in the service I had come to love.

By Christmas the boat was approaching some sort of efficiency. We had done our torpedo trials at Arrochar in Loch Long, we had done our radar trials, our deep dive to 400 feet off Ailsa Craig, our depth-charge trial which involved the dropping of depth charges on us at various, but of course non-lethal, distances, and depths. This latter experience added to my growing unease. We had been over to Larne in Northern Ireland for exercises and returned with two empty torpedo tubes stuffed with goose and turkey carcases for Christmas leave, and it would not be long after Christmas that we would have to sail in deadly earnest.

Half the ship's company went on leave for Christmas and half for New Year. I was on duty for the Christmas period and found myself in charge of *Tradewind* lying alongside the *Forth* in Holy Loch. Diana and I were living ashore in the Linwood Guest House on the outskirts of Hunters Quay, together with a number of other officers from other boats and their wives. Duties were light; just routine visits to the submarine morning and late afternoon, otherwise the time was my own.

On Christmas morning I went off to take the ship's company to morning service on the depot ship. It was a fine day and pleasant to be standing on the quarter deck singing carols. Following the service, another tradition was observed. Each mess in the boat (everyone ate in their own quarters so that there was a stokers' mess, a torpedo-men's mess, etc.) had its own party. In bigger ships it was customary for the officers to do the waiting but with us it was just expected that the captain, or in this case I as the senior officer on board, should visit each mess in turn and take a drink with them.

The rum ration was still being issued in all H.M. ships in those days. A good big measure, neat for the older and senior hands, watered into 'grog' for the more junior, was issued daily at noon. In submarines at sea the issue was made on surfacing for the night, and the combined effect of the rum and the men's first gulp of fresh air for perhaps twelve hours meant that the boat's efficiency was impaired to a greater or lesser degree for as much as the first hour after surfacing. Watch-keeping officers did not as a rule drink at sea; that was left to doctors and parsons. The rum ration had to be consumed straight away (extra pay of a few pence a day could be taken in lieu but not on a day-to-day basis) and it was strictly forbidden to 'bottle your tot'. Nevertheless the bottling of tots did go on and the one day on which their revelation carried little risk of retribution was Christmas.

Proceeding from mess to mess I was regaled with rum and felt it my duty to toss back each tot with a smile, one that no doubt got broader as I made my way down the length of the submarine. I had promised to be back in Linwood for our landlady's special Christmas lunch which centred round a Larne turkey, but I felt it incumbent on me to have one or two more drinks in the wardroom of the *Forth* before disembarking. The liberty boat was not very prompt in leaving for the shore and it was obvious that I was going to be ten minutes or so late for the one o'clock kick-off in Linwood. Diana was somehow expecting me to be late and had placed herself, sherry in hand, in the bay window which gave a view down the front garden to the gate. With relief she saw my cap appearing behind the hedge and then horror struck her; instead of opening the gate and proceeding up the path I climbed slowly and carefully over the fence beside the gate and started somewhat unsteadily up the side of the path.

She rushed to the front door and, recognizing my condition, said: 'Quickly, go up to our room and lie down. I'll say you're not feeling well and bring you up some food later. You beast!' I obeyed, she followed me and surreptitiously locked me in, then returned to the dining room, made my excuses and sat down to the feast.

Our room was on the first floor at the back over the window of the dining room. After some minutes Diana was startled to see my uniform cap go hurtling over the back garden. No one else seemed to notice but then it was followed, at regular intervals, by every piece of my apparel, right down to the last sock which floated on to the bushes below. The rum had repeated its peculiar effect on me of inducing a strip-tease.

After the New Year things began to get more tense. We finished with practice torpedoes and loaded live ones. My state of mind was giving cause for worry, my usually cast-iron digestion was playing tricks and I suppose, with hindsight, that I was showing signs of anxiety neurosis. I stoutly declared that I was all right but tests were made and I was sent to a head-shrinker in Glasgow, who apparently said that I was suffering from delayed reaction to former experiences and that I should temporarily be taken out of seagoing boats. Just before *Tradewind* was sailed away on active service on 29 January 1944 I was discharged to the *Forth* awaiting reappointment.

At the time I was angry and my pride took a big knock. I did not want anyone, least of all myself, to think that I had funked anything but I knew I was edgy, unfit and depressed. Lynch Maydon was very kind to me, as was everyone else on *Tradewind*. Some sort of dysentery was the official reason for my being left behind; I couldn't help the feeling that I was really just plain 'shit-scared'.

EIGHT

On the lunatic fringe

On my brief New Year's leave I had taken Diana back to Kent and
installed her in a furnished thatched cottage not far from her
mother's house while I, as I thought, went off to the Pacific. Now
all was changed. It was clear that I was going to remain shore-
based, at any rate for the immediate future, but where?

The answer came quickly. I was reappointed in February as
Additional Staff Officer 2 to H.M.S. *Ambrose*, the shore establishment in Dundee that housed the Ninth Submarine Flotilla. The
base occupied two groups of buildings, an infirmary and an orphan-
age, on either side of the road that led to Monifieth through
Broughty Ferry. Below these were the docks occupied by the submarines of the flotilla.

It was a mixed flotilla, and besides several Royal Navy boats
there were others, some of which had escaped from what were now
enemy waters, manned by Poles, French, Dutch and Norwegians.
The work of the flotilla was concentrated on the area from the
North Cape and Spitzbergen down to the upper North Sea. Denmark and Norway were both in enemy hands and the main effort
was to blockade access to the Atlantic and to carry out raids on
coastal shipping, particularly in the Norwegian Fjords.

I found life in the operations room fascinating. As the junior
watch-keeper of three my task to begin with was to keep track of
the boats on patrol, read all signals as they came in from the cipher
room, and decide who should see them and whether they needed
immediate attention. With many of the routine ones it was just a
matter of keeping the operations charts up to date. One of the vital
jobs was to see that bombing restrictions were constantly and
accurately applied. When a submarine was on patrol it was essential
for her and for us to know exactly the area in which she could surface by night to charge batteries and transmit radio signals without
fear of being attacked by our own Coastal Command aircraft that
were busy by day and night over the same waters. The R.A.F. of
course had to have the same information and the restricted areas
had to be kept to the minimum.

Within two weeks of my arrival two things had happened. First I had been promoted to second in charge of the operations room; secondly, Diana had come up to join me. We anticipated that I would be in that job for some months, perhaps even 'for the duration', and our baby was due in two months' time.

Diana was quite ready to leave the cottage in Kent, for she was alone in it most of the time and there were nightly air raids on London. Returning enemy aircraft had a nasty habit of jettisoning bombs over Kent; Diana's aunt was killed in this way in her home not many miles away. One night when Diana was alone a bomb was dropped into the woods near enough to the cottage to lift the thatched roof bodily and drop it back, superficially undamaged but a few inches out of true. In her state of pregnancy this was something she had not enjoyed.

When she first came up we stayed in a private hotel in Broughty Ferry named Cambustay but known to us as Mortuary Manor. It bore a marked resemblance to one of Charles Addam's establishments in his *New Yorker* drawings and it was inhabited, apart from the two of us, entirely by the aged. Meal-times were torture because we had to restrain our desire to giggle and dared not talk above a whisper. Not only was rationing in full swing but the cooking was ghastly. Everything was accompanied by ice-cream-scoop dollops of mashed potatoes and/or swedes innocent not only of rationed butter but also of salt. What is more, the rigidly applied rule was two dollops for a man and one for a woman, despite Diana's evident condition and greater hunger. The main implement provided for eating with was a 'sponk', devised by some man of genius out of a cheap metal spoon the top of the bowl of which had been cut into three prongs like a blunt fork. One side of the bowl had been rendered slightly less blunt to act as a cutting edge. Amongst the other inmates ear-trumpets were the rule rather than the exception. One old lady asked to have her table moved as 'the ceaseless passing of the waitress makes a draught and gives me earache.'

After a week or two of Mortuary Manor we moved into an unfurnished ground-floor flat in one of the jute-kings' mansions built in Broughty Ferry at the height of the affluence produced by that trade towards the end of the last century. The mansion bore the inappropriate name of Reres Cottage. Our flat consisted of two huge rooms and a draughty, primitive kitchen, originally the scullery, with the shared use of a gas-geysered and unheated bathroom on the floor above. Diana's mother got together a load of furniture and linen and had it sent to us. We were hard up, living only on my pay which was always months in arrears. Diana ran up curtains for the vast windows out of, appropriately enough, jute sacking which was obtainable without coupons and which she dyed a russet red.

On the whole we enjoyed ourselves. It was good to be together again just when we had feared to be separated for an indefinite period, and the social life was highly diverting.

I enjoyed my work too. The Wren officers who did the deciphering – 'cipherines' – were charming and two or three of them very pretty indeed; also we had a little wardroom bar next to the operations room. It became a habit of the commander of the base, Charles Stack, to put his head round my door at 1100 or so with the words, 'Come on, Staffy, gin time!' If my duties allowed – and by that time in the morning most of the important daily work had been done – I would join him in the wardroom. Here we drank gin, twopence a tot, from glasses made by sawing off the bottom half of small soda-water bottles. Between sips these fitted conveniently into the breast pocket of one's uniform jacket. The little ritual lasted about twenty minutes. It began with Charles raising his glass and giving the well-known Scottish toast: 'Here's to us, none like us.' One day I replied by saying, 'And why the bloody hell should they?' So witty did he find this response that I had to repeat it daily – and it always got its laugh.

When the baby was due we moved into the Stacks' house and when things were imminent Diana was whisked off to a nursing home on the other side of the city. Pre-natal standards were abysmally low by today's criteria. Diana, never tremendously robust physically though of indomitable spirit, was ill-prepared for the birth and had a terrible time. I was not there for the delivery (nor have I been for that of any of my children, for the father's presence was not encouraged then as it now is and I have always been and still am squeamish in these matters), but by all accounts it was less than skilfully managed. When I was called in a hurry from the operations room where I was on night watch it was all over. Diana was in a bad way, and the boy baby lived only a few hours – mercifully, perhaps, for the doctor and midwife feared brain damage. The bomb near the cottage was held responsible, but we think that inadequate midwifery had more than a little to do with it.

Both my senior officers in the operations room had now left and I found myself doing the job of Staff Officer Operations (S9).

About this time another of the odd Naval exercises in which I was a pawn took place. This was the handing over of a number of our ships on loan to the Russians. Rosyth on the Firth of Forth to the south of us was the centre for the operation. A battleship, a cruiser and a few destroyers were, I believe, part of the package, but we at (S9) were concerned with the training exercises for the handing over of four submarines to our allies.

The four boats, *Sunfish* (renamed B1), *Unbroken* (B2), *Unison* (B3) and *Ursula* (B4), turned up with skeleton Royal Naval crews and full Russian crews already on board. Communication was difficult. The interpreters seemed to have no grasp of technical terms in either language.

The programme was simple, and not unlike our take-over of the American destroyers in Halifax. The Russians would get to know the boats by coming out with the British crews on a series of man-oeuvres in the exercise area off Arbroath. Then the British crews would leave the boats, and the Russians would have two or three days of shake-down exercises by themselves before pushing off for Murmansk, each proceeding separately according to careful routing instructions.

Things went well at first. The Russians learnt fast and were friendly. They would have been more friendly still if the political commissars in each crew had allowed it, but any attempt on our part to provide personal hospitality was quickly stamped on. For instance, one of our commanding officers whose parents lived near-by tried to take his opposite number home at the weekend, but this was not permitted. The sailors were not allowed a free run ashore, only conducted tours. The officers did manage to get pretty high one night at a mess party, however. The Georgian captain-to-be of *Sunfish* excelled himself: an out-going fellow with Stalin-like moustaches except that they curled up at the ends, he became known as 'Handlebars', a name which he lived up to by riding a bicycle round the mess after dinner with his hands to his face. But this night of jollity was obviously not approved of; thereafter the Russian discipline became tighter as the Russians themselves became less so.

Having taken over the submarines the Russians clapped on the most stringent security: not a single British person was allowed on board again and an armed sentry was posted at the inboard end of each gangway. We responded by putting one of our own sentries, unarmed, at the landward end. They put in exorbitant demands for spares of all kinds including medical supplies. We did our best to satisfy them nonetheless.

All four submarines were due to sail at staggered intervals, starting early one morning. The evening before we had had a briefing session, at which I had given the crews the most detailed instructions about their courses, speed of advance and bombing restriction areas, which should take them safely, as far as our forces were concerned, round the North Cape into their own waters.

At around midnight that evening our sentry on the end of the gangway of one of the U class boats was startled to hear shouting coming from the submarine and even more startled to see a Russian officer come staggering down the gangway with a knife sticking out of his back. For some reason the officer was not followed and our sentry quickly got him to the guardhouse at the dock gates from where he was whisked up to the Naval hospital not far away. Our doctors pounced on him, withdrew the knife and reported that he was in a dangerous condition and could not be moved. He certainly could not sail as planned at first light. He turned out to be one of the Russian captains. After an hour or so a Russian delegation with an interpreter came to say that he must be returned to the boat and it must sail. Our doctors refused; they said that to move him might be fatal and they were not going to discharge him from hospital. The Russians withdrew. Shortly before dawn an armed party of Russian sailors arrived at the hospital with a stretcher. They walked straight to the room where the injured man was, bundled him on to the stretcher, marched back to the docks and the boat duly sailed. Whether he survived or not I do not know, nor how he came to be stabbed in the first place.

We were glad it was not our extrovert friend Handlebars, of whom we had grown quite fond. Alas, however, he became the victim of his own rashness. Having called as ordered at Lerwick, he hurried his boat ahead, disregarding his instructions and the safety areas provided, and two nights later was sunk, hopelessly out of position, by an R.A.F. Liberator. The three surviving Us were returned to Britain at the end of the war.

Diana mended fast and by July 1944 she was again pregnant. Apart from taking her for long walks during a few days' leave at Blair Atholl and making her slide down a mountain on her backside I treated her with great care.

I realized that I was now doing a job which, had I the qualification, would carry more money – badly needed – and advancement in rank. Accordingly I put in for the Staff Course at Greenwich and, with the recommendation of Captain (S), was accepted for the autumn term, somewhat to my surprise.

We moved down from Dundee with mixed feelings. We had become fond of the place and of our colleagues, and life there was peaceful compared to London where the V1s were about to give way to the even more lethal V2s. Diana went back to her parents at Hodges Place. I was resident in the Royal Naval College where the windows of my third floor 'cabin', already consisting of cardboard rather than glass, were more than once blown in by the blast from bombs of one kind or another.

I enjoyed the ten weeks of the course itself and loved living in the mess, with meals in the Painted Hall – shored up with protective scaffolding but still preserving its atmosphere at dinner-time with aged vintage port at fourpence a glass (limit two glasses per head, three on guest nights!) – skittles in the ancient alley in the bowels of the building, visits to the Yacht Tavern just outside the gates, and getting home to Kent for thirty-six hours each weekend.

Apparently I gave satisfaction in the course and was then given a little leave, which included Christmas, while they decided what to do with me. Of course I wanted to go to a submarine flotilla again, but there didn't seem to be an immediate vacancy and I was packed off at the beginning of January to Greenock as Staff Officer (Administration) to Captain (D). I really knew little about destroyers and the administrative side did not interest me greatly after having been used to the vicarious thrills of the operations room. What is more, Diana and I moved at first into the officers' annexe of the Seaman's Hostel at Greenock which was desolate to a degree. Our attempts to warm our otherwise unheated room by collecting driftwood from the beach and burning it in the empty fireplace were singularly unpopular, producing toxic smoke from the tar-impregnated wood and little in the way of heat. Diana was miserably uncomfortable. There was a record-breaking cold spell that year, and I had another of my tonsillitis attacks and had to go to hospital for a few days. We then moved into a comfortable hotel which cost us far more than we could afford.

I was not sorry to receive a sudden summons in mid-February to return to London and report to the Second Sea Lord's Office. The fact was that the war in Europe was nearly over, and though the V2s were still plunging into London the Germans were in full retreat. Someone had thought of the logistical and psychological problems involved in the imminent return of a large number of prisoners-of-war, some of whom had been taken early on in the war. As an ex-P.O.W. and with staff training I was selected to look after the return from Germany of all the Naval P.O.W.s. I was by now a lieutenant-commander and joined the Admiralty with an office of my own high up in Queen Anne's Mansions overlooking the ruins of the Guards Chapel.

Diana was still with her parents and I was able to commute. As the arrival of our child got nearer Diana and I went to stay with a cousin of hers in Dulwich, whose husband was an anaesthetist at King's College Hospital. On 25 April she gave birth to our eldest daughter Simone in King's; this time, although it was again not an easy birth, all went well.

My task was made easy by good documentation and I was able to draw up a scheme for repatriation and rehabilitation. Events moved fast, however, and even before the surrender was signed on 4 May prisoners began to be flown in to Northolt. From there they were packed off on indefinite leave. The war in the Far East was still on and demobilization had not yet got under way.

When plans for demobilization were at last announced they laid down that all non-regular personnel would be demobilized progressively according to what was called their 'age and service group', the oldest with the longest service first and so on. For many people this meant months' if not years' more service until their turn came. Some of the returning P.O.W.s had been in the bag so long that their repatriation leave would have to be followed by a considerable period of retraining before they could be of much use. With my commanding officer's blessing I drafted an Admiralty Fleet Order which, in brief stated that ex-P.O.W.s could be demobilized immediately if, in the opinion of their senior officers, there was no point in keeping them on. This order was approved and promulgated.

Soon all the Naval P.O.W.s were home or accounted for, and it was decided that, as the war with Japan looked like being over in a measurable time, I should be sent out there to make liaison with the Americans and set up machinery for the recovery of our Naval personnel in Japanese hands. Information was scarce, the Red Cross not having any organization there and the Japanese in no way subscribing to the Geneva Convention. In order that I could keep my end up with the Americans it was recommended that I should be given an acting brass-hat for the mission and rise from lieutenant-commander to full commander. While all this was in preparation the atom bomb was dropped on Hiroshima on 6 August and the Japanese surrendered on 14 August. My trip to the Far East, and my brass-hat, were cancelled, as the speed of events did not provide time to set up any special organization.

I had little to do and my department was winding down. I began to consider my future, something that I had hardly done before. I did not want to go back to being an actor. In my heart of hearts I knew that I would never be a great one, just someone with a superficial talent. I was tempted to stay in the Navy, having enjoyed every aspect of Naval life. But Diana was not and would never be the stereotyped Naval wife – so what?

Coasting along at the Admiralty, wondering what to do next, one day in early September I got a wholly unexpected letter which said, briefly, that Glyndebourne was getting itself together again, that Rudolf Bing was resuming his pre-war job as general manager, and that he was looking for an assistant. Would I, if I were interested, go for an interview with him in an office in Canada House in Trafalgar Square? The letter was signed by one W. E. Edwards from an address in Lewes, Sussex. This gave me a clue.

My Aunt Freda had married a certain Leslie Turner who was an estate agent. They had lived for most of my young life in the third castle, Braemar, and had had three children. In the first war, Leslie had served as a dashing motor-cycle dispatch rider, and his colleague and great friend had been Walter Edwards. At some point Edwards became John Christie's agent for the Glyndebourne and Tapeley estates. Edwards offered Leslie Turner a job as his assistant at Tapeley (in North Devon) and then when, in about 1933, Edwards became John Christie's man-of-business and was set up in an office in Lewes, my uncle was promoted to estate manager for the Ringmer and Glyndebourne estate. John Christie was busy expanding his local interests at this time and with Edwards's assistance set up a building works based on the old estate repair yard, a motor works (a rather grand name for a garage-cum-electrical workshop), and, of course, the opera. Edwards did not like music, still less opera, but he was involved in the finances as a sort of *éminence grise*, and thus Uncle Leslie, who knew nothing about the conduct of a theatre, found himself box-office manager for the first Glyndebourne Festival in 1934. The Turners now lived in Ringmer and I as a dutiful nephew had been to visit them now and again, principally in the winter months when I was not sailing.

Well, I thought, why not? Though I was not interested in opera and indeed despised opera singers for being rotten actors, I was interested in the continual development of the stage and backstage facilities at Glyndebourne. Hamish Wilson was the designer in residence at that time and something of a household pet of the

Christies. On a number of occasions he had proudly showed me over the buildings but I never actually attended a performance there in pre-war days. When Glyndebourne was starting up again Bing consulted Edwards, whom he liked and respected, about finding an assistant, or rather two. Edwards knew of me as my uncle's nephew with several years of theatrical experience and, furthermore, as someone to whom he thought the Navy had given the potentiality to be an administrator – hence the letter.

I went to see Bing. He seemed a bit puzzled to be interviewing a Naval officer in uniform but did not turn me down out of hand. Indeed he arranged for me to present myself to the Christies two days later at 5 p.m. (still 1700 to me) in the foyer of the Savoy Hotel. This I duly did, and they took me into the bar on the left up a few steps from the entrance hall which seems to be just the same today as it was then. I put my cap, gloves and silver-headed ebony stick – we were a bit dandyish at Queen Anne's Mansions – under my chair, tea was brought and conversation began. Audrey was charming and drew me out. John said little, as I recall. I took my leave, went home, and told Diana that I had no idea what it was all about but everyone seemed very nice.

Three days later I had another letter from Edwards, offering me the job of Rudi Bing's assistant at £750 per annum plus train fares. I was required to start work, as soon as I could free myself, at the new London office. The whole thing was a surprise, but it offered an immediate solution to the problem of what to do next and after discussing it with Diana I decided to accept, thinking that it would provide me with employment while I cast about for a more obvious opportunity.

I went to my commanding officer. 'I've been offered a job,' I said. 'They want me to start as soon as possible. Would you, sir, be so kind as to sign me out under the A.F.O.' (the one I had drafted). 'Of course, dear boy,' he replied. 'I've just bought a farm in Scotland. I'm off myself next week.'

So I finished my Naval career. On Friday I went to Olympia to collect my 'demob' outfit of civilian suit, raincoat, hat, shoes, etc. I didn't flog it, as many did, to the black-market touts waiting outside the door. The next week on 1 October 1945, my twenty-ninth birthday, I joined the good ship Glyndebourne.

NINE

In limbo

What follows is a very personal account of, as Stanislavsky put it, 'My Life in Art'. When I told my old friend George Malcolm Thomson, no mean historian himself, that I was about to launch upon an account of this, the longest section of my life, but had a bad memory for the sequence of events, he advised: 'Bugger history, write about the girls.' I hope I shall not take unseemly liberties with history; I shall try to heed his advice in the second part, though with discretion, and I shall not be able to avoid bringing in the odd, or not so odd, male here and there.

Post-war Glyndebourne had set up its London office in 66 Great Cumberland Place, behind Marble Arch, only a few doors away from the house in which John Christie had been born. Rudi Bing had been released by Spedan Lewis, the chairman of the John Lewis Partnership and a good friend of John Christie's, from his war-time job at Peter Jones to resume his old post as general manager, and he had two irons in the fire with which he hoped to get Glyndebourne going again. He realized, as did John and Audrey, that the pre-war days when untaxed money could be made available to run the Glyndebourne Festival as a private venture were gone, nor had private sources been replaced by a more or less heavily funded Arts Council and large-scale sponsorship such as exists today. Other solutions must be found. Objective number one was to get Glyndebourne open again, to clear away the minor additions that had enabled it to be used as a home for children evacuated from London, and to rebuild the basic organization.

Fortunately Glyndebourne had escaped the attention of the Services. Fortunately also Jock Gough, the stage foreman whom John had taken over from the Tunbridge Wells Opera House to help him build Glyndebourne, had remained as resident caretaker, being too old for military service. The Ringmer Building Works with its joinery shops still existed, as did the Motor Works, and their skilled staff were coming back from the war. What is more, while Audrey and the children, Rosamond and George, had been packed off to Canada and America, John had stayed on at Glyndebourne and exercised his meticulous care and interest in every aspect of the place, doing daily, and indeed nightly, rounds of supervision.

Some event had to take place at Glyndebourne itself, and as soon as possible. After various kites had been flown, as Spike Hughes has so fully and well described in his history of Glyndebourne, Bing was able to conclude an agreement with the coterie of artists surrounding Benjamin Britten to combine in launching the latter's *Rape of Lucretia* for a short season in 1946, to be followed by an extensive provincial tour and some performances abroad. John Christie personally was to give the financial backing and Bing his professional advice, but the artistic direction remained in the hands of Britten, his collaborators and his publisher.

The hopes of Glyndebourne were mainly pinned on an international artistic festival on the lines of Salzburg to be started somewhere in the British Isles wherever money could be found. This, it was hoped, would enable Glyndebourne to carry on its pre-war work within the Christies' financial limitations. This idea had been discussed in the early days of the phoney war in 1940, when Glyndebourne mounted a tour of *The Beggar's Opera* in which Audrey sang Polly Peachum. One evening when the tour was in Edinburgh, Audrey and Bing stood on a traffic island in Princes Street. The castle, looming against the lurid sky and racing clouds, made them both think of Salzburg and it was Audrey who said: 'This is the place for our festival.'

The idea was left to simmer as the war became more intense, but as soon as its conclusion seemed to be a measurable distance away the Christies and Bing returned to the scheme with renewed enthusiasm. The approach to Edinburgh was fruitful, and thus was born the Edinburgh International Festival. At the time I enter the story both *The Rape of Lucretia* première and the first Edinburgh Festival of 1947 were irons glowing nicely in the furnace and ready to be beaten into shape.

The second assistant whom Bing took on was Ian Hunter. He had been a conductor-pupil of Fritz Busch before the war and was still in the Army; he didn't get his discharge until several months after me. Since I was there first and the *Rape* was more advanced than Edinburgh, since my theatrical experience was greater, and since Ian was an Edinburghian anyway, it naturally came about that I got the Glyndebourne side of Rudi's work and Ian the Edinburgh part, my concern with the Edinburgh Festival being restricted to Glyndebourne's physical contribution of presenting opera in the King's Theatre.

For my first year I commuted from Kent to Great Cumberland Place and spent one day a week at Glyndebourne. For the 1946 season of the *Rape* at Glyndebourne, Diana, the baby Simone and I stayed with my widowed Aunt Freda in her cottage in Ringmer. I went out on tour with the *Rape*, and in the autumn Diana and I bought a little terraced house in what was then a quiet back-street of Lewes; it cost us £740, most of which we got on a mortgage.

The Rape of Lucretia was my first experience of opera and opera singers. Glyndebourne's contribution artistically was twofold; first, in suggesting Kathleen Ferrier to Britten for the title role and second, by pressing upon him the great Swiss conductor Ernest Ansermet, to alternate with the young Reginald Goodall. All the important parts were double-cast and Nancy Evans shared Lucretia with Kathleen. I went to meet Nancy on her arrival at Lewes station and was overwhelmed by her beauty. Kathleen on the other hand was a jolly, earthy, North Country person, and I found that all the company were just like the actors I had known so I speedily lost my awe of them. Only Joan Cross and Peter Pears continued to overawe me, probably because of their nearness to Britten, who seemed to me a remote, withdrawn figure who obviously did not see eye to eye with John Christie. Flora Nielsen alternated with Joan Cross in the soprano part, and the Danish tenor Aksel Schiötz with Peter Pears. Otakar Kraus shared Tarquinius with a young American, Frank Rogier; I struck up a warm friendship with Otakar which was to last for many years. The sets and costumes were designed by John Piper, and most of the fabrics were hand-dyed. I well remember the impressive hand-dyed dress that John's wife Mfanwy wore on the first night.

My involvement with the Britten group lasted until the next year, 1947, when they came to Glyndebourne again – now as a separate company, the English Opera Group – and repeated the *Rape* with the addition of the first performances of *Albert Herring*. Glyndebourne in the same season presented Gluck's *Orfeo*, with Kathleen Ferrier singing the role for the first time.

Relations between Britten and Christie had become strained. Christie thought that the previous year's *Rape* had cost him far more than it was worth and made a number of criticisms about some of the cast who were Ben's friends. Richard Lewis had come into the cast in place of Schiötz and Christie considered him to be a Glyndebourne find. Altogether there were many small frictions, and I found myself in a somewhat difficult position. I was more or less one of the company as far as the artists were concerned but still in fact Christie's man. The last straw came when the English Opera Group, in the person of their general manager Anne Wood, offered me a more responsible and better paid job as their company manager. I thought it over and turned it down, but John was furious that they had offered it to me without consulting him or Bing. My choice was to prove the right one eventually, but I was given cause to doubt this by hearing from Audrey that she had seriously considered suggesting to Bing that he got rid of me as I did not seem to be giving enough attention to Glyndebourne's affairs. My decision to stay proved a turning point, and for the rest of her life Audrey gave me the greatest help, encouragement and indeed affection.

During the winter I continued to have my one day a week at Glyndebourne, usually a Tuesday or Wednesday, and there were regular meetings with Edwards, who had an office in Lewes, and with Bing, often over lunch in Shelley's Hotel. Bing spent the occasional weekend at Glyndebourne, almost always alone, his wife Nina, somewhat of a recluse, preferring to stay in their flat in Maida Vale with the dachshund Pip.

One Monday in the Baker Street office, to which we had moved in order to accommodate the expansion needed for the Edinburgh Festival, Rudi said: 'When you go to Glyndebourne next will you please go up to the bedroom I was in for the weekend. I think I left some handkerchiefs, a tie and socks in the chest of drawers beside the bed.' I found the room, one on the top floor overlooking the garden, collected the minor haberdashery and duly bore it back to London. Rudi was a heavy smoker and the Christies did not like smoking in their company. 'I've brought back your things and removed the evidence of your smoking in bed,' I told him. 'What do you mean?' he asked. 'Well, the box you'd used as an ashtray I put in the dustbin. I suppose you'd got rid of the cigarette ends.' 'Box!' he exclaimed, 'what box?' 'A plain cardboard box with metal corners with a lot of ash in it.' 'My God,' said Rudi. 'That was my father.'

His mother and father had come to live in Lewes just before the war and had loved it. When his father, by then a widower, died, Rudi could think of nowhere more suitable to scatter his ashes than on the downs between Lewes and Glyndebourne where he had so often walked. Without saying anything to anyone he had taken the ashes over to Glyndebourne. Unfortunately the night had been moonless and the scattering, obviously, not a complete success.

Regular trips to Edinburgh were made by Rudi, Ian and myself. All three of us went up together on the night sleeper train. On one occasion, as was our habit, we met for breakfast in the dining car. Three cups of coffee were produced and a small saucer with three lumps of sugar; food rationing was still strictly in force. The lumps were not of uniform size. Looking nonchalantly out of the window Rudi stretched out a hand and popped the largest lump into his cup. Spotting his action I speedily followed suit and got the next largest. Too late Ian found himself with the smallest. Blinking rapidly, he said: 'You two aren't gentlemen, grabbing the largest lumps like that.' 'All right,' said Rudi. 'Suppose you'd had the first choice. Which would you, as a gentleman, have taken?' 'The smallest, of course,' said Ian. 'That's exactly what you've got, so why make a fuss?' In retrospect I can't help feeling that that was a lesson well learnt by my friend who has since seldom ended up with the smallest lump of the sweet things in life.

Theatrical costumes were also still subject to coupons, a special ration being made which was far from adequate. In an attempt to alleviate the situation for *Orfeo* John Christie donated a pair of his own long underpants to provide part of the costume of one of the fiends in the Hades scene. It was an easy sacrifice for him, as he bothered little about underclothes.

With Ferrier in *Orfeo* were a charming American girl Ann Ayars as Euridice and an equally charming Greek girl as Amor. Carl Ebert had come back from self-imposed exile in Ankara to direct (or to produce, as we termed the function until recently), and Zoë Vlachopoulos from Athens was his choice for the part. Besides her big round eyes and ready smile I chiefly remember the most deliciously dimpled knees revealed by her costume as Eros, erotic knees if ever I saw any, and the one phrase of English she had learnt from Rudi Bing: 'Don't be Vaig, arsk for Haig.'

I had my first managerial experience of an industrial dispute. As assistant manager I was in effect house manager and responsible for the day to day running of the opera house and its ancillary services, which included the catering. This was being done by Glyndebourne itself, as it had been in pre-war days, and had its own manager, 'Buster' Brown. All the wine came from the firm of O. W. Loeb, supplied by the great Otto himself; much of it had passed through the same hands twice, as Christie had sold up the cellar during the war at a considerable profit, only to find that he had to buy a large part of it back again after the war at a correspondingly marked-up price. The chef was none other than the redoubtable Trompetto, who went on to take charge of the Savoy Hotel kitchens in London and to become one of the first of radio and television's great cooks.

The dispute that arose was not over the food or drink, however. The trouble was with the male waiters and arose because they regarded themselves as casual labour and were paid by the night, together with a share of the tips, the 'tronc'. With new and tighter post-war tax controls, the ruling was given that these payments should be subject to P.A.Y.E. On the first Friday of the season, when the waiters arrived by bus from Lewes and Brighton, they found that their pay-packets reflected the ruling and promptly refused to serve dinner in the interval, then only about an hour away; the curtain had already gone up. Buster reported to me, I reported to Bing, the accountant Dennis Gardiner confirmed the correctness of Buster's action, and the waiters dug their toes in. Bing, Gardiner and I prepared to do the waiting ourselves, seeking recruits from the gentlemen of the corps of ushers – then as now a splendid body of local devotees who, in return for a small daily rate and the chance to hear the opera several times a week, provide that atmosphere of unhurried calm and efficiency which ensures that Glyndebourne audiences do as they are told without resentment. At the last moment, however, Buster achieved a settlement acceptable to all, and the audience never discovered how near they were to having their cold salmon and cucumber and strawberries and cream all on one plate.

Amongst the waitresses were two girls who sunbathed topless in the car-park as the first of the audience was arriving. Several drivers were seen to be making repeated circuits of the area before parking, but eventually formal protest, or perhaps just a deterioration in the weather, brought the practice to an end. It was the same two girls, either together or in turns, who used to pay nocturnal visits to an Italian member of the music staff occupying a room in the house immediately above Bing's. 'I don't care what he does with the girls,' Bing said to me, 'but why the hell has he to move the furniture about to do it?'

After the last and unhappy joint season with the English Opera Group we started rehearsals at Glyndebourne for the first Edinburgh Festival, in which we were to present *Macbeth* and *Le nozze di Figaro*. Both were essentially revivals from the last Glyndebourne festival in 1939, with a number of members of the old casts returning. The biggest snag was that Fritz Busch could not be asked to return as conductor. During the war he had remained in the Americas, both North and South, while Carl Ebert had chosen to go east to Turkey. Busch had alienated the Christies' affection as well as Ebert's. He had mounted several operas, notably *Macbeth*, with his son, who had been Ebert's assistant, in charge of the productions, but without, in Ebert's or Glyndebourne's opinion, having given sufficient reference to the productions' origin. As a result of this tiff he had not been as helpful to Audrey while she was in America and in need of both moral and financial support as his normally kind and generous nature would have led one to expect.

Glyndebourne needed names for its début at Edinburgh. Greatly daring, Bing offered the job to Georg Szell, a Hungarian of difficult temperament but undoubted talent and recommended by no less a man than Bruno Walter. He had also conducted the Scottish Orchestra, which Bing felt Glyndebourne was under obligation to use at Edinburgh, and would therefore be prepared for its undoubtedly ropy state in those difficult post-war years.

The casts assembled at Glyndebourne for the statutory four weeks' rehearsal: one week of musical preparation, with individual artists and their coaches at the piano, leading to ensembles and a full sing through with the conductor, then production rehearsals and the slow build up to orchestra, stage and costumes.

Macbeth had Francesco Valentino and Margherita Grandi from the pre-war cast and *Figaro* had John Brownlee, a veteran from the second Glyndebourne season of 1935, as the Count. Italo Tajo, who had been in the chorus in 1935 and 1936, sang both Figaro and Banquo, and Eleanor Steber and Giulietta Simionato each made their début with Glyndebourne as the Countess and Cherubino respectively. It seemed altogether a promisingly starry cast for a new international festival.

My indoctrination into the facts of operatic life was speedy. First the Susanna fell by the wayside. She was American, a presumably talented girl whom Rudi had 'discovered' and succeeded in selling as a prospect to all the top brass concerned. Only Szell was suspicious, and his suspicions were vindicated. She turned up for rehearsals not knowing one note of the part and wearing a sexy pink satin pyjama-suit, by no means standard gear in those days. However talented she was in other ways, her rate of learning notes was slow and Szell insisted that she be dismissed. A hurried search was instigated for an adequate replacement at short notice, but Szell was hard to please. Tatiana Menotti, who had sung Despina at Glyndebourne in 1936, was available, but she could not come for several days and Szell didn't know her anyway.

Walter Midgley was Macduff; not the most experienced of operatic actors at that time or the most accomplished ever. At the end of one morning's rehearsal Szell, a tall, lean, saturnine figure, turned to him and said: 'Tell me, Mr Midgley, when are you going to sing *some* of the notes Verdi provided?' Walter, unabashed, replied in his high-pitched voice with a good Yorkshire accent: 'It's all bloody well for you, you've got the score in front of you.' 'Don't you know, Mr Midgley, that I never conduct from the score?' Szell stalked coldly away. Midgley turned to me and gave me his opinion of Szell in one short word. 'But,' he went on, 'that man Ebert's a genius. I didn't know what to do in my aria except stand and sing but he told me to lift my sword in front of me like a cross. It's a bloody marvellous gesture. I shall use it in all me parts.'

The next day at ten o'clock, with rehearsals due to begin in half an hour, there was general consternation. Szell had packed his bags and silently stolen away without a word of explanation to Bing or anyone else. So there we were, with less than a fortnight to go, without a conductor for either opera (Tullio Serafin had originally been engaged to share with Szell but had refused to accept the British income tax regulations), and with Susanna still on her way from Italy. Excellent though hardly world-famous conductors were found from close at hand and Tatiana Menotti turned in a charming performance which went particularly well with Simionato's Cherubino.

Szell and Bing never made it up. Szell's career with the Cleveland Orchestra is world famous but his austere reputation persists. Bing never engaged him again, and on one occasion when someone said to Bing that Szell was his own worst enemy Bing is reported to have replied: 'Not while I'm alive.'

Margherita Grandi was a formidable lady and undoubtedly the most convincing operatic Lady Macbeth of my experience. Although born in Tasmania she was Italian by blood and her English was more Latin than 'strine'. In Edinburgh she was assigned a room in the North British Hotel which straddled the railway line. There were still a lot of steam trains about. Early next morning I was summoned to her presence. I went bearing roses. 'I cannot rehearse today, I cannot stay in this room. The weather is warm [it was; the first Edinburgh Festival began in wonderful weather], it is *un*breathable with the window clos-ed and with it open the *rumore* and the *carbone* are *impossibile*.' I got her moved to the Caledonian Hotel, another station hotel but less intimately affected by the trains.

One evening I made my way to the stalls bar at the King's Theatre during the second part of the opera to meet the manager and get the figures for the audience that evening. The bar lady told me that the night before had been her evening off and she had gone to see some elderly relatives 'outwith' – as they say in the North – the city. 'What have you got on this week?' they asked. 'Oh, still the opera,' she had replied. 'We heard the broadcast last week,' they told her, 'and we thought they sang marvellously, but how the puir wee things manage to learn it all and perform with their handicap we can't imagine.' 'Handicap?' said my friend. 'What handicap?' 'The announcer said they were all born blind. We heard him distinctly say the Blindborn Opera Company.'

John Pritchard joined the music staff in 1947, recommended to Audrey Christie by Roy Henderson. Audrey and I went to hear him conduct the Derby String Orchestra in a concert performance of a Handel oratorio in Derby one wet and cold winter's night. I think this was the first bit of 'talent hunting' I ever did on Glyndebourne's behalf, but not the last and by no means the least rewarding.

That autumn ended my first two years at Glyndebourne, the period I had given myself in which to cast around and think what my future, our future, should be. I had done reasonably well, not financially but in the agreeableness of life. Diana seemed happy in a musical and not too rigid background. I found the mixed experience of the theatre and the Navy helpful in providing clues to handling people. Glyndebourne's future seemed to be expanding despite the financial damper on the festival itself. Only one other job had been offered and I had turned it down. Our little house in Lewes was adequate if primitive, and marriage seemed to be worth it. I had only one serious regret – there was no sailing.

TEN

On the ladder

The 1948 season began with the Bath Assembly, a junior offshoot from the Glyndebourne team. Bath had been one of the cities on the original Bing list for a festival and the venture stemmed from that. Ian Hunter ran it and I looked after the opera – in this case an English version by Basil Ashmore of Mozart's *Die Entführung aus dem Serail*. It was presented by 'the Assembly Opera under Glyndebourne direction'. The Assembly as a whole was an artistic success, but the burghers of Bath took against the idea of culture being thrust upon them by a bunch of outsiders and decided that they would henceforth run a more 'popular' festival from their own resources.

The next event was the inauguration at Glyndebourne itself of 'A Festival of Mozart Concerts under the direction of Sir Thomas Beecham, Bart. [he always insisted on the suffix] and in association with The Arts Council of Great Britain'.

It was now clear to all concerned that Glyndebourne Opera had no hope of performing under its own aegis in Glyndebourne, for there simply wasn't the money, but that the ploy of finding a new venue at Edinburgh, even if inadequately housed, was working. How to keep a path trodden to Glyndebourne was the question, and the answer seemed to be to rekindle the old love-hate relationship between Sir Thomas Beecham and John Christie which, though barren till now, still showed signs of possible fecundity. Beecham's latest orchestra, the Royal Philharmonic, was interested; indeed it had agreed to replace the frankly sub-standard Scottish Orchestra at the King's Theatre for the next Edinburgh Festival and, who knew, perhaps Sir Thomas might even at last one day conduct a Glyndebourne Festival Opera performance. The first step was the concerts, and I was appointed manager on the basis of fools stepping in . . . For me this was the start of several happy years with Sir Thomas.

He and the then Lady Beecham, Betty Humby, herself a concert pianist, came to live as John Christie's somewhat unsatisfactory tenants at Delves House on the village green at Ringmer. Lady Beecham was in delicate physical and nervous health. On occasions I would lunch with them and she would then retire to rest while Tommy and I sat down to discuss programmes. This generally meant making few decisions but it produced from him an endless stream of anecdotes which got louder and louder as he enjoyed himself, and the port, more and more, until there would come a thumping on the floor of the room above and the sound level would fall abruptly. Sadly I kept no notes of the anecdotes, and now so many of Tommy's have been swapped amongst his friends and acquaintances that it is difficult to remember which that I know are original and which apocryphal. Once, in the midst of some philosophical flight of rhetoric, he declared: 'As Goethe said to me...' with a quick look to see how I took this statement of his own venerability (1949 was Goethe's bicentenary); then, with just a twinkle in those lively eyes and a pull at his cigar, off he went again, enlarging the theme and increasing the decibels before the inevitable thumps.

The 1948 concerts were spread over a Wednesday to Saturday in mid-July. The first afternoon Tommy delivered a 'lecture'. It was publicized as being 'on Mozart with reference to works to be performed at the Festival'. In fact it was a public performance of my Delves House afternoons but without the thumps and with much laughter from the audience. There were four evening orchestral concerts by the Royal Philharmonic, with Clifford Curzon, Gerald Jackson, Dorothy Bond, Dennis Brain, Jean Pougnet and Frederick Riddle as soloists, and four afternoon chamber recitals by the Philharmonia String Quartet with William Glock, three of the four players who were soon to become the Amadeus Quartet, and Harold Craxton, Leon Goossens and Arthur Grumiaux. Not a bad line-up, as history has proved.

In the last concert one of the items was Brahms's 'Four part songs for female voices, horns and harp'. I stood with Tommy in the wings. The stage had on it the curious 'concert set' of scenery designed for John Christie by his friend 'Bear' Warre to echo the panelling of the auditorium – part of which, as was the existing *trompe l'œil* panelling at the back of the gallery in the organ room, was painted by John himself under instruction from the scene-painter. The seating having been suitably arranged, on went the horn players. Tommy turned to me and, in a resonant stage whisper on a rising tone, said 'The horns!' Next came the harpist. 'The harpie!' Finally the twelve girls (selected from the Glyndebourne chorus). 'And the whoors!' Chuckling, he toddled – Beecham never walked – on to the stage. The 1949 concerts were extended to three weekends. The Haydn chamber recital was to include, at Tommy's insistence, the *Divertimento for two hurdy-gurdys*, and Tommy also insisted that John should be one of the soloists. John reluctantly agreed, thinking that the instrument had simply to be held under one arm and cranked with the other hand. Too late he realized that the playing required fingering of the strings as well. Saying nothing, he turned up at the rehearsal not with the instrument (indeed great difficulty had been found in tracing one, let alone two, playable instruments) but with the current Glyndebourne pug dog, called Sock, held under one arm while he twiddled its tail with his other hand. Beecham did not find this funny – it wasn't his joke. Finally the piece was played by one of the orchestra on one instrument only.

While the concerts were still on, unexpected developments on the managerial side were afoot. Edinburgh had found Glyndebourne, in the person of John Christie, too seignorial for their Scottish civic pride and had sought to drop the recognition of Glyndebourne as their 'Artistic Management'. Bing insisted for a time that he was Christie's man, and even when in early 1949 the divorce between Edinburgh and Glyndebourne took place, Bing still managed to serve both parties and be at once general manager of Glyndebourne and 'Director of Festival Organization' at Edinburgh. The Edinburgh London office continued to be, as it was for some years afterwards, in the Glyndebourne offices at 23 Baker Street.

During the early months Bing had gone, at Glyndebourne's expense, to New York to do some scouting, ostensibly on behalf of Glyndebourne and Edinburgh. He had, however, got wind of impending changes at the Metropolitan Opera and not the least of his effort was spent in pressing his own suit. In this he was successful. The Met somehow got agreement for his release from Edinburgh after the 1949 festival and Bing coolly announced to the Christies that he was leaving. They were, not unnaturally, incensed. John was furious after all he felt he had done for Rudi before, during and since the war, and Audrey felt genuinely let down as her affectionate nature had extended itself in his direction and she had thought this feeling to be reciprocated. That he should go to the Met was not contested – who better to run the world's most important opera house (*pace* three or four others) than Glyndebourne's man? – but it was the manner of his going, or perhaps the lack of manners, that hurt them so much.

For the opera at Edinburgh in 1949 Bing's name was dropped from the Glyndebourne masthead and my name appeared as general manager just four years after I 'came ashore'. Ian Hunter was given the Edinburgh job and we two continued, one in each of Bing's shoes, to tread happily together up and down Baker Street, and have remained close friends ever since.

Working with Rudi Bing was a valuable experience; his ruthlessness was impressive, his ability to write the most cutting letters a talent of a high order, but he never imposed on either Ian or myself that aloofness which was to characterize his long tenure at the Met. There he was never anything but Mr Bing; to us he was always Rudi. More than once I took letters back to him saying, 'Look, if you want to make an enemy send this, if not I suggest . . .' Sometimes he wanted the enemy, more often he was surprised that anyone should take his remarks ill. His sense of humour I found sardonic and there was little that was overtly generous about him. His human weaknesses seemed then to be an over-solicitous care for his dachshund Pip and a penchant for ladies who were unhappy.

The 1948 Edinburgh Festival was a consolidation of the first. We again took two well-tried operas from the pre-war repertory, *Don Giovanni* in its old sets by Hamish Wilson and a newly mounted *Così fan tutte*. Rafael Kubelik conducted the *Don* with great success, alas his sole appearance with Glyndebourne to date. Paolo Silveri had the title role, a Don Juan to the life. At the end of a morning rehearsal I heard him say to one of the girls in the chorus, 'Queek, before lunch.' This became something of a catch-phrase. Ljuba Welitsch was the Donna Anna, my first, but by no means last, encounter with the Bulgarian temperament. At that time unknown outside Vienna, Ljuba was of a fiery and vivid mettle. She addressed her aria, *'Or sai chi l'onore'* directly at Don Ottario, sung by Richard Lewis, transfixing him with an extended arm and a bayonet of a forefinger. One evening I stood in the wings at this moment and she moved her aim half an inch from Richard to me, invisible to the audience. I felt the full power of her personality and stood, like a rat in front of a mongoose, incapable of movement until the laser beam of her basilisk eyes switched back to poor Richard, who had to endure the treatment at every performance.

Ian Hunter and I shared furnished accommodation not far from the King's Theatre. Ian, still a bachelor, was not unmindful of a need to remedy that situation, only unsure of where the best chances lay. The establishment was not far from the King's and belonged to a lady of undoubtedly strict views who, having locked up one of the major rooms and filled the keyhole with wadding (I know because I tried to peep into the sanctum), as well as firmly lowering the blinds and drawing the curtains, retired to the Outer Hebrides to ride out the salacious storm of 'festival' in more austere surroundings. We were constantly mindful of her unseen presence about the house; never more so than when Ian, having reserved the sitting room for a little suit-pressing on a young lady from our company, was at the height of his ardent approach when rudely disturbed by the door being thrown open violently. I was asleep, there was no gale blowing, so who could it have been but the spirit of the owner at its vigilant duty? It really need not have wasted its time because it transpired that the young lady was temperamentally better equipped to defend herself against Ian than against one of her own sex.

We had an unofficial, and improper, racket on the side; since we were both in need of ready cash we ran a gossip column in one of the two Edinburgh evening papers and continued to do so for first one and then the other for several years. We had to have our copy ready by 9 a.m. This made breakfast an anxious time, as we were often not as clear-headed as we might have been nor as early out of our respective beds when a small messenger boy would arrive on a bicycle and ring the doorbell with great punctuality. But we managed to find something every day for four weeks and to right several wrongs of omission, disregard or inaccuracy by our professional rivals, who never found out who the columnist with all the inside information was. When Ian was elevated to being director of the Festival and I to general manager of Glyndebourne these nefarious practices had to cease; the evening papers were never the same again for festival gossip and foresight.

The year 1948 was also notable for the arrival in the chorus of two young sopranos, April Cantelo and Tatiana Preston. There was a young clarinettist in the stage band of *Don Giovanni* who, so rumour had it, lived in a tent on the wilder slopes of King Arthur's Seat. April became his wife and their daughter was named Susanna, as April was by then singing Barbarina with ambitions to sing Susanna herself. The clarinettist was Colin Davis.

Tatiana, the daughter of a distinguished diplomat and a Russian mother, wielded her charm through large and liquid eyes and an endearing stutter, which left her entirely when she was on the stage. She was fond of telling people, and I certainly never tired of hearing, that she 'was b-b-born in V-V-Vladivostok where the t-t-tigers come from'. The naturally rather low and husky voice, inherited no doubt from her mother, rose to a ravishing squeak when she got to the t-t-tigers.

The Edinburgh Festival of 1949 was somewhat of a marking time as far as we were concerned. Perhaps Bing's main attentions were elsewhere when it came to the planning. But the great find was Sena Jurinac. She had been recommended by Ljuba Welitsch, who said: 'This Croatian girl is really something, for Glyndebourne she would be ideal.' Ljuba was not wrong. Sena started as a mezzo, or rather a second soprano singing Dorabella. Within a year she was singing Fiordiligi at Glyndebourne, and for me she was and remains the supreme Fiordiligi. At a Highland Ball in the Assembly Room one evening Sena sang Tosca's *Vissi d'arte* as a party piece. It was so shatteringly beautiful that her transition to soprano was confirmed on the spot. She certainly, if one may be allowed to say so, left the Highlanders reeling.

It was clear that the immediate need was to expand and re-establish our contacts in Europe. A tour of auditions and contact-making in Germany, Switzerland and Austria was planned for Audrey and myself by Freddie Diez, a swashbuckling Viennese agent whose command of English was sufficient, if somewhat more colourful than he always realized.

It was early in 1950 that we set off by plane to Düsseldorf where we were met by Diez. Düsseldorf had been terribly battered and Diez had arranged rooms for us in a modest hotel (we having only a correspondingly modest amount of money to spend, since the business allowance was then only some five pounds a day), which had not been badly damaged and was undergoing renovation. A great luxury was a private bathroom to each room; my bathroom, oddly, had two doors, one from the bedroom and one into the corridor. On the first morning I was in the bath when the corridor door was lifted off its hinges from the outside and carried away by two workmen who seemed oblivious of my presence.

We called on the opera and had audience with the Intendant, who was courteous in defeat but clearly had little hope that England would ever cut a figure in the operatic world. Here at Düsseldorf began a habit that I maintained for many years thereafter: to commemorate my first, and sometimes subsequent, visit to a particular city by the purchase of a necktie. I still have a large collection and can name the provenance of most. I also appropriated coat-hangers if they had the name of the hotel on them. Not only did this provide myself and my immediate family with a great many coat-hangers but resulted, to the benefit of most of the hotels and the detriment of only a few, in providing names which led to return, and less acquisitive, visits.

Apart from the opera productions seen, the singers heard and the personalities met, these trips greatly extended my education in the matter of food and drink. In Düsseldorf, at Diez's recommendation, I made my first, but by no means last, visit to Zum Schiffchen – an old, 'typical' restaurant in what had been a warehouse on one of the docks off the Rhine. It had heavy tables of scrubbed wood, benches, and waiters dressed in the traditional breeches and smocks of the Rhine bargee. To me, coming from victorious but poorly victualled and heavily rationed England, the menu was exciting and very German. Beginning with a pair of Frankfurter sausages with mustard and horseradish and going on to boiled beef and dumplings with a curiously acid, to my taste then, salad of a root vegetable (since identified as celeriac, and now grown by me), I paused for breath before considering the choice between a *Käseplatter*, which I knew to be a large wooden dish full of slices of cheese, black bread and gherkins, and something with the portmanteau name of *Apfelpfankuchen*. Since I am insatiably curious about new dishes and will usually go for the unknown rather than the known, I opted for the latter. 'Was ist das?' I said in my best German to the elderly waiter, pointing to the word. 'Mein Herr, das ist ein Apparat.' I ordered the 'apparatus' and it duly arrived, a huge apple pancake, light and fluffy and the size of a football pitch.

From Düsseldorf we went to Hamburg, where the opera had reopened under Günther Rennert in the old opera house with the auditorium in ruins. Rennert and his team had most ingeniously contrived a small opera house entirely on the stage area which, due to the iron safety curtain having remained down, had escaped the incendiary damage suffered by the rest of the theatre. They had used the set for Act II of *Der Rosenkavalier*, which also had remained unburnt, for the walls of the new auditorium and created a small stage at the end, and by dropping one of the old stage lifts had been able to provide an orchestra pit also. It was an almost miraculous bit of improvization which lasted for several years while the theatre was transformed and rebuilt round it. Finally the theatre closed for only a few months, while the company went on tour and the stage was reinstated in its full size. Thus the present impressive theatre was created in the busy centre of Hamburg without the opera losing any of its momentum. Rennert spoke quite good English even then, having been taken as a German prisoner-of-war to Canada. He and I got on well together.

From Hamburg we flew to West Berlin down the 'corridor' over Soviet-occupied East Germany, landing at the military airfield on the north-western outskirts. Here Diez met us again and took us to the Hotel Stephanie which was situated on the upper floors of a large house just off the Kurfürstendamm. It had large Biedermeier rooms and furniture, and only provided bed and breakfast – ersatz coffee and bread and honey with a boiled egg or cheese if required.

It was here that I suffered one of the most terrifying experiences of my life. Audrey Christie was a beautiful and fragile woman – Dresden china is the image that springs too easily to mind. Mentally she was as tough as old boots; her charm, both natural and when consciously used, was infinite; her sense of humour could always be aroused; but physically she was frail. Her later career as a professional operatic singer was affected by this, for she had not the stamina either to project the full strength of her very pretty voice, even aided by her innate musicianship and sharp intelligence, or to sustain her through the gruelling programme of rehearsals and performances. Something as yet undiagnosed was sapping her vitality.

It was the early part of the year when we went to Germany in 1950, and it was cold. Her chief protection against the elements was a black astrakhan fur coat of elegant cut but terrific weight. I have never considered myself to be a weakling but that coat weighed a ton and every time I helped her on or off with it and hung it up I wondered how so frail a figure could carry it. She ate appreciatively but little. She drank with enjoyment but never beyond the limits set by her strict self-discipline. She suffered from migraine. When this started I do not know, but I suspect that it was well before the war and that most of the last-minute cancellations of those days and a consequent reputation for unreliability were attributable to this.

On this occasion, having arrived in Berlin, been to the opera and returned to the cosily shabby calm of the Stephanie, I awoke next morning with the knowledge that we had another day before us of meeting the unknown. My breakfast was brought to me. Diez telephoned with details of the day's appointments: a meeting with the Intendant and some auditions in the private house of a voice coach of his acquaintance. Could I please have Mrs Christie on parade by 11 a.m. and could we meet for coffee at Kempinski before going on? Freddie Diez never stayed in the same hotel as us; he always had alternative accommodation elsewhere, but then he had a wide circle of friends. If he were not such a confirmed landsman he would have made a good sailor.

At about 9.30 I enquired on the house telephone whether Mrs Christie in Room 23 had called for her breakfast yet. 'No,' I was told. At 9.45 I got the same answer and asked them to connect me with her room; no reply. Ten minutes later and again I tried – still no reply. I went to her door, knocked and got no answer. The hotel had double, virtually soundproof, doors, no doubt provided in its original role as a luxurious but discreet haven for those who wished to enjoy Berlin's famous delights. I waited till noon, cancelling appointments via Diez, and tried again – nothing.

Audrey had gone to her room the night before in good health and spirits. Should I alarm the hotel and have the door opened? I decided against this as I felt confident that she would surface from whatever malaise had struck her, but as the day and then the evening wore on the strain increased. At last, late in the evening, my tap and ear to the door elicited a muffled sound from inside and I went back to try the house telephone which I had so far purposely not used for fear of disturbing her. A faint voice told me that she was all right but tired and wanted to rest.

Next day I went through much the same procedure but got no great response, other than a reassurance that she was alive, until the early evening when, on the telephone, she said she was waking up and would like something to eat. I went out to a shop in the Kurfürstendamm and bought some smoked salmon and German champagne. When I knocked on the door she opened it, pale and fragile in her négligé. On her bed was spread, despite the heavily centrally heated room, the closed windows with heavy curtains and the double door, that astrakhan coat. She had no idea of the day or time or for how long she had been 'out'. I left her for the night, telephoned Diez to say that I hoped tomorrow we could continue, and found dinner at a little restaurant nearby. In the morning she had ordered her breakfast before I ordered mine and was as fit and resolute as ever.

I was to return to Berlin on many other occasions under easier circumstances but this time I was glad to be off, by way of Frankfurt and Munich to Zürich.

Frankfurt was another war-torn city, with a really ropy small hotel – our money was only just holding out – and food of memorable badness. The opera had moved from the bombed opera house to the Grosse Schauspielhaus and was struggling; the town was overrun with American G.I.s and the atmosphere was one of expediency and callousness. We were glad to go on.

Then came Munich and another back-street hotel, but a spacious and more gracious city, in parts damaged or destroyed but still with much to admire, including a little restaurant, again Diez-recommended, Zum Kannchen. There, a few years later, I was to be offered Irish coffee – the proprietor, like Diez, being a keen fisherman and having been to Ireland – long before that pernicious beverage had become as widely known as it is today.

There were then no performances of opera in either the Munich Opera House or the Cuvilliès Theatre as both had been destroyed. All performances were given in the Prinzregenten, a clanking tram ride out of the centre of the city. Built as a precursor of Bayreuth, it was a big semicircular auditorium of raked seats with a semi-buried orchestra pit. Reverberant acoustics and a noise like machine-guns as the audience rose from the unpadded spring-loaded wooden seats which then banged upright are my chief recollections.

Leaving Munich *en route* for Zürich provided another small drama. In the early evening Audrey Christie and I arrived by a decrepit taxi at the airport building, a triumph of Nazi architecture – huge, pretentious, with doors showing all the signs of having been blasted open by the advancing American army, and round the perimeter a sort of turf wall of grandstands remaining from the political rallies and military march-pasts held there. The assembly hall was crowded and the call system to departing flights difficult to hear, and the departure board was not one of the electronic marvels we know today. The crowd in the hall was distinctly odd, old, heavily dressed, and clanking like the Munich tram. We found ourselves in the midst of a Jewish refugee party on their way to Israel with all they could carry of their scanty possessions hung about them. The heavy dressing, despite the overheated hall, was explained by the fact that they were wearing two suits or two dresses and two overcoats each, plus an imagination-boggling supply of underwear; the clanking came from the pots, pans and cooking utensils with which they had draped themselves – the regulations apparently limited the size and weight of baggage taken but put no restrictions on personal wear. I shall never forget the experience, nor fail to appreciate the emotions of the children of Israel by the waters of Babylon.

Zürich was another world. All the lights were on, the Bahnhof-strasse was a glittering row of jewellers, shoe shops, dress shops, pastry cooks, of which we had not seen the like since 1939. There was no rationing, no apparent shortages, lots of money – except for us, still on five pounds a day. The opera house, small but elegant in a heavy Swiss-German way, was full of smartly dressed people, and I well remember my shock at the all-pervading odour of garlic in the buffet such as I had not encountered since pre-war days. Suddenly it was peace time again, as though the war had never been.

Here I had one of the few experiences in the opera house that have reduced me to tears of emotion, rather than rage or boredom. Lisa della Casa was singing Butterfly and though she was about as Japanese as a Rolls-Royce (and just as sweet sounding), at the moment when she went behind the screen to die and the scarf slowly slithered down on top of her I was overcome. But perhaps it was the garlic after all!

From Zürich to Vienna – my first time ever in that city. Even in its occupied state it had that air of dilapidated gaiety and run-down grandeur which everyone still seems to feel there, something quite different from the German cities we had just been in and much more real than the neutral survivor's gloss of Switzerland. The only hotel open to British visitors at that time was the Astoria off the Kärntnerstrasse, shabby and by no means the equal of the big hotels in the Ringstrasse that had been commandeered as head-quarters for the occupying powers. With its carpets dingy and stained, and its wash-basins cracked, it was far from the pleasant hotel it is today.

The first person to call on us, within minutes of our arrival, was Sena Jurinac. Before setting off on this trip Audrey had said to me: 'You know, you look far too young and baby-faced to meet your foreign colleagues with any authority!' 'Very well, I replied, 'I'll grow another beard,' and thereupon once again stopped shaving my chin and upper lip. I have worn that one ever since. Sena had never seen me bearded, and as she came through the revolving door of the Astoria and spotted my two months' growth she burst into laughter and went round in the door two or three times before falling into the hall to embrace us.

We went to pay our respects to Dr Hilbert, the famous Intendant who ruled the Vienna Opera of those days. All performances were being given either in the old Theater an der Wien where *Die Zauberflöte* had had its first performance and where the original drop-curtain for that opera was still in use, or in the Volksoper some way from the centre.

Egon Hilbert's office was in the main building, on which

reconstruction had already begun. He received us rudely with an open half-hunter watch in front of him to indicate that his time was precious. One of his staff interpreted as he did not speak, or did not deign to speak, English, and Audrey's German could not keep pace with Hilbert's high-pitched rapid delivery. (I have always been able to understand German fairly well, especially spoken with an Austrian accent, but have never managed to speak it for anything but the expression of my basic needs.) What, in short, he told us at considerable length was that Mozart belonged to Austria and especially Vienna, and that no one in England understood, or ever could, what Mozart's music and operas really should be. It was therefore ridiculously presumptuous of Glyndebourne to declare itself a shrine to Mozart in the barbarian countryside of Sussex. We left, Audrey enraged and I astounded by his arrogant rudeness. In later times I found this attitude to apply to everything he did, and we never had any willing co-operation from him.

Freddie Diez, a Berliner by birth and a Viennese only by adoption, took us to all his favourite haunts, the *heuriger* at Feuerwehr Wagner's (Fire Brigade Wagner's) and the Zum Weissen Rauchfangkehrer (White Chimneysweep's, a restaurant much favoured by singers after performances) among them.

That he was at home in Vienna was soon demonstrated. Our travel allowance was running pitifully low by the time we reached there and the exchange rate against the Austrian schilling was frightful. Rumour had it, however – and all Viennese rumours are invariably correct – that in a week or so, some three or four days after we were due to leave and our business permit would have run out, there was to be a devaluation of the schilling by some very large percentage. Diez took us to see a personal friend of his, the manager of one of the most prestigious Viennese banks in the Graben. We entered by a side door and were shown into the manager's private office. He was most courteous and un-Hilbert like, sent out for delicious coffee, and proceeded to cash our remaining traveller's cheques at the future rate: a totally illegal transaction, of course.

The sequel to this occurred in London some months later. John Christie, having been told by Audrey of Freddie Diez's help, asked me to let him know when Freddie was next to be in England so that he could thank him personally. This I duly did and Freddie was invited to lunch with John at Brooks's, a club of which Freddie had never heard and which on entering he mistook for the English equivalent of one of those Viennese coffee houses that are somewhat club-like. The sight of members reading at table did not surprise him and he did not recognize, nor did John point out, the distinguished political figures by whom he was surrounded. The lunch he was given did somewhat disappoint him, however – shepherd's pie and rice pudding lubricated with a modest amount of English pale ale was hardly what he as a *bon viveur* really appreciated, though it was John's favourite sort of menu.

What they talked about at lunch I never found out but I doubt if either understood the other too well. The final misunderstanding took place on the pavement of St James's Street, when Freddie thanked John for luncheon and John, conscious of the great honour he had done to a foreigner in taking him to so prestigious a place, said: 'Oh, you were so very kind to my wife and my manager in Vienna that I thought this was the least I could do in return.' It was several years before I could persuade the literally minded Freddie that he had not been insulted.

Freddie, alas no longer with us, was a great womanizer, well known in Vienna for his fondness for opera singers of a certain majesty of bearing. The sight of an attractive woman entering a restaurant or bar was enough to send his head whizzing round to follow her with his eyes – indeed Diana said that he was the only man she had met whose head could turn through 360 degrees.

ELEVEN

On the make

In the autumn of 1949 plans for the Festival of Britain to be held in 1951 rapidly took shape. John Wilmot, a Labour M.P. who had been a minister in the coalition government and who was a staunch supporter of Glyndebourne, urged that Glyndebourne should reopen its doors with an opera festival for the great year. We were asked to give an all-Mozart season of four operas, and a special grant of £25,000 was promised, not through the Arts Council but direct from the Treasury.

I protested that to mount four new productions in one season was, if not impossible, at least undesirable because of the strain on all concerned. I asked that we should be able to have half the grant in advance, so as to enable us to put on two operas in a short season in 1950 and to run ourselves in for the major effort the next year. Unfortunately the Treasury could not see its way to meeting this request; the whole grant had to be paid in the one financial year.

The Christies saw my point very well. The two short seasons in 1946 and 1947 had been put on in a fairly austere fashion and no performances of opera had been given at Glyndebourne since. To run a full-scale festival on the pre-war lines would involve a big expansion of staff, most of whom would perforce be new. There was every reason to set the machine going in 1950 with a comparatively modest start.

Plans were laid and we drew up a scheme to present a new production of *Die Entführung aus dem Serail* and revive the *Così* of two years before. Even this modest ambition could not be achieved without help, and John Christie turned to his old friend, the chairman of the John Lewis Partnership, John Spedan Lewis. I was despatched, bearing my budget and detailed proposals, to see the great man at his house near Stockbridge in Hampshire. He gave me lunch and asked many questions; he then took me for a long walk in the garden while he delivered a monologue on his political and social beliefs and the principles on which he ran his store, a monologue frequently punctuated by his sudden disappearance behind a bush with the remark, 'Sorry, old man's ailment, you know.' His flow of words was, however, unbroken. We then repaired to the house and he dictated a long paper to John Christie, using two secretaries in relays so that he could read over each page in turn without waiting for the whole to be typed. After tea I was packed off, bearing the promise of a guarantee which would cover the estimated deficit on the festival. We were back in business.

As a newcomer unconcerned with the old disagreements my next mission was to ask Fritz Busch to return to reopen the Glyndebourne Festival as conductor. He accepted. The festival went well, Busch's return and Sena Jurinac's assumption of Fiordiligi being the highlights, and our sights were firmly set on 1951. Thanks to Spedan Lewis's generosity, and with our grant from the Treasury available, we were able to plan adventurously.

Mozart's *Idomeneo* had never enjoyed a professional performance in England since it had been written 170 years before. Hans Gal now prepared a performing edition to the dictates of Fritz Busch. Oliver Messel designed the sets and costumes, still the designs best suited to the music of the opera that I have ever seen. One could listen with one's eyes open and look with one's ears open, which is not always the case with this piece of *opera seria* whose complexity leads people so often to miss its effortless balance.

We had the perfect cast 'ready-made' for two of the principal roles – Sena for Ilia and Richard Lewis for the title part. In Léopold Simoneau, the Canadian, Busch had found the ideal tenor for Idamante. Birgit Nilsson, then totally unknown and another Busch find, came straight from Norway to sing Electra; she sang the two dramatic arias magnificently, the lyric central aria less well, but her acting was rudimentary and Ebert's best efforts were needed to persuade her that her arms could be held in more elegant positions than as two bananas loosely connected to her ample shoulders. She went on to make a highly successful career in the most important roles and theatres, as well as earning a reputation for a hard-headed appreciation of the value of money. During one of the Edinburgh festivals when she was singing in concerts and already famous I took her on a tour of the antique shops. She found everything too expensive until, in one of the junkier emporia, she unearthed an attractive English pottery plate priced at a shilling. Because it was cracked she got it knocked down to ninepence.

Busch, as in pre-war days, was the principal conductor of all the operas, with only a few performances going to John Pritchard. I wonder how many of today's conductors would approach so big an assignment with the confident ease shown by Busch. He was a brilliant musician, and one of the most urbane conductors; liking good wine and pretty women, he knew how to relax. His orchestra loved rather than feared him. Nothing appeared to him too serious to be turned into a joke, but he had a stubbornness of purpose sufficient to keep his end up with Ebert, and the quality of musicianship to keep Ebert, no mean musician himself, ever respectful of his demands. But by the time he came to *Don Giovanni*, our other new production, late in the season his stamina was flagging, and one hot July evening he was in obvious difficulties during the long first act. He got through it but felt he could not continue for the second act after the customary prolonged Glyndebourne dinner interval.

John Pritchard, as was customary, had checked that Fritz had turned up for the performance and then gone off to Eastbourne for a swim. By a stroke of luck I managed to ring someone who found him lying on the beach. He jumped into his car and hurtled down the twelve-mile road to Glyndebourne. Half-way there the engine of his car caught fire, and though the fire was not serious he had to abandon it; a garage provided a taxi and, hot and bothered, he arrived in the pit just in time for the second act. Here his customary coolness reasserted itself and the performance was unblemished. The audience, of course, were unaware that anything untoward was occurring.

This should have been a warning to us all, but it went unheeded. Busch went on to conduct both operas at Edinburgh, though again Pritchard had a few performances of *Don Giovanni*. I had been back home in Lewes only a few days when, in the early hours of the morning, the telephone rang. It was Ellen Morgenthau, Fritz's secretary, to tell me that he had just died, quite suddenly; she was with his wife Greta at the Savoy where he had been staying, preparing to give some London concerts. What should she do, she asked. She had told no one. Greta was distraught and she was very upset herself. 'Do nothing,' I said. 'Take Greta back to your room if she'll go with you and I'll take over.' That was easily said but I hadn't the faintest idea what to do. It was two o'clock in the morning. I put down the receiver, thought for a minute or two, and then rang the Savoy and asked for the duty manager. From that moment everything was taken out of my hands; the hotel's wonderfully smooth machine sprang into action and even the making of a death mask was organized. Fritz's death was a great shock for everyone. It was particularly tragic that, having got him back to

Glyndebourne, working again with Ebert and with Messel and Piper as collaborators, his new term of office should have been cut so short.

I had asked John Piper, who had designed the two Britten operas, to design the new *Don Giovanni*, and very magnificent it was. We gave the opera in those sets some forty-six times, the last being in 1954. Then it went out of our repertory until 1960, by which time Günther Rennert had replaced Carl Ebert. He naturally, as all directors do, wanted to reshape the work with a designer of his own choice. The Piper sets have long since disintegrated; only one of the backcloths, the street scene, still exists, rolled up and carefully stored. A number of sketches for other scenes remain and I still hope that someone will one day recreate those designs and give a new audience a chance to see John's realization on the stage again.

Lisa della Casa, who had so moved me in Zürich as Butterfly, came to sing the Countess in *Figaro*, bringing with her her handsome husband. They were a striking pair. When asked by an interviewer what her husband did, Lisa turned her big, beautiful eyes on him and replied, 'He loffs me.' Quite a sufficient occupation for any man.

On my way down from Edinburgh I went to Rosehill, near Whitehaven in Cumberland, to stay a night with Miki and Agi Sekers. Miki was a Hungarian refugee who had founded the West Cumberland Silk mills just before the war. Shadow factories, as they were called, were then being built with government grants and Whitehaven had serious unemployment and therefore plenty of spare labour. Miki had personally taught the locals how to operate the weaving machines. During the war they had manufactured parachutes, but immediately the war was over Miki turned his own skills in weaving and design to great effect in making a successful onslaught on the fashion trade with fabrics for *haute couture*, and on the world of interior design with furnishing fabrics of new and challenging textures and patterns. He and his wife Agi, also a Hungarian, were great lovers of all the arts, particularly music and the theatre.

One day in late 1949 or early 1950 Audrey Christie had passed a letter to me. Couched in enthusiastic terms, it said that the writer had so enjoyed performances by Glyndebourne at Edinburgh that he would like to provide all the fabrics necessary for a new production at Glyndebourne. Neither the signature at the end nor the name of the firm meant anything to Audrey or myself, but we agreed that I had better reply somewhat cautiously on her behalf and see what there was in the offer. This I did and met Miki for the first time. It was clear to me that the type of fabric he was producing was stunningly suitable for stage use and I quickly put him in touch with both Messel and Piper. The result was immediate. Some of his material went into *Idomeneo* and most of the *Don Giovanni* costumes were made of material he provided, specially woven and dyed.

Miki swam strongly into the lives of everyone he came in contact with, and immensely so into mine. It was not surprising therefore that, after the curtain was down on our last performance at the King's Theatre, I should drive down with them to Rosehill. In two hours of fast driving we discussed the future of Glyndebourne and how, now that we had used Spedan Lewis's generosity to get going again and the Treasury's Festival of Britain grant to re-establish a full-scale festival, other sponsorship or help in kind might be found.

A few weeks before, the Sekers had been to the Aix-en-Provence festival, then only a year or two old. Miki had brought back with him an elegantly produced programme, which carried a great deal of advertisement. 'Why,' asked Miki, 'couldn't Glyndebourne do something similar?' 'Why not indeed,' I said. Up till then programmes at Glyndebourne had been free handouts, and in the early years there had been a large gold-covered brochure without advertisements, which again was free.

We agreed that if Glyndebourne were to publish something it should be even better than Aix's, and that we should not mess about with half, quarter page or even smaller advertisements but insist on full pages only (double-page spreads came later). Also we felt that the cost of a page should not be set at a commercial rate but should represent a contribution to the running costs of the festival. Five hundred pounds per page, Miki said, should be possible; a far larger sum than it now sounds. Forty pages should be aimed at, bringing in £20,000 – close to the sum that the Treasury had provided. The programme should not be given away but sold at a realistic price, which would cover the costs of printing the book itself. A book, we decided, it should be, not just a programme, and thus it got its title of *Glyndebourne Festival Programme Book*. The contributions must be of high standard; nothing too boringly erudite, but also nothing too cheap should go in. Miki showed me copies of *The Ambassador*, an export trade monthly for the fabric and fashion industries, produced very magnificently by a friend of Miki's, Hans Juda. Why not ask his help and advice?

All this was heady stuff and I eventually retired to bed to think about it. At breakfast Agi joined in our discussion enthusiastically, and I departed with an appointment to call on Hans Juda so as to try to arrive at some costs, with a great deal to tell the Christies, and with Miki's assurance that he would immediately begin looking for advertisers. By the time I reached London he was on the phone to say that he had got the first two, his own firm and his next door neighbour, High Duty Alloys, of which Geoffrey Herrington was then chairman. By the end of that week I was able to report back to Miki that if he were to guarantee six pages sold at this juncture I could give the go-ahead. 'I've already got eight,' was his reply.

Lord Wilmot, as John Wilmot had become, was now involved. Not only had he helped to get us the Treasury grant but he had had a great deal to do with the setting up of the Sekers factories in Cumberland, loved music and painting, and lived near Glyndebourne. Miki in his drive for advertisers started throwing parties in his London house, 1 Harriet Walk. Oliver Messel lent his beautiful house in Pelham Crescent for more events, and out of all this came the foundation of the Glyndebourne Festival Society.

Deprived of Busch's services as principal conductor we approached Vittorio Gui. I had struck up a happy relationship with him in 1948 and 1949; he was, I think, the man I most admired and for whom I have the most lasting affection in my entire operatic experience. To my great joy he agreed to come. I had visited him regularly in Italy and we had already thought that it was time Rossini came to Glyndebourne. The success of *Don Pasquale* in 1938 had shown that the lighter Italian operas had a place there, but Gui was not keen on Donizetti. On the other hand he was tremendously pro-Rossini. Our first choice fell on *La Cenerentola* as being less hackneyed than *Il barbiere di Siviglia* and virtually unknown to a post-war audience. Gui had conducted it often but Ebert had never produced it before; there was, however, a German version that he knew. Oliver Messel was the obvious choice to design it. The problem was to find a coloratura mezzo-soprano who could sing that long and taxing role with its vocal fireworks, particularly in the two finales. Nowadays there are plenty of such voices about, but Gui could not find anyone who pleased him enough in Italy and we went on hearing every singer who asked for an audition, as our custom was and has remained.

One winter afternoon in the Wigmore Hall there turned up a Spanish girl living in London, called Marina de Gabarain, with an intelligent face, splendid dark flashing eyes and that prideful

169

stance that is particularly Spanish. She was, in fact, a Basque from San Sebastian. She sang Carmen to us, and instantly Audrey Christie and I pricked up our ears. The voice had that indefinable Spanish huskiness that is so appealing and the coloratura, although by no means perfect, was there. Jani Strasser, then Principal Music Coach, was back at Glyndebourne for the season but working in Strasbourg in the winter and not immediately available. We decided to send Marina to Rome to have a week or so of coaching under anyone Gui thought fit, and then let him decide if he could accept her. There was no doubt in our minds that if she could manage it technically she had everything else that the part required. She went in mid-February and at the end of the month I went to hear Vittorio's verdict. She had improved but was not yet perfect. If she would continue to work hard on her intonation problem Gui felt that she would make it in the end. Anyway, there was nobody better to hand so Marina got the job.

She never achieved complete consistency. When she was nervous, as on a first night or when making a gramophone recording, or if she was temperamentally disturbed (and she had lots of temperament), she did sometimes disappoint, but she went on to sing Cenerentola in nearly all the many performances Glyndebourne gave of that opera for the next five years, including the ones in Berlin. She had other successes with us as Preziosilla in *La forza del destino* and as Baba the Turk in *The Rake's Progress*.

Marina had no shortage of male admirers while she was at Glyndebourne and eventually married and gave up singing for a few years. She tried unsuccessfully to make a come-back and then, very sadly, died after a short illness, far too young. I had become very fond of her and her funny ways. John Christie used to introduce her as 'Her Majesty the Queen of Spain' and many did not at once disbelieve him. She was definitely one of the memorable girls of Glyndebourne.

Living in Lewes was quite an ordeal for Diana. She had always lived in the country before, with a garden and space round her, which the tiny terrace house in East Street with three floors, an attic and a cellar did not provide. She had one child, then two and finally three to cope with, inefficient help to start with, and a tight budget. East Street now is a busy one-way thoroughfare but then it was a quiet backwater. Our first-floor sitting room looked out across the street at a tall, mellow, brick and flint wall, over the top of which one could see the fine trees, in particular a huge copper beech, and the taller shrubs of the walled gardens that backed the big houses in the High Street. Now the wall and gardens have gone and there are garages and a bus station in their place. Albion Street, with its terrace of rather larger houses, joins East Street at right angles, and on the corner there stood a gas lamp post which a man on a bicycle used to light with a long pole every evening and turn off every morning, and under which the Salvation Army band used to play on Saturday nights.

The big excitement of the year, apart from Lewes Bonfire Night on 5 November, was the early autumn day when a troupe of gypsies, bound from east to west on some annual migration, would assemble at the bottom of the steep hill, unharness the horses from all but one of their caravans and attach the spare animals to that one, even tethering them to the sides. Then, with all the troupe down to the smallest toddler pushing and uttering wild encouraging cries to the horses, they would get the caravan to the top, where the whole propulsion system would be dismantled and return to the bottom to bring up the next one. Repeated four or five times, it was as good as a circus.

During the Glyndebourne season I left early and returned very late, seven days a week, so I saw very little of Diana or the children. In the late summer there was Edinburgh which took me away for a month, though as the children got older they and Diana did join me for some or all of the time. In winter I commuted to the Baker Street office or went on trips abroad, so that the time we spent together in peace and quiet was pretty minimal. After a year or two we went in for au pair girls – Swiss, French and Danish – and most were a success, thanks to Diana's ability to emulate the oyster in its technique of working steadily on the grain of sand within the shell until it turns into a pearl.

John Christie was great on writing letters to *The Times*, mostly on the subject of Covent Garden and the iniquities of the Government and the Arts Council. Usually he would show them to me before posting so as to make sure that I was prepared for any reactions they might, and usually did, arouse. He didn't like the telephone and used it only to summon me or for very brief messages. The last post was cleared at the sorting office at Lewes Station at about 8 p.m., and John would sometimes drive in to catch it.

One dark and cold night in mid-winter we were sitting in our first-floor room listening to the wireless while Florence the au pair girl, who was a straight-laced Swiss, was ironing in the kitchen on the ground floor. There was a knock at the front door, an unusual event. We heard Florence go along the passage to the door which opened ditectly on to the street. A silence followed. I put down the tapestry chair-seat that I was working on and went to the head of the stairs to see what was happening. Florence, who had opened the front door, turned round to me ashen-faced, then fled into the dining room and slammed the door behind her. On the doorstep was a strange figure, back-lit through the mist by the street lamp and dimly front-lit by the hall light. It had on *lederhosen* – Bavarian leather shorts with decorated braces – white stockings and patent-leather evening pumps; it wore a patch over one eye, and through a triangular tear in its white cricket shirt its left nipple was projecting, this last effect heightened by the cold and frosty air that was sweeping in. It was John Christie on his way to the post with a letter he wished me to see before it went. I don't think Florence ever recovered from the shock; she certainly never again opened the front door to a knock at night.

The evening pumps and cricket shirts are ancillaries to the picture of John Christie, a man who believed in not doing anything unless he did it for all he was worth. Having found, in pre-war and pre-marriage days, a style of white cotton-flannel shirt that he liked, he ordered a gross, all identical, only stipulating that the tails should be somewhat shorter than was then customary. After that he wore them, with or without an ill-knotted tie, on every day-time occasion and often in the evenings too. When not in more formal clothes for dinner he preferred to change into his beloved *lederhosen*. One Saturday afternoon in spring, he lent the lawn in front of the house for a Morris Dancing display. Tiring of the sport, he wandered off round the ponds with his pug dog. The dog, whether in chase of something or merely missing his bandy footing on the verge, fell into the water. John waded in and retrieved it. His trousers were now both wet and muddy, so he removed them and placed them dripping over one arm. He held the pug, also dripping, under the other and set off back for the house. The assembled dancers stood aghast as this strange figure, mini-shirt tails flapping over a total absence of clothing beneath them, strode purposefully through their midst and back into the house.

The evening pumps were one of his good ideas to help both mankind and Glyndebourne. At the end of the war, shoes, like all clothing, were rationed and such things as patent-leather evening pumps with grosgrain bows on the toes were unobtainable. John felt that every gentleman would dearly love a new pair, and he conceived the idea of asking Spedan Lewis whether John Lewis's could persuade a manufacturer to introduce them as a new line, to be sold exclusively through and for the benefit of Glyndebourne. Two major snags appeared. The first was that patent leather was unobtainable. That was soon overcome; the new 'plarstic' could substitute. The second proved insurmountable. Clothing coupons and trading restrictions meant that the pumps could only be provided for sale on the open market and not to Glyndebourne's benefit. The open market did not appear to be large enough to warrant manufacture on a sufficient scale.

John did not give up easily. He persuaded Lewis's to have several dozen pairs in two or three sizes made up out of a thick shiny black substance. These unfortunately proved to be the cause of very hot feet when they were worn. John distributed the pumps to a wide circle of friends and I got a pair which I dutifully wore whenever evening dress was called for at Glyndebourne, including private dinners in the house.

One such occasion was the première of the film *On Such a Night* which the Rank Organization had made to publicize Glyndebourne. It was directed by Anthony 'Puffin' Asquith, and a distinguished audience gathered for the première, which in deference to John was held in the Odeon cinema in Lewes. We met and drank at Glyndebourne and then made our way in convoy to the cinema. It was winter or early spring and the night was cold. The cinema manager, who stood at the door with the mayor to greet John and Audrey and their guests, had turned his central heating up to full pitch and the place was like an oven.

Diana and I had seats at the end of the front row of the circle and I was against the wall. The film went well but the temperature continued to rise. My feet felt red hot, particularly the right one. At the end we rose for the loyal anthem and only then did I realize that my right foot was stuck. To my horror I found that the material of the shoe had welded itself to the hot-water pipe which ran along the wall. Visions of limping out with only one shoe on through the little gaggle of townsfolk who had gathered on the pavement to see the swells and celebrities flashed through my mind, but with a desperate effort I prised myself loose and spent the rest of the evening hoping nobody would notice that a rat had apparently consumed a large part of the right side of my right foot. What was worse was that the nylon sock I was wearing had also fused, so that it was bare flesh that was exposed. I did not ask John for another pair.

In 1982 on the centenary of John's birth I was asked to write a short piece for *The Times*, which I did gladly. In it I painted a personal picture of a man whom I respected and greatly liked. I make no apology for repeating two of the anecdotes here.

After the war and the end of clothes rationing, John decided that he needed some new suits and went to Mr Povey the tailor in Lewes. (John always called him 'Puvvy', just as the village of Selmeston nearby was always 'Simpson' to him.) He ordered a dozen suits, all to be of exactly the same ample cut, single-breasted and of course with no waistcoat. John never wore a waistcoat or an overcoat. All were of different weights of cloth from very light to very heavy, and most of them were tweedy. When the time came to try them on, 'Puvvy' was commanded to do up the fly buttons, attach the braces and concertina the trouser legs into two rings on the floor of his shop, which incidentally was clearly visible to passers-by in Cliffe High Street. John, without touching a button, dropped his own trousers by slipping off the braces, revealing that he was clad only in a short-tailed cricket shirt, and stepped into the new pair. If he could pick up the braces and pull up the trousers without touching a button and the waist was pleasantly loose, the fitting was over.

John, despite having only one eye for most of his life, was a keen and good shot. The late Sir David Webster told a story of coming to *Don Giovanni* as John's somewhat uneasy guest during a lull in the sporadic warfare that John conducted with the authorities at Covent Garden. Sitting in John's box, he found himself next to someone whom he judged by his visage and bearing to be a local country gentleman. They had not been introduced and in a pause between scenes David asked him 'Do you come to Glyndebourne often?' 'Oh yes,' was the reply. 'John has me for the opera and I have him for the shootin'.'

TWELVE

In the air

My friends and erstwhile colleagues who have read this far will be wondering how long I can go on without bringing Jani Strasser into the picture. The answer is, no longer. To write about Glyndebourne without including Jani would be like writing about Elsinor without including either Rosencrantz or Guildenstern.

When I joined Glyndebourne, Jani and his wife Irene were living in Priory Road in Hampstead. Jani was teaching and helping Michel St Denis with his school at the Old Vic. He was not called in to help with *The Rape of Lucretia* or with *Orfeo* the next year, largely I think because Hans Oppenheim, who was assistant conductor to Ernest Ansermet, did not get on well with the voluble and volatile Hungarian. But he was called back for the two pre-war revivals in the first Edinburgh Festival.

He was assiduous in getting his pupils into the chorus for *Orfeo* and in recruiting the bigger chorus for Edinburgh. Indeed, he was virtually chorus master for 1947 and 1948. When I took over the reins, however, I succeeded in persuading him that we really could not have a singing teacher in the influential hire-and-fire position of chorus master. With a good grace because he liked him, Jani accepted John Pritchard's taking that position while he, Jani, remained principal coach. This move I made on the advice of Audrey Christie, who, though she loved and admired Jani, advised me that he should never be allowed to have too much authority as his Central European turn of mind often led him into devious paths.

Jani was never quite satisfied with his title on the programme which had to be, to use one of his own words, 're-caboodled' at frequent intervals. He started in 1934 as Hans Strasser, Professor of Singing, Vienna, Budapest and Glyndebourne; became Principal Coach in 1938; went on successively to be Chief Coach in Charge of Musical Studies, Head of Music Staff, Director of Musical Preparation and Chief of Music Staff, Head of Music Staff and Preparation; and finally Consultant Specialist in Singing and Interpretation.

175

During his time he had a number of 'satchel-bearers', assistants so called because Jani always went about at Glyndebourne with a leather school satchel which contained the scores he was currently working on, his notes and his constantly re-caboodled prognostications of the next day's rehearsal schedule. The satchel-bearers were a talented lot; one at least became an agent for singers while another, Brian Dickie, moved steadily up the Glyndebourne hierarchy, taking in a successful stint as artistic director of the Wexford Festival on the way, to become my successor as the fourth of Glyndebourne's administrators. Yet another is a respected and volatile figure in contemporary music in Paris.

When Jani and Irene were eventually given a grace-and-favour house in Ringmer they decided to call it Satchels. Unfortunately they did not get the spelling quite right. The name board read Sachell's, and so it remains to this day, with newcomers to the village speculating on Sachell's identity and the part this foreigner could have played in local history.

As the years went by Jani and I went on dozens of audition trips up and down Europe and behind the Iron Curtain. He loved making the arrangements with the agents for the auditions and running the auditions themselves. I was delighted to have this spade work done for me and only made sure, after a few experiences, that the final choice of hotels and restaurants was left to me. Jani was the travel agent's despair. He obtained every flight and train timetable that he could lay his hands on and the more complicated he could make the journey the better he was pleased.

I came across this side of his character the first time the company assembled at King's Cross for the train to Edinburgh. Though everything had been perfectly arranged by the stage manager, with tickets distributed, seats reserved and meals arranged, Jani flew up and down the platform waving his gloved hands – he was a great one for gloves, special grey cotton ones which could only be right if bought at a certain shop in Florence – and behaving for all the world as though he were an over-excited sheepdog. It was clearly very enjoyable to him and I soon learnt how to keep him happy by making him feel responsible yet at the same time quietly double-checking the arrangements myself.

My memories of Jani are mostly connected with travel. He would always have the maximum weight of luggage allowed, and carried an immense selection of gadgets with him. He had a passion for office sundries, paperclips, pencil sharpeners, supplies of string, and also insisted on taking many changes of clothes, being pleasantly vain about his personal appearance. He did not trust hotel laundries and carried with him a huge block of common washing soap weighing several pounds.

Unless forced to I never shared a room or a sleeper with him. He was a fidget, and the laying out of a special folding tray on which to put his bits and pieces beside the bed, his unpacking and packing, seemed to go on all night, however late he went to bed and however early the next day's plane or train might be. One time in Wexford in the Talbot Hotel, which was overcrowded as always during that delightful festival, we were obliged to share a small room and bathroom at the back. On our third night we went to bed at about 2 a.m. – rather early for Wexford – knowing that we had to get up betimes to drive to Dublin to catch the first plane to Paris. Jani had gone to the room some time before me, I having waited deliberately to give him time, like a bride on her wedding night, to get undressed and into bed before I entered. Having judged the time to be right I ascended, only to find him bent over the bath washing some shirts and smalls. 'They'll never be dry by six o'clock', I said. 'Oh yes, they will. They're nylon and I've got a new drier to hang them on.' With that he produced a complicated plastic gadget consisting of a series of coat-hangers cantilevered out from a large rubber suction cup designed to stick to the tiles over the bath. He proudly erected this, hung up his washing and we both retired to our beds. After I had read a few pages of my book and he had entered up his accounts and other notes in the selection of ledgers he kept for the purpose, the light were put out.

I was almost asleep when a noise which could best be described as a succulent pop was followed by a rustle of falling nylon and the rattle of light plastic objects in an empty bath. On went the light, Jani leapt from his bed, rushed to the bathroom and resecured the whole contraption. We settled ourselves again. Ten minutes later the same thing happened. 'What did you wet the sucker with?' I asked. 'Water, of course.' 'Try spit this time.' He did, and it was quite half an hour before it happened again. Not willing to be defeated he tried once more, with no longer-lived success. We did get two hours' sleep before they called us. The washing was bundled into a plastic bag and taken wet to Paris where Jani reported complete success. Either the tiles were more porous or the room was not so hot and steamy as at Wexford.

Jani's wife Irene was a character in her own right and they were a wonderful double act. Both spoke heavily accented but fluent English, but they would switch into Hungarian, German, French or Italian in mid-sentence with equal ease and wonder why their companions did not always understand what they were talking about. Irene had some splendid malapropisms and would talk of 'ramshackling' her drawers to look for a mislaid object and of being committed to some action not 'hook, line and sinker' but 'hook, sink and knickers'. Knickers (or drawers) were a strange preoccupation, because she boasted, like my Greek princesses in Alexandria and John Christie, that she didn't wear any.

Jani and Irene went everywhere at home and abroad in a succession of little cars beginning with a Fiat 'Topolino'. She was the driver. Jani mercifully never learnt to take the wheel. When the cars got too old Irene was adept at filling the gearbox with sawdust to deaden the dreadful grinding noises and then flogging them to some unsuspecting victim in north London. The Strassers had one or two little mishaps on the road but it was never, of course, their fault, and somehow the other person's insurance always coughed up to their eventual advantage.

There was one accident, however, which could have been serious and which more or less put a stop to their Continental motoring. One dark and nasty evening on a busy road in Belgium, hastening to the Hook to catch the ferry, the windscreen wipers packed up and Irene pulled in to the right-hand side of the road and stopped. Jani, who was sitting in the left front seat, began to open the door to get out in order to wipe the screen by hand. Before he had put a leg out a lorry tore by, caught the door and, sweeping it forward, broke its hinges. Jani got out, and the lorry having very properly stopped some yards ahead, went to remonstrate with the driver. While he was doing this another lorry came along, saw them too late, braked and skidded into the back of the Strasser car, pushing it over on to its side in the ditch. Jani described how he and both lorry drivers rushed to Irene's aid, to find her literally backside up in the driving seat; a sight to make even Belgian lorry drivers blench.

After Jani retired from Glyndebourne, Irene having died rather suddenly of lung cancer, he went on with his teaching and made annual visits to Sydney where he coached in the opera. Eventually he was overcome by Parkinson's disease; mercifully he died quickly and quietly in Lewes, before old age and failing health had had time to make him really miserable.

On his last visit to Sydney he was under treatment for his illness and the pills he took had the effect of colouring his water. One day, so he told me, he was in the backstage gents when one of his favourite burly Australian stage-hands came in and took the position beside him. Glancing down he said in sudden surprise, 'Christ, Jani, yu're pissin' blew!' 'And vot colour,' retorted Jani, 'do you suppose my blood is?'

For several winters Jani worked at the Centre du Nord in Strasbourg, teaching and coaching. He and Irene had a small flat there which became, like all their habitations, a little bit of Central Europe. When I was making my one and only trip round Germany with John Christie we called on them. Irene, in John's honour, had cooked one of her special Viennese dishes and produced a rich and splendid dessert. They had got some Strasbourg goose liver to start with. Jani, who was not a great drinker or very knowledgeable about wine, had taken local advice and produced a first-class bottle of each of three Alsatian wines made from the Sylvaner, the Riesling and the Gewürztraminer grapes. Alas, the dinner was not a success. I thoroughly enjoyed it but John pronounced each dish in turn too rich, too mucked-about or too sticky, and refused to do more than take a sip from each bottle which he pronounced to be nothing like good German wine. If I make him sound boorish, he was not. He had great charm but complete honesty, and would not dream of disguising his opinion just to save people's feelings.

Another tour of Germany with John and Audrey was planned for the winter of 1952 but Audrey was not well. The fatal disease that had been the undiagnosed cause of her migranes and blackouts, a brain tumour, was developing and she spent a lot of time in bed or in hospital. She still kept as firm a grip on Glyndebourne as she could and even from a wheelchair could deliver some severe strictures. It was said that in those last months it was the ones she loved best to whom she gave the hardest time. If that was so, then John came first in her affections and I was certainly included. Both he, I know, and I in my place loved her and did our best to help. That tour never materialized; however, a year or two after her death, John and I set off.

The trip was an eventful one for me, beginning with a night spent at the Grosvenor Hotel on Victoria station, necessitated by doubts about fog and an early plane to Düsseldorf the next morning. We travelled to London on an after-dinner train from Lewes and went straight to bed in adjoining rooms. John did not like central heating and opened his window which, like mine, overlooked the glass roof of the station several floors below. He took out the glass eye he wore on public occasions, rather than the more usual and homely black eye-patch, and placed it on the external window-ledge to make sure that it would be nice and cool for insertion in the morning. Then he closed the window and went to bed. Some time in the night he found the heat of the room too much and opened the window, having forgotten all about the eye. In the morning he went to get it from the window sill and could not find it. He came and called me, wondering where it could have gone. Could it have been stolen by some jackdaw? I leaned out of the window. There, far below in the lead gutter between the glass roof and the wall of the hotel, the eye gazed up at me with an unwinking stare. It was retrieved undamaged through a lower window by an obliging member of the hotel staff and off we went.

In Düsseldorf it was snowing. Because we had a certain amount of baggage I was allowed to take a taxi to our hotel, the same hotel in which Audrey and I had stayed before but by now fully renovated and with no danger of bathroom doors being removed. It was, however, some distance from the opera house. We had a light lunch, I made some telephone calls to confirm auditions for the next morning, and while John rested I went to pay my respects to the Intendant of the opera and get our tickets for the evening performance, which was, I think, *Don Carlos*.

John insisted on wearing a black tie, though it was not a first night – in any case the German rule was just as strict, if not more so, than ours; a plain dark suit, a shirt with stiff or soft turn-down collar any colour one liked, so long as it was white, and a long or bow tie, also any colour one liked, so long as it was silver grey. I asserted my independence by wearing a blue pin-stripe suit, a pale blue shirt and a dark blue watered silk tie, hoping to offend nobody.

We set off for the theatre. No taxi was deemed necessary, despite the wet snow that was blowing along the street, since we were on a direct tramline. John of course did not have an overcoat. Legend (sponsored by him) went that he had only ever had one and that he had given it to an impecunious old Eton schoolmaster, A. S. F. Gow – a delightful eccentric, if not quite of John's magnitude. John was wearing a woollen scarf and also a felt hat, though not the famous Coke hat that he wore on more formal occasions deliberately to impress. He also surprisingly had galoshes (overshoes known to Americans as 'rubbers', a word which to us has at least two very different meanings).

It was fully dark as we walked through the slush to the tram stop and boarded an already crowded car. The windows were steamed up and we had to stand, peering out as best we could to find the right stop. Having recently been that way before I spotted the stop before the opera and told John that ours was the next one. As the tram drew to a grinding halt and the doors began automatically to open, John was the first to descend. The tram cars were high above the street, the landing platforms were at pavement level, and as the doors opened so did two or three steps automatically obtrude to provide a safe descent. John, however, beat the system. Somehow he got through the doors before they were fully open, missed the steps and fell to the street, where his rubber shoes slipped in the slush while at the same time his scarf caught in the door. By a miracle the scarf unwound itself and he was not strangled, though his hat flew off, never to be recovered. I leapt out after him while through my brain, like the flashes that are said (erroneously I think) to come to a drowning man, shot thoughts about regulations for getting a corpse crated and on to the next available plane for England.

John lay prone for only a second, however, and before anyone had time to help him was on his feet again, looking round for the culprit who had pushed him. The tram moved on, the crowds were indifferent, and we made our way to the opera house. Once in the foyer I realized that John had torn both the knees out of his dress trousers and that he was quite badly grazed. I suggested that we return to the hotel but the bells were ringing for the first act and he refused. We took our seats and he sat there, dabbing at his knees with a large white cotton handkerchief. What his neighbours thought was not revealed nor, obviously, did John care. He sat the opera out but did consent to take a taxi back as he had lost his faith in the efficiency of Düsseldorf trams. Next morning he was stiff but undaunted and our tour continued as planned.

John's attitude to injuries was simply to disregard them; had one not known him to be kind, considerate and indeed soft-hearted, one might have thought him callous. One evening during the lighting rehearsals of *Don Giovanni* in 1951 I was sitting with John Piper having supper in the canteen. In came John Christie, who asked if we minded if he joined us. As he sat down I saw that his white shirt was heavily bloodstained and then I saw that his hand, wrapped in a handkerchief, was bleeding freely. 'A dog,' he said. 'It's nothing, just playing.' Piper was silent but began to look a little green. John went on as if nothing unusual had happened and Piper made an excuse and left the table. Finally I got John to admit that it was more than a scratch and packed him off to Dr Rice in the village who had to put several stitches in his thumb. In fact John had been teasing a dog that someone had left in a locked car with a bit of the window open. Delighted by its barking John had made faces at it and then put his hand through the gap – just playing, as he said. After John had left for the village, driving himself of course, Piper rejoined me and admitted that he felt squeamish at the sight of blood. Not so John, for half an hour later he rejoined us, with his hand properly bandaged but still wearing his blood-boltered shirt, looking like an apparition out of *Macbeth*.

On our tour John's eye continued to bother him, though it was not again mislaid. He much preferred the patch for comfort and would regularly ask me when preparing himself for some meeting: 'Moran, do I need to put me eye in?' In one hotel we had adjoining rooms with a connecting door which was anything but soundproof. I found it touching, and think it no breach of confidence now to reveal, that he regularly said his prayers out loud, concluding with a personal message to the Almighty, with whom he felt himself to be on intimate terms, and most touchingly of all a little conversation with Audrey who was clearly, to him, not very far away.

In Frankfurt in the grandest hotel, the Frankfurter Hof, we sat down to dinner. John scanned the wine list for the name of a grower that he knew he liked. He found a Maximin-Gruenhaus from the von Schubert estate that Otto Loeb had introduced to him and it was duly brought. John had one glass and decided that it was good but that the price was ridiculous. The restaurant was very hot, so he ordered *Orangensaft*. What he really wanted was orange squash, and he asked for a large jug, describing the size with his hands. The waiter looked surprised and disappeared, returning ten minutes later with a large container full of freshly squeezed orange juice. On the bill this appeared as the equivalent of three bottles of the good wine to which I had fallen heir after John's one glass. Dinner over and the bill signed, we left the dining room, all the very proper German diners looking open-mouthed at the large figure of John, with eye patch, marching out holding a ewer of unconsumed orange juice followed by his small bearded companion wearing a bland smile.

After Frankfurt we went to Munich, then back to Cologne and on to Hanover where Peter Ebert was working. By this time John's energy was beginning to flag and he elected to stay in the hotel and not go to the opera. I went alone, and returned to find him less than enthusiastic about the plan to go back to Cologne the next day before returning to London the day after. I knew there were direct flights from Hanover to London by B.E.A. but that they were with small slow aircraft and mostly used by service personnel from the

British forces in Germany. I rang through to the airport and was told that there was a flight at 11 a.m. next day. Could two seats be made available, I asked, and said that they were for Mr John Christie of Glyndebourne who wished to get home in a hurry. The duty officer confirmed that two seats would be available and we turned in.

Early next morning my telephone rang. It was the senior B.E.A. official in Cologne in a great state. Could Mr Christie not be persuaded to stick to the original plan? Comfort and safety could be guaranteed that way, but the Hanover to London flight was not suitable. The aeroplane was inadequately heated, as all the front part of the seating had been removed for freight and the passengers sat behind it in the rear five or six rows of seats. Also it was not pressurized and had to fly at a low altitude, and the weather forecast was bad, with violent thunderstorms predicted over the North Sea.

This I reported to John, who said that all aeroplanes were overheated anyway, and that he didn't mind what height he flew at and wasn't concerned about a bumpy ride. I told the B.E.A. man that, despite his misgivings, we would like to be on the eleven o'clock flight. He got on the phone to head office in London and gloomily reported that if Mr Christie insisted he could not be refused, but they still did not advise it. The more opposition was put up, the more determined John became.

The local representative told us that our aeroplane would be coming from England and that it would need a forty-five minute turn-around before departure. As it would probably be late he would send a car to pick us up from the hotel when he knew the arrival time. We sat in the hotel packed and ready; ten-thirty and eleven came and went, and at about eleven-thirty Mr B.E.A. himself arrived to escort us. The aeroplane would arrive at any minute and they hoped to speed up the turn-round, so could we please come now.

It was not a nice day: it was blowing hard and there were icy showers out of racing clouds. We arrived at the airport to find that the plane was in, a four-engined propeller-jet Viscount. We were ushered quickly through Customs and passport control before the next hitch developed. The plane needed some attention before being able to return and there might be a delay of up to an hour. Meanwhile, said Mr B.E.A., would we please have lunch in the airport restaurant – at B.E.A.'s expense, of course.

So we sat in solitary state. The lunch was not particularly good and John ate and drank sparingly. I found that *viertels* of a drink-able Moselle turned up whenever I raised my eyebrows at the young waiter and so looked to the future philosophically. Out of the window I could see a good deal of activity around the tail of our aircraft and at one point a shower of sparks that looked like welding. I said nothing to John, however.

At last they came to take us to the plane. The other passengers and our baggage were already embarked and it would take off as soon as we were ensconced. We found the back rows fully occupied by servicemen and a few wives, all obviously a little apprehensive and over-excited. Two, as it were, first-class seats had been specially installed and in front of us there was an enormous pile of freight. We were strapped in and given blankets which were tucked carefully round us, like travellers in an early motor-car.

Off we went, and flew bumpily but without seeming trouble south-west over Germany and Holland to Amsterdam, with good visibility but gale-force winds. From Rotterdam we turned further west to cross the North Sea. Soon big thunder clouds became visible ahead. The captain of the aircraft came back to talk to us and apologized for any discomfort. There were, he said, heavy thunderstorms between us and London which he could not climb above, but he hoped to be able to dodge between them. The London area was clear.

The plane droned and bounced on. The pilot edged round the first few clouds but suddenly they were too dense and we flew straight into what seemed like midnight darkness. There was a literally blinding flash, a colossal cracking bang and I thought the end had come. In what seemed a long time, but was in fact only seconds, vision returned and I realized that we were still flying straight and level and had in fact broken out of the other side of the cloud. The passengers behind us, after a stunned silence, burst into a mixture of curses and shrieks. I looked at John, who sat quite impassive, looking straight ahead wrapped in his blanket like a prophet on a mountain, but a very pale-faced prophet. A minute or two later the captain came back to report that all was well and tell us that we could expect an easy landing at London. We had, he said, not been struck by lightning as we might have thought, but had been the cause of an electrical explosion and a clap of thunder and flash of lightning because of the discharge of static electricity built up in the airframe. It was unpleasant, he said, but not dangerous. On the way out, he told us, they had really been struck by lightning, and that was the cause of the delay in setting off.

They had been welding a new bit on to the tail. John received this explanation with equanimity born of his own scientific background, but as far as I know he never set foot in another aeroplane for the rest of his life.

We were met, as we had requested through B.E.A., by the Glyndebourne Armstrong Siddeley driven by Arthur Howell from the Ringmer Motor Works, the nearest to a chauffeur that the Christies ever had. John insisted on taking the wheel for the drive home for which he chose an eccentric route through Windsor (not so eccentric for him, I suppose, as it was the route he would have taken in the old days from Eton). The night was upon us. John did not judge distance well with one eye and was easily dazzled. He swore that none of the oncoming cars had dipped and so kept his headlights full on. He had a pet theory that it was safer to go round left-hand bends well out over the middle of the road because 'you could then see further round the bend and spot oncoming traffic earlier'. How we got home without mishap can only be explained by John's undoubted pull with the Almighty. Arthur Howell sat sweating in the front seat; I had chosen the back thinking it was safer and that I might manage to sleep off not only the *Viertels* but the stress and strain of the last fortnight. Nevertheless it was one that I would not have missed for the world.

In 1953 Bernard McNabb became Glyndebourne's press officer. Bernard, who came to us from the B.B.C. and had been in the R.A.F. in the war, was sent down to Glyndebourne for a confirmatory interview and lunch with the Christies. He was told to take the local taxi from Lewes to Glyndebourne. John was horrified to hear that he had come by taxi and insisted that after lunch he would himself drive him back to Lewes for the train.

The lunch apparently went well, the Christies thought him a nice fellow – high praise – and I rang him next day to confirm his engagement and ask him how he had got on. Very well, he said, apart from the race back to the station. Being driven by John in the old grey Standard Nine with loose steering and worn out suspension, known to those of us who drove it from time to time as the 'Grey Jelly', was, commented Bernard, 'The nearest thing I've experienced since the war to low flying.'

THIRTEEN

In Auld Reekie

Glyndebourne Opera was part of the Edinburgh Festival for eight years from its inception in 1947 until 1955, missing only 1952. It returned once more in 1960, after which Edinburgh no longer found it possible to afford the expense, since they had to bear the whole cost whereas the foreign opera companies that replaced it were heavily subsidized by their own countries. But Glyndebourne Opera is not forgotten in Edinburgh, and certainly Edinburgh is not forgotten by those members of our company who spent so many hectic but happy weeks there.

The staging of the first version of *Ariadne auf Naxos* in 1950 I considered to be a great personal triumph, in that it brought together and succeeded in maintaining in harmony the biggest circus of operatic, theatrical and balletic talent to work together in recent times. Beecham had conducted this version on its first and only London presentation at His Majesty's Theatre in 1913 and it was he who suggested it for Glyndebourne at Edinburgh. The opera was written to follow Molière's play *Le bourgeois gentilhomme* as the entertainment the *nouveau riche* Monsieur Jourdain provides for his guests, and on this occasion the Molière play was given in a specially reduced English translation by Miles Malleson who also appeared himself in the title role and directed the play, the distinguished cast being drawn largely from his colleagues at the Old Vic. The opera was directed by Carl Ebert and the ballet scenes within the play choreographed by Marie Rambert with dancers from the Ballet Rambert. The whole show was designed by Oliver Messel, working for Glyndebourne for the first time.

That Beecham, Ebert, Messel, Malleson and Rambert could all cook in the same kitchen seemed a miracle – any two of them could be expected to work successfully together, but all five at once . . . Nevertheless, it came off, and a thoroughly enjoyable show it was. Of course those who knew the second version, which replaces the play with an operatic prologue, bemoaned the absence of the great musical highlight of the composer's aria; on the other hand, those who found in that version the second half to be over-long and over-serious, here in the first found it somewhat shorter and interlarded with comic interjections from M. Jourdain, who sat on the fore-stage as a spectator throughout.

Messel was a completely new type of designer as far as Carl Ebert was concerned, and to begin with Carl found him difficult to take. Accustomed to the German tradition which gave the producer exactly the practicalities that he wanted at the expense, if necessary, of correctness of style, he found instead a creative decorator who provided a setting into which he was obliged to adapt himself. He was also more used to being addressed as Herr Professor than as 'Carlie dear'.

Beecham concerned himself solely with the music and in this field was his autocratic self. He and Messel understood each other instinctively and were able to avoid any difficulties – that is until the moment of Bacchus's appearance, when the inevitable problems, in the days before closed-circuit television, of the singer being able to see the conductor and at the same time be hidden from the audience, caused a memorably agitated rehearsal in the King's Theatre. It happily ended in laughter when the German tenor Peter Anders, in answer to a bellow from the pit of, 'Bacchus, where the hell are you?', bobbed up from behind a rock with a mellifluous 'Yoohoo, Sir Beecham.' Malleson and Ebert respected each other as actors but their relationship developed no further, and Marie Rambert chuckled her way through the whole thing. She treated me with motherly affection born of my time in her husband's company at the Mercury Theatre fourteen years before.

For 1951 the new production was Verdi's *La forza del destino*. I was able to persuade Ebert to take yet another British designer, Leslie Hurry, who had recently been responsible for outstanding sets for the ballet *Hamlet* at Covent Garden. Hurry's style of painting suited the music splendidly, being tumultuous and tortured, and his costumes were wonderfully colourful. He was not best pleased, however, when John Christie, on seeing one of the wings representing a rocky defile, remarked in his habitually outspoken way that to him they looked like nothing so much as a rabbit's entrails.

At the end of the 1951 festival the Edinburgh committee decided to invite the Hamburg Opera for the following year. We at Glyndebourne were not as dismayed as we might have been because we had our own festival in Sussex to occupy us and a tour of two Mozart operas in America, under Sol Hurok's banner, in prospect.

The tour foundered like so many other similar plans, but relations were re-established with Edinburgh and our return in 1953 was announced in time to still the storm of protest that our exclusion had brought.

When we returned it was with two operas from our then current repertory, *La Cenerentola* and *Idomeneo*, and a new production, the stage première in Britain of Stravinsky's *The Rake's Progress*. Glyndebourne insisted to Edinburgh that it was not interested in appearing at their festival merely with works brought up from the same year's festival in Sussex. Our suggested formula for the future was one popular success from the current festival, one revival of a similarly proved piece from a previous year, and one new and relatively unknown work that would excite interest in the operatic world, bring out the best efforts from the Glyndebourne team and, with luck, justify its choice in popular opinion. One such had been the original version of *Ariadne*.

Naturally everyone's thoughts turned to a contemporary work, if a suitable one could be found to fit all the criteria. Ebert had directed the world première of Stravinsky's *The Rake's Progress*, for which W. H. Auden and his collaborator Chester Kallman had provided the libretto, at the Teatro Fenice in Venice in the autumn of 1951. Although it had had a splendid cast, including Elisabeth Schwarzkopf, and had been conducted by Stravinsky himself, it had not really jelled as a production and all concerned had felt unhappy about it. Ebert wanted a chance to do the *Rake* again, so we proposed it to Edinburgh and, particularly since it had a libretto in English, it was accepted.

The Fenice had insisted that Ebert should use a particular Italian designer for the *Rake*. This man produced drawings based on a romantic Italianate view of Hogarth, with none of the bite and satire that the piece demanded. Ebert showed them to me at the time and I was very critical of them, and he was extremely disappointed in the final result. Indeed Ebert attributed the lack of success in Venice almost as much to them as to the unsatisfactory rehearsal conditions and internal bickering.

When he suggested the work for Edinburgh I put in the strongest possible plea for the designs to be by a contemporary satirical cartoonist who could enter fully into the wonderfully successful amalgam of the eighteenth and twentieth centuries, treating the nineteenth as though it had never been, which both score and libretto had achieved. 'Who?' asked Carl. 'Osbert Lancaster,' said I, and Carl agreed that I should approach him. Osbert's work was of course already well known, but he had done little in the theatre except his one remaining, and as I write happily still frequently visible, stage work, the ballet *Pineapple Poll* for the Royal Ballet.

'But,' said Ebert, 'a ballet is one thing, just backcloths and wings; opera is another, particularly with nine changes of scene, furniture, stairs, windows and all manner of props and effects.'

When consulted on this aspect of the problem Osbert brushed it aside with a sideways wag of his heavy moustache. 'I was trained at the Slade. The theatre holds no terrifying mysteries for me.' He rose to the occasion magnificently. He caught the feel of the piece and wit flowed from every line he drew. Many comic artists, with a subtle twist or an unexpected curve, can turn a serious subject into something risible; Osbert is unique in being able to draw a dead straight line and confer upon it the ability to raise a smile. His choice of colour always imparts that slight suggestion of the ridiculous that even the most beautiful prospect invokes in the light-hearted.

Richard Lewis again proved that he could outdistance other more flashy tenors in musicality, mellifluousness and subtle grasp of character. In this particular case Carl Ebert had been keen to have an American tenor, David Lloyd, for the role, but Lloyd fell ill in New York in mid-July, with rehearsals due to begin in a week's time. Richard Lewis was already an established Glynde-bourne favourite and had been singing the principal male part in Gluck's *Alceste* in June, but he had not been seriously considered for Tom Rakewell as it was thought that he might be a little too solid in texture for that volatile and insecure young man. In this emergency the solidity of his talents and his innate musicality came to everyone's aid. He asked for a score, took it to a beach in the south of France, and in a week came back with it memorized note and word perfect, an almost incredible feat with such a long part in so short a time. His method of memorizing is photographic — he sees each page before him as he sings. That is why his singing is so accurate and why, if he makes an inadvertent mistake, instead of floundering until the conductor or the prompter can pull him back, he sees it immediately and corrects automatically. None of this makes him less sensitive than the 'learn-it-by-ear' school, and his performance in the *Rake* was proof of his artistry.

The following year older productions of *Così* and *Ariadne* were set off by a sparkling new production of Rossini's virtually un-known opera to a French text by Scribe, *Le Comte Ory*. Gui, Ebert and Messel were at the top of their form. Oliver went to *Les Très riches Heures du duc de Berry* for his sets and costumes. Ebert's gift for the handling of chorus scenes managed to steer a hilarious but safe course around the fact that the male chorus, dressed as nuns, had to get highly intoxicated in Act II. This was something that neither the Protestants nor the Catholics of Edinburgh could easily laugh at. Sesto Bruscantini, Juan Oncina and Ian Wallace were a trio perfect in their timing, precision, enjoyment and sense of their own and each other's character. The ravishing Hungarian, Sari Barabas, was not only a brilliant singer but was also able to walk in a medieval gown, with her (albeit taut and trim) tummy stuck forward and her skirt bunched in one hand just below it, in a wonderfully seductive way. Together they formed a cast for this opera which has never been approached, let alone surpassed anywhere else that I am aware of.

The outstanding event in Edinburgh in 1955 was Verdi's *Falstaff*. Carl Ebert's somewhat Germanic production of the work had been seen at the Cambridge Theatre in London and he was no stranger to it, or to Shakespeare, before that. I had had my usual discussions with him about the designer and had put the point strongly that *Falstaff*, though not a Shakespeare play in itself, was in its essence English. Verdi and Boito had realized this marvellously and had not in any way Italianized either the plot or the emotions, except perhaps in the final tormenting of Falstaff. It was a comedy; why then should not the scenery reflect the fact, and who better with his architectural background and wit than our mutual friend Osbert Lancaster?

Carl was a little nervous that the more moving moments might get sent up, but took to the scheme with alacrity when he heard Osbert's simple suggestion that Ford was a *nouveau riche* merchant of Windsor, then a 'desirable' suburb, and that his house should therefore be of the period and brand spanking new with no patina of time upon it. The Garter Inn, on the other hand, must be an old pub of a hundred years earlier. The Thames is the Thames and Windsor forest Windsor forest, and they should remain so. Within this simple premise the sets came out just right, never too heavy, never too frivolous, and always romantic where required. Indeed the last scene, with Herne's oak and the river glinting in the background, had a real magic. There were no gimmicks. Carlo Maria Giulini conducted and brought freshness and a young genius's sensibility of touch to this last flowering of Verdi's genius.

Falstaff was rehearsed at Glyndebourne and Fernando Corena, singing the title role, stayed in the White Hart Hotel in Lewes. His room looked out over the roofscape towards the railway station with the Downs and Newhaven in the distance. He spoke little English at the time and was clearly bored and found the evenings long. He took to spending long stretches in his room and, as he was naturally a gregarious and extrovert type, his colleagues wondered what he was doing. Reading or studying hardly seemed likely. Then the cat came out of the bag, if one may put it that way. At last Corena was seen at his window with an air rifle with which he was whiling away his time taking pot shots at the local moggies. The matter was satisfactorily hushed up and shortly we moved up to Edinburgh; whether he resisted his anti-feline impulses there I do not know.

After the first year or two at Edinburgh, when my family were old enough to travel easily, we used to take a furnished house for a month, generally out in the direction of the Braid Hills. I would go ahead by car and open up the house, Diana and the children coming up by train a couple of days later. We usually found a house big enough for us to have a lodger or two, particular friends of ours from the company. During each of the three weeks of the festival we would throw a supper party after the performance. After some experiment Diana found a successful menu which, as the guests were different at each party, we did not need to vary: fresh shrimps potted at home the day before, cold grouse and salad, raspberries and cream and plenty of cheap Italian wine. Grouse, too, were cheap, because Diana bought the previous year's birds which the poulterers were selling off to make way for the new season's bag, but very good they were after she had done with them.

Our car in those days was a curious one, a Minerva, a Belgian car made in Liège just before the war. It had a German Adler engine and front-wheel drive like an early Citroën. I had acquired ours second-hand one Sunday afternoon in Hastings to replace an elderly Hillman Minx. It had come to this country as a one-off show piece for the immediately pre-war Motor Show. It was beautifully built, with doors that shut like a Rolls, splendid veneered dashboard and thick leather seats. Its chief drawback was that if one went over a severe bump with the brakes on the shock caused parts of the brake mechanism to bend and seize up, necessitating the help of the nearest blacksmith. Also the universal joints for the front-wheel drive were enclosed in heavy leather gaiters which had to be kept packed with grease, otherwise the vibration practically took the steering wheel out of one's hands. We learnt to cope with both problems, however, and Mrs Miniver, as we called her after the war-time heroine, did us wonderful service for several years. We even took her to Italy and back.

Fortunately for Diana, Mrs Miniver had another virtue; her wheel-base was exactly the same as that of an Edinburgh tramcar. One morning Diana was on her way after a latish night to the centre of town to collect the shrimps and grouse. Somewhat sleepily she followed the tram in front, stopping and starting when it did. Suddenly she was conscious of being shouted at and became aware that she had missed a diversion sign and was now following her tram on its rails propped up over the six-foot deep trench of a road excavation. There was nothing to do but pray and go on until she reached solid road some twenty yards further on.

Anthony Besch, then Ebert's assistant, was one of our lodgers. One night we went to a party at Compton Mackenzie's which went on until daybreak. On leaving we found we were more than a little merry. Anthony agreed to ride in the boot, holding the lid open for air. On the way back we were overtaken and stopped by the police. Did I know, they asked politely, that I had a man in the boot? Oh yes, I replied, and they waved me on. How times have changed!

In 1955 we told the Edinburgh committee that we intended to have a special Mozart bicentenary festival at Glyndebourne the following year, with six of his major operas in the repertory, and that we would not therefore have the time to prepare a new work for them. We did not want to go to Edinburgh without a new production and therefore proposed to skip a year. Edinburgh turned once again to the Hamburg Opera. Robert Ponsonby took over from Ian Hunter as the third director of the Edinburgh Festival to come from the Glyndebourne stable, but even his goodwill was unable to overcome the financial problems that beset the funding of opera, and for the next four years he had to depend on foreign subsidized companies. By 1960, however, one year before he was to hand over the direction to Lord Harewood, we managed a return that had long been lobbied for by our friends and supporters.

The pattern was somewhat different from previous Glyndebourne visits. There were performances of two operas from the preceding Glyndebourne Festival, *Falstaff* with Geraint Evans, and Bellini's *I Puritani* with Joan Sutherland, both works conducted by Gui. The 'novelty' was a triple bill conducted by John Pritchard consisting of Wolf Ferrari's *Il segreto di Susanna*, Busoni's *Arlecchino* and Poulenc's *La voix humaine* with Denise Duval in the solo part and Jean Cocteau as designer and director.

All this added up to the cheapest package Glyndebourne could provide for the money that Edinburgh could afford.

The incoming director, Lord Harewood, could not be claimed to have come from the Glyndebourne stable, though he has always been a frequent and welcome visitor there and in the early Britten seasons was in more or less constant attendance. Not even his wide knowledge of opera and strong personal views, however, could bring about Glyndebourne's return to the scene which it originally set in 1947. Nor, several directors later, has this happened yet. One can only hope for a return in the not too distant future. But Glyndebourne progresses and keeps its equipment and techniques firmly up to date; the sad lack of any such progress with an opera house in Edinburgh makes it less and less likely that Glyndebourne or any other company will be content to take cut-back versions of its productions to present on what should be an international platform.

FOURTEEN

In the Emerald Isle

I first went to the Wexford Festival in 1953. It started under inspired leadership in the same year that the Glyndebourne Festival
reopened, 1951. I have returned seventeen times since with never
decreasing pleasure.

I was invited by its begetter Dr T. J. Walsh (Doctor Tom to his
many patients and friends in the town). Diana and I made it the
excuse for a short holiday in Ireland. Diana had never been before
and my acquaintanceship was confined to my experiences in Dublin
at the Gaiety Theatre and a peep out of the galley of *Phryna* when
rounding the Fastnet rock.

Dr Walsh and his principal collaborators, Dr Des Ffrench, Dr
Jim Liddy, and the proprietor of White's Hotel and Secretary of
the Irish Lifeboats, Eugene McCarthy, performed a miracle – but
then almost all creative efforts in the theatre are miracles. As a result
of playing gramophone records and listening to opera broadcasts
(Wexford was in a good area for European broadcasts), and egged
on by Tom's consuming passion for opera – particularly of the
nineteenth century – they decided that they could in that town of
some eleven thousand inhabitants put on a festival that would
produce operas at a standard that Dublin itself was not seeing and
probably had never seen. The venerable Dublin Grand Opera
Society was in the habit of hiring established productions from
abroad and slapping them on miserably unrehearsed, with singers
ranging from the excellent to the execrable.

At Wexford they decided to do everything from scratch; the
programme grew from one opera a year to two and then to three,
at which it has remained. Its list of participating artists is impressive for novelty and discovery, and Glyndebourne has borrowed as well as lent.

On our first visit we stayed in White's Hotel, the old White's in
the Main Street. The Talbot was not so important then, but
quickly developed, as has White's itself, into a complex mixture of
grills, restaurants, art galleries, dance halls, bars and comfortable

bedrooms. The little entrance hall of White's was the hub of the festival; that it gave directly on to the narrow street in which I one day met a large pig which had strayed from the market beyond, was just one of its charms.

The charming Georgian Theatre Royal was rescued from being a run-down cinema and little by little lovingly restored. Its natural acoustics have always been a help, its steep line of sight and terribly cramped backstage facilities disadvantages. But, though no one in their right mind would think of building a new opera house exactly like it, in that narrow little street with no room either for the audience or the performers to swing the proverbial cat, equally no one could now think of the Wexford Opera Festival taking place in any other building.

All the doctors were equally delightful in their different ways and equally hospitable in the best Irish way. They tried to keep their practices going despite the hectic life of festival week, with opera every night, a party or a dinner before it and always a party after. As the curtain was not down until well after midnight the night was still young as the morning began. Somehow a few drinks at White's led to a half-mile walk along the Main Street to the Talbot for a few more, then a walk back, the many pubs on the way providing handy, if noisy resting places. I have known the walk to be repeated several times between curtain down and breakfast, and in both hotels and in any bar the conversation is always good – possibly more brilliant one feels, than anywhere else in the world.

After breakfast a short stroll along the quay is obligatory, followed, particularly in the days of Dr Hadden, a Protestant missionary doctor, by one of the conducted tours in the town or countryside, back for a Bloody Mary before an oyster lunch, then a film in the Cinema Palace, tea, more drinks and dinner before the opera.

How the doctors managed to keep this up I don't know. I actually heard Tom Walsh say to a patient on the pavement outside his consulting room: 'Oh you're fine, till after the festival anyhow. Come back and see me then.' One day I met Des Ffrench, wellington-booted, coming out of a cottage on the road to Kilmore some miles outside Wexford when I was on a Hadden tour, and he, I knew, had a vital committee meeting in ten minutes' time. Another time, Diana, getting into the back of Jim Liddy's car, sat on something hard. Pulling it out from under her she revealed the doctor's stethoscope. 'Throw it out of the window,' said Jim Liddy. 'I've never heard a damn thing through it yet.'

Dr George Hadden's conducted tours began early in the history of the festival. He was a tall, fine-looking man, with flowing white hair and beard, who had returned from his work in the Far East to his native Wexford and made a study of local history from its beginnings. He was dressed, whenever I saw him, in hairy tweeds, with heavy brogue shoes, no hat, no tie or socks. He had a grand way of striding round the town, with his party keeping up as best they might, declaiming the history real or imaginary of anything in sight. One day we were going along one of the narrow streets in the upper town and I was admiring their simple Georgian portals when I noticed that the numbers on the doors were somewhat haphazard. Not only were they not in numerical order but there were numbers repeated here and there in the most casual fashion. I said to Hadden that I found the system a bit odd. 'Oh, sure,' he replied, 'everyone has the number he likes best.' 'But,' I asked, 'isn't that confusing for the postman?' 'Not-at-all, he knows exactly who lives where.' All perfectly natural of course.

The long-distance tours gathered on the Crescent Quay by the statue of Commodore John Barry, the father of the American Navy. Those with cars gave lifts to those without. In 1955 I gave a lift to a distinguished-looking couple who, from the international air about them, were obviously not natives of Wexford. They had a house, they said, some distance from Wexford in the Dublin direction and this was their first visit to the festival. He introduced himself as Alfred Bite (or was it the less rapacious and more nautical sounding Bight?). They were clearly knowledgeable about opera and interested in my Glyndebourne background, and we had a pleasant morning. I for my part did my best for my Wexford friends by extolling the festival and all its doings. I cannot have been a total failure, for the next year they appeared in the list of patrons and two years later Sir Alfred Beit was vice-president, succeeding Compton Mackenzie as president in 1970.

I hope it was on the same tour that George Hadden led us to a windswept hillock overlooking the South Slob (slobs are marshes in Ireland) and the grey shallow waters of the Slaney estuary. On the top of the rise, which we had reached by a muddy, cow-patty walk from the cars, were a few scrubby trees and bushes distorted by the wind and an outcrop of large grey boulders, with no sign that any of them had ever been worked by the hand of man. Perching himself on the largest, looking like a prophet with his white hair and beard blowing in the wind, Dr Hadden held forth on the fact that this had been the site of the palace of some ancient Irish king, renowned for having tried but failed to repel the Danes who had landed and founded the town of Wexford. It was a poetic and evocative performance and when he had finished, leaving us looking misty-eyed out to sea in search of the upswept prows of the invaders, he said: 'Well, that's what I like to think. I've not a bit of evidence to go on, of course.'

Fintan O'Connor was a great character. A lawyer practising in Wexford, he lived in bachelor magnificence and enjoyed, and I use the word advisedly, a wide circle of friends. His main contribution, apart from his presence and wit, was to organize a Festival Forum. This was the time when the Brains Trust was flourishing on television in England. Fintan selected his panel with care, as did the B.B.C., but he personally supplied accommodation for anyone who needed it, and treated his panel to a full Hallowe'en feast cooked by his excellent housekeeper.

I was fortunate enough to be invited to appear on the Forum in 1955 and 1956. For the first, besides myself, the panel under Fintan's chairmanship consisted of Osbert Lancaster, Eoin O'Mahoney ('the Pope O'Mahoney', billed as 'barrister and Irish controversialist'), Brigadier-General Edward Dorman O'Gowan, known more widely as E. E. Dorman-Smith and also as the O'Gun, and a local hurley champion.

We met at three in the afternoon for the feast – oysters, roast turkey, plum pudding, mince pies and Stilton washed down with stupendous quantities of excellent burgundy and crowned by great beakers of port – after which we were encouraged to rest our brains, taxed by the brilliance of our own conversation, by a short nap. We were then invited to meet downstairs at seven o'clock fully kitted in black tie or tribal gear, for a bite and a glass before repairing to the Cinema Palace for a short rehearsal at eight o'clock. At eight-fifteen the doors were opened to the avid public, who had been invited to send in their questions with the promise that these would not be disclosed in advance to the platform group, and bully-off was at eight-thirty. Some of us napped more successfully than others. Fintan was waiting below with champagne and smoked salmon, both in more than adequate supply. The questions – we were not on the air, much less on television – were carefully selected, and I suspect augmented by Fintan, and covered a wide range of topical subjects treading on thin ice but always treated with good humour and wit.

Fintan's care for his guests was far from over. He had obviously come to the conclusion that, as the evening wore on, the platform group might be inclined to flag. He had therefore arranged for three large jugs of iced orangeade to be placed on the table before us, together with frosted glass tumblers. The Cinema Palace heating followed the local pattern of being initially over-abundant and then dwindling to none at all, and the nervously sweating panel found the cold orangeade welcome, only realizing, and appreciating, the high proportion of rum in it as the hall cooled and the questions hotted up. That night's big question was whether Nelson's Pillar in Dublin should remain (it has of course since been blown up), so you can understand that I had every need of the Navy's blessing.

On the second occasion my fellow members of the panel were Compton Mackenzie, Christopher Hollis (then on the editorial boards of both *Punch* and *The Tablet*), John Raymond of *The New Statesman*, and 'the Pope O'Mahoney' again. We enjoyed the traditional feast, rested gently, and reassembled for the champagne and smoked salmon, Monty Mackenzie resplendent in a kilt. Only Christopher Hollis was missing. At seven-thirty John Raymond led us to the foot of the stairs and we gave a polyphonic rendering of A. A. Milne's 'Hush, hush, whisper who dares, Christopher Hollis is sleeping upstairs.' Christopher appeared slightly huffily and off we went to meet our public. The question that took the longest time was: 'Did the panel approve or disapprove of women in trousers?' Comprehensive replies were given, not least by Monty Mackenzie from the safety of his kilt. It was another great night, surely.

Fintan always chose 1 November, All Saints, for his shenannigan. After the first of my Forum nights, when I was again staying in the old White's Hotel, it was imperative that I should be at Dublin airport for the first London flight the next day. Fintan said that was fine, he would send his aged and cherished Alvis with his driver, a personable young man who had been doing the ferrying for the Forum, to pick me up at 6 a.m. at the hotel. Having learnt always to pack the night before an early departure, however chaotically, and having asked for a call with tea (what a hope!) at five-thirty, I fell into bed at about three. I was awakened at six-fifteen, not with tea but by Fintan's driver, Brian O'Kennedy, standing in my room and shaking me. By six-thirty we were on the road, I sitting beside Brian in the front.

It was still pitch dark and the Alvis's powerful headlights cut a path up the narrow hedge-girt road towards Arklow. Suddenly out of nowhere appeared the gaunt white figure of a ghostly horse. The car skidded to a stop and the animal, seeming ten feet high, turned its skeletal head and red-rimmed eyes on us and then stalked off through a gap in the dark hedge – frightening enough to any punch-drunk traveller, but now made the more so by eldritch screams coming from the back of the car. Brian turned on the interior light to reveal two terrified girls. 'I'm sorry, sorr,' he said, 'but they wanted a lift to Dublin and I didn't think you'd mind' – pause – 'I didn't mention it to Mr O'Connor though and I trust you won't.' I didn't, of course, but I wonder if those two young ladies have ever forgotten their sight of the white horse of the Apocalypse walking on the night when the graves are said to open.

Once at Wexford I had the opportunity of saving the life of a prime minister. The circle of the Theatre Royal at Wexford is raked at a steep angle and in the old days had only one gangway down the middle. Those in the front row had a low parapet in front of them and looked precipitously down to the orchestra and stage. When standing up they would find the rail just above knee-high and were in danger, if caught off-balance, of capsizing over it.

It was on the second night of one festival that the *Taoiseach*, Mr John Costello, graced the occasion. He was naturally given the best seat in the house in the front row of the circle on the gangway. I was seated in the third row, also on the gangway. Unbeknown to the *Taoiseach*, and to me, a certain journalist from Dublin, who wrote beautifully when sober and even more beautifully when not and was therefore famous for the extreme beauty of his writing, was seated on the gangway too, some four or five rows back.

At the interval the *Taoiseach* rose and began to make his way up the gangway while the audience around him remained respectfully standing in their places; all, that is, except the journalist who, suddenly awakened from the somnolent satisfaction of musical appreciation, thought quickly of the need to be first out of the circle and down to the Tower Bar in the Main Street. Unmindful of the august presence making its way up the gangway he leapt to his feet, missed his step and fell backwards on to the figure behind. Quick as a flash I leapt forward, put one hand on each of the seats to right and left of me and supported their combined weights for long enough for the *Taoiseach* to regain his balance and the over-inspired one to be pulled out of the way. Without my prompt action, I like to think, yet another politician might have gone to join that short but select list of those who have met their death while attending the opera.

FIFTEEN

On the playing field

I have never been any good at ball games. Football, rugby, hockey –
field and rink – tennis and squash I have had mild flirtations with in
my time, but it was I who cooled, and quickly. Indoor ball games,
billiards, snooker, billiard fives, have all tried me and found me
wanting, nor have I taken to bridge or any other form of cards.
Golf I have never felt drawn to.

Only with cricket did I have a slightly longer affair; due, I think,
more to the euphoria of the clunk of ball on bat, the cawing of the
rooks in neighbouring elms and the enticingness of the tea ladies
than to the thrill of achievement. But my cricket career did not last
long. It culminated one hot August afternoon well before the war
when I was playing for a scratch side in an away-game at Birchington. I was known to be useless but a full eleven was hard to come
by and I went along for the ride and, as it turned out, for the beer.

We assembled in a pub adjoining the ground. The match was due
to begin at one-thirty. I arrived with my captain and one or two
others in good time but the rest of our team was late and I had
rather more beer while waiting than was good for me at my tender
age. By the time the game was ready to start there was only one
chance for my captain, and that was to put me in to bat early on in
the hope that my artificially induced elation would lend accuracy
to my eye and boldness to my strokes. The trouble was that the
inept fellow then lost the toss and we were sent out to field.
Realizing that I would not be stimulated by this turn of events he
put me out in the deep field, in such a position that I had only to
walk a few yards to left or right at the change of the over. With luck
few if any balls would get as far as me.

For quite a long time all was well. I dozed, piece of long grass
from the boundary in mouth, standing like a sleeping horse. The
sun beat down, the soporific sounds of cricket and caws became
more and more distant, and my eyes, narrowed to slits by the glare,
were soon closed entirely by the somnolent effects of the beer.

Suddenly there was a great shout as ten voices bellowed my

name; opening my eyes with a jerk I saw to my horror a cricket ball coming straight towards me at great speed. With no curve in its trajectory it grew in size like a surrealist object drawn by Dali. With a scream of terror I threw up my hands to protect my face, the ball hit them with such force that I was knocked backwards on to the sun-baked earth and passed out. I came round to find myself the hero of the game; my hands had held the ball and I had caught out the opposing team's most vigorous batsman, miraculously stopping a drive that any sensible person would have avoided. But I had a nasty headache and when later I went in to bat I was out first ball. I have never played cricket, drunk or sober, since.

I returned to the playing fields once more, with equally mixed success, in 1955, the year which marked the hundred and fiftieth anniversary of Nelson's victory at Cape Trafalgar. Ian Hunter was by then managing director of Harold Holt Ltd and general manager of the Bath May Festival. It occurred to him that, because of Nelson's strong connections with Bath through Emma Hamilton and the large and continuing Royal Naval presence there, it would be a good idea to make that anniversary the central theme of the festival. He discussed this with me, and what started as a pageant of the more conventional kind evolved into a sort of *son et lumière* before that name or technique had become known in this country.

We sought someone to write the script of the pageant and with great good fortune hit upon Jackie Broome. I had met Captain Jack Broome D.S.C., R.N. when I was doing the staff course at Greenwich in 1944, and knew of his talents as a writer, comic artist, draughtsman, naval historian, sportsman and raconteur, as well of course as his having been a protagonist in the P.Q. 17 drama on one of the Russian convoys. He came up with the suggestion of dramatizing the pageant and re-enacting the Battle of Trafalgar on the playing fields of Bath. The site of the Bath football ground in the centre of the city hard up against Poultney Bridge and the river was selected. Naval co-operation was sought, and help with personnel and bands readily promised. The Navy appointed a liaison officer who did much of the co-ordinating work with the local populace.

Jackie turned in a script that was really exciting. It ran from Nelson's departure from Portsmouth in *Victory*, through several episodes in his career to the moment of the great battle itself. There it switched to the French and Spanish side and back again, followed the battle in realistic detail, recorded the death of Nelson, the hour of victory and the news reaching Falmouth and the

Admiralty, and culminated in a great parade and a spoken tribute to Nelson.

I had long admired Nelson and had read most of the standard works about him. I found the subject very moving. We obviously needed a team of first-class actors; but how could we afford the 'stars', would they be prepared to perform in the open air, and how would we amplify the voices? Thinking of my early days in radio plays, I came up with a solution: to make a recording of the dialogue with the voices we wanted and many of the sound effects, and then to get local amateurs to act the parts in dumb-show.

I arranged for stands to be built in the corner of the football ground nearest the river in an L shape with a platform stage in the middle, and we investigated the possibilities for scene changing and having the ship scenes on moving trucks further out into the field. Alas, a major snag appeared, one that should have been an omen of worse to come: the ground was soft and would not bear the weight of the proposed trucks and their rails. Another problem was that the variety of short scenes meant that, with even the simplest scenery and furniture on a single central stage, there would be inevitable breaks in the action. To overcome the latter problem I decided to have three stages set in echelon between the stands, the central one to be used for all the general scenes and the two outer ones for the English and French sides respectively. By rapidly switching the lighting, which was to be mounted on two big towers behind the stands, from one stage to another, it would be possible to keep the action continuous as scenery could be changed while a particular stage was in darkness.

To overcome the first and greater difficulty of the nature of the ground Jackie proposed making use of perspective; instead of having moving ships, why not have ships made to different scales set out deeper in the field and illuminated as and when necessary? From this evolved the final and successful solution, to have two-dimensional cut-outs of the ships with billowing sails, all properly disposed according to plans of the action as it happened. Each cut-out would be manoeuvred by one or two people, according to the size of the ship. The ships and their crews would start lying flat on the field, and would rise and move about as required. In the area closest to the stages but some hundred feet behind them were the biggest ships, to be used for the close-ups of the battle. Seventy or eighty feet behind them were the smaller-scale ships, almost the whole battle array of both fleets so that long-shots of the action could be shown.

Low fences simulating the sea stood in front of each area to hide the lighting troughs and cables and conceal the ships when lying flat. Effects men were to be provided, controlled by Naval walkie-talkie from the control room, to make smoke and fire from the ships and so reproduce the tumult and heat of the battle. The principal ships in the foreground appeared in several versions, each successively more battered as the fight progressed.

It was a conception so brilliant that we, its progenitors, began to feel that it rivalled Nelson's own genius in handling the battle in the first place. I can't claim that all my staff were as visibly overcome as Nelson's had been when the plan of action was explained. His captains, Hardy, Collingwood, Blackwood and the rest, are on record as crying with emotion at the time; mine reserved their tears for later shedding.

Music was provided in two ways. On the tape all the sea-shanties were sung by the Admiralty Male Voice Choir in an arrangement made for me by Raymond Leppard. Live music was to come from the Royal Marine Band, Plymouth. H.M.S. *Drake* from Devonport provided the marching guard. The miming actors came from the Bath Operatic and Dramatic Society, and the ground workers were provided by the same source, together with the Boy Scouts, youth clubs and other local bodies.

The all-important tape of the dialogue and sound effects was made at the now famous E.M.I. studios in Abbey Road, supervized by John Allen who had been director of the Glyndebourne Children's Theatre and had since joined the B.B.C. Nigel Patrick played Nelson perfectly, his rather light, insouciant delivery matching exactly the character of Nelson as I, at least, felt he must have been. Nelson, like other geniuses, remains an enigma, but he has long fired the imagination and continues to do so, and every sensitive soul has his own mental picture of him. Jack Hawkins was my Hardy, who also spoke the linking commentary.

Nelson was fortunate with his weather; the gale he warned of did not strike until he was dead and the battle won. For us the elements were less kind. Mid-May one might have thought was pretty safe, but not that year. First it rained a lot and the playing fields became sodden; so did the Boy Scouts lying prone under their ships on the grass, and they had to be kitted out with waterproof clothing. Nevertheless the show went on and both audience and players braved the rain. Apart from the weather it was accounted a success, and with ten days to play in we felt that the weather must help sooner or later.

On the day the show was to be transmitted by the B.B.C. on television, an eagerly sought and triumphantly negotiated coup for the Bath Festival, the evening started dry but wild and windy, with a forecast of worse to come. The performance began as planned just as dusk turned to dark. The initial pictures, black and white only of course in those days, were good considering the state of technical equipment and the problems of lighting, and we had just reached the start of the battle proper when the heavens opened up. The picture was being beamed from the B.B.C. van behind the stands up to a portable dish aerial on top of Solsbury Hill and from there to the B.B.C. at Bristol. The elements entered the battle with a tremendous lightning strike and a clap of thunder which put the B.B.C. aerial out of business. Despite the storm the show went on, and I sat dismally in the B.B.C. van looking at the pictures the cameras were getting but which were going no further. Nor were they, in those times, being recorded.

The weather went from bad to worse. One night the rain actually turned to snow, in mid-May in Bath if you can believe it. Each night at the end of the show the salute was taken by a distinguished visitor: on the first night by the mayor, then the Second Sea Lord, the Lord-Lieutenant, the First Lord, the Controller. The summit was to be reached on the sixth night when the salute would be taken by the First Sea Lord, Admiral The Earl Mountbatten of Burma K.G., no less.

On Tuesday, after a night of rain, the morning broke with a promise of better weather. The First Sea Lord was on his way, with a schedule of sundry visits to Naval establishments, a luncheon, more visits, and the culminating thrill of the Battle of Trafalgar for the evening. The rain had stopped. However, not from on high but from below came a new menace. Inexorably the river Avon rose, and little by little the battlefield of Trafalgar disappeared under the flooding waters. The show could not go on. The waters had engulfed us and the greatest naval sea battle of all time could not be re-fought because there was water a foot deep over the pitch.

So it was that I, ex-Lieutenant-Commander Caplat R.N.V.R., found myself in the ballroom of the Navy-commandeered Imperial Hotel, backed by a blackboard, chalk in hand and with a machine to play our precious sound tape, facing an audience centred round the great Dickie himself and including the contemporary Lord Nelson and all the local top brass of the Navy, to give a discourse on the brilliance of Nelson's strategy and in effect tell them how battles ought to be won.

No performance in my acting days was ever preceded by stage-fright of such a degree, but I had the courage of my, and Nelson's, convictions and sailed into the thick of it. It went gratifyingly well and everyone was complimentary at the end, not least the First Sea Lord. Naval hospitality took over, which I willingly accepted, and after the second or third drink Lord Nelson came up and congratulated me. 'There's just one thing,' he said, 'that you got wrong – the "Kiss me, Hardy" bit.' Now I was particularly proud of the way we had handled that on the tape; the relationship between Nigel Patrick and Jack Hawkins had been just right and neither of them could be thought to have other than normal feelings for each other. After all, as I said to Nelson, it was an age when strong men showed emotions freely. Had not the captains wept at the battle conference, even before the rum had gone its rounds? 'No,' said Nelson flatly. 'Nelson wasn't like that. He was a fatalist. What he said was *"Kismet,* Hardy".' End of conversation. But I know what I think and I reckon I know what Hardy did.

SIXTEEN

In rural Sussex

Out of the Festival Society Committee and in a sense out of the programme book was born the Glyndebourne Arts Trust, one of the pioneers, if not the pioneer, of all such bodies designed to raise money by voluntary means and to support its object. It was steered into being by an impressive array of prominent people, and Spike Hughes's *History* tells the story fully.

For me it was an interesting time. I greatly enjoyed the diverse characters of the trustees and found myself more and more drawn in to the hub of the wheel. Robert Ponsonby was made the secretary of the Trust and of the Festival Society. Neither of these bodies had any artistic or administrative powers; these were vested in the 'Executive', consisting of John Christie, Carl Ebert, E. Scott Norman as financial adviser and myself. As general manager I found myself responsible for practically everything, and when Robert Ponsonby moved on to succeed Ian Hunter at Edinburgh I found it simpler to take on the three posts Robert vacated. I must confess that it was nice to have all the reins in my own hand.

Glyndebourne in those days was by no means the vast rabbit warren it has become. Office space has always been a problem and still is. I think a certain Professor Parkinson has propounded a law about it. I started, as did my predecessors, by using the former potting shed in the old garden wall – now unrecognizable as the Information Office. From there I moved to a room overlooking the walled garden, built on as an afterthought when the Mildmay dining hall was built; and thence to the old smoking room in the house itself, a semi-basement room now used by the production staff. Originally it had been a ground-floor room and gave access to the oldest part of the cellars behind it; then, when the terrace was constructed thus raising the level outside, it lost all but the top part of its window. It was damp, but cool in summer, and in winter we worked from the London office in Baker Street. The old smoking room holds happy memories for me, social and otherwise.

We were fortunate in those days in being able to furnish the offices in London and in Glyndebourne with Christie furniture, some of it too good for the purpose but a pleasure to be with. When I moved to the smoking room John installed several noble pieces and a painting depicting the rescue by Captain Daniel Béat Christie, Bombay Lancers, of the harem of Surdah Cawn from a fate worse than death at Tellicharry on the Malibar coast in 1782; a feat the reward for which did not a little to swell the family coffers. The picture did not show the gallant captain himself but only a bevy of seven insipid Victorian virgins, not at all what one would expect a well-run harem to be stocked with. I told John that though I appreciated the historical importance of the picture, I was afraid I should find it rather hard to live with. 'Well,' he said, 'you'd better have something there; the wall is damp and the plaster keeps on breaking away.' 'Do you mind, sir,' I asked, 'if I have that big sea-painting that's in the cellar?' John was astonished; he had forgotten it was there and anyway he didn't think much of it, as it had no historical significance for him nor was it signed or dated.

I knew what the picture was, however – or rather, though I could identify neither ship nor artist, the reason for its being painted. It is a triple portrayal, such as was common in the days before photographs, of a cutter under full sail on three points of sailing, accurately painted from the seaman's point of view and attractively, if rather naïvely, from the viewer's. Behind the three aspects of the cutter the whole might of Nelson's warships could be seen on the horizon. I like to think that it was painted for some young officer enjoying his first command in one of those small, fast, yacht-like vessels that ran messages for the fleet, perhaps one of those that from close inshore spotted the Franco-Spanish fleet coming out from Cadiz before Trafalgar and carried word to Nelson, or one that sped off home and brought the news of the tragic victory to Plymouth.

I was allowed to carry that picture to my next office in the new buildings behind the little boxes in the theatre, and from there to my last office in Childs' Sitting Room above the kitchen in the house. Childs was the butler of pre-war days and obviously knew how to make himself cosy. Up under the roof, overlooking the front drive, his room somewhat resembles an upturned boat, and when I and the picture moved there it was dubbed Peggotty's.

I have never spent an entire night at Glyndebourne in all the years I have been connected with it. Very late home I have been on numberless occasions, but never have I brushed my teeth in the morning there. Early on Audrey Christie suggested that we should occupy one of the cottages at Glyndebourne itself, and subsequently her late father's house in Ringmer. Both offers we gratefully declined; living over the shop didn't appeal to us and to settle in Ringmer would mean, as we already knew from our short sojourn in Aunt Freda's house in Harrison's Lane, living in a hotbed of largely inaccurate gossip. So we stuck to our terrace house in Lewes, built a better kitchen and another bedroom on to the back and counted ourselves lucky.

By 1953, however, the Lewes house had become too small, even with the extension. We decided to look for somewhere larger. Diana wanted to get back into the country, but all the houses we were offered were either unsuitable or far too expensive. We began to lose hope but slogged on. After Christmas, not having had any satisfactory offers for 12 East Street, we virtually gave up, and told the agents that we would sell our house only if we could get a price which they thought impossibly high. I think it was £1,750. We had bought the house nine years before for £740 and had spent about £350 on the extension; it doesn't sound much now but in those days it was real money.

I went off on one of my trips abroad in early April and on my return rang Diana from the airport. 'Any news?' I asked, in the way one does. 'I've sold the house.' 'You've what?' 'Got the price we asked and we've got to be out in six weeks.' 'Where are we going?' 'Don't know.' Hurriedly we got particulars of all the houses on offer in the neighbourhood. It was the same old story. The desirable ones were out of our reach, the cheaper ones were not to our taste. Just one seemed possible; at Barcombe, equidistant from Lewes and Glyndebourne, with the right amount of accommodation, and at more or less the right price. We had been offered it before and had got no further towards inspecting it than stopping in the lane, peering down the overgrown drive and getting a squint at the end of a late Victorian, early Edwardian, red brick and tile pile looking decidedly dank. That had been in November. Now in April we went to have another look. Neglected and overgrown the garden certainly was but aglitter with daffodils.

Once inside we realized how wrong we had been to dismiss it. Every room except the kitchen and two of the four attic bedrooms had a wonderful view across open farmland to the long line of the Sussex Downs five or six miles away. The only signs of human activity apart from the cultivated fields were a beautiful and ancient farm and its outbuildings half a mile across the fields and beyond that, every now and then, the sight of the little toyland engine and train of the Bluebell railway puffing itself along with neat gobbets of white smoke.

Inside, the house was delightfully neglected too. William Morris curtains hung mouldering from verdigrised brass rings on wooden poles, ivy had come in through an open window and grew on the ceiling in the dining room, but the sitting room was full of daffodils and included an elderly lady sitting by a wood fire, sewing away, the natural daylight augmented by a neon striplight screwed to the ceiling. She was looked after only by her husband's old batman and was keen to move to smaller accommodation. Our son Marc, then five, fell for her at once and she for him. His great sorrow when we moved in was to find her gone; he had thought she was part of the fittings.

At £3,250 with an acre of garden, a garage for two cars, loosebox, potting shed, three big and four small bedrooms, two bathrooms, the house was a snip. A survey showed that it had been built like a fortress by Judge Grantham of Barcombe and that all the newel posts and mantleshelf uprights were turned teak staunchions from old sailing vessels. All the Grantham houses in the neighbourhood bear this trademark. He must have bought up such fittings from wooden ships being dismantled at Newhaven or Lewes about the turn of the century. They have, to those who think that way, a slightly phallic look and it has been suggested that curious fertility rites used to be practised here.

Only the name depressed us: 'Yewhurst'. We thought it boring, and there was only one yew of any size on the property, that being a magnificent one several hundred years old. We decided to rename the house and I instigated a competition amongst our friends to find the right name. To make it more attractive I offered a first prize of a week's free gardening on the premises. Strangely nobody entered. Studying the ordnance maps I found that the big wood which then started a few hundred yards away was named Slut Garden Wood (slut is a variation of sluice and refers to a weir and pond on the river by the farm below; garden in Sussex means any enclosed area and in local use is applied to the vegetable plot rather than the flower area). I suggested to Diana that, in view of the house's somewhat Chas Addams' style, we should rename it Slut's Garden Priory. She objected, so we dropped the 'hurst' (which means a small wood) and it became The Yew Tree House. The only friend to accept some free gardening was Robert Ponsonby, once. His height and the strain on his back, the inadequacy of our implements and the state of the ground soon put him off.

After all these years I do not regret Diana's having accepted the offer for East Street, nor our willy-nilly move here. As I write this I look out from one of the attic windows at the wonderful view, unchanged except that the railway has gone, the edge of the wood and the nightingales within it have withdrawn, and a new pond has appeared. Certain attempts at suburbanization that have been made along the lane are mercifully invisible, and although this afternoon is one of driving south-westerly wind and rain and the Downs are nearly out of sight, I know they are there and will reappear from Black-cap at one end to Chanctonbury, on a clear day, at the other.

There were many causes of late nights over the hill at that time and one was a roulette school run by a friend of John Pritchard, Basil Horsfield. Basil was a talented cook (which perhaps contributed to his later position as one of the more successful artists' agents). He produced delightful suppers for John, who was never unmindful of the pleasures of the table and, as a late-night extension, he set up a private, friends-only roulette game in John's room on the top floor of the house. Much to my surprise I began to win; not a lot, for stakes were low, but I came away each night better off than I had gone in. I had discovered a system which seemed to be guaranteed to pay off, not spectacularly but regularly. Diana was justifiably getting pretty fed up with my late hours, not for the first time, and did not, I sensed, quite believe my explanation that I had found a system which I could apply to the tables in Cannes casino and thus make our fortune.

Alas the bubble burst; Basil discovered that he had been paying out marginally the wrong odds on one particular fall of the ball. I had, quite accidentally, discovered the error before him. Basil lost a few bob, and I lost any faith I might have had in my gambling luck. Indeed, I have often thought that if anyone wanted a horse 'stopped' without risk of detection the only thing they need do was pay me a small sum to back it.

A local figure of that time, the fifties and sixties, was Harold Williams. He had been a member of the chorus in pre-war days, and had gone on to become not only one of the best character actors in roles such as the innkeeper in *Falstaff* and countless vignettes drawn by producers from his presence in the chorus, but also chorus manager, with a good no-nonsense authority and a sincere belief that the show came first, the chorister second and that the management had to make the best of it. A man of many parts, he not only sang all over the county in smoking concerts but was also a town councillor, the local masonic top-dog, the chauffeur of the judge at the Lewes assizes, the confidante and driver for the most successful of Lewes's race-horse trainers, a knowledgeable dealer in second-hand cars and a keen gardener.

It was in the last three capacities that Diana and I came to know him best. He several times helped Diana to pick a car from a bewildering selection of old bangers, and had an unerring eye and ear for the sawdust-in-the-gearbox botch up. He gave me advice on placing bets, advice I seldom took and never made any money on, for if I didn't back his tip it won, if I did it didn't – but that, according to Harold, was always because of some stupidity on the part of the jockey.

As a gardener Harold prided himself particularly on the quality of his vegetables. Every year at the beginning of rehearsals I would find parcels of superb asparagus deposited on the driving seat of my car. Any expression of thanks drew a blank stare; he was certainly not going to be caught sucking up to the management. After one of Diana's and his expeditions to find a replacement for Diana's ancient Austin eight, they walked together round our garden at Barcombe. Diana showed him our asparagus bed, established long before our time and yielding well, but with nothing like the quality of the spears produced by Harold.

'Why,' she asked him, 'can't we grow such good asparagus as you?' He replied in his gruff Sussex accent: 'You know I 'ave certain connections in the racing stables?' 'Oh, of course,' said Diana, 'all that horse manure.' 'Yes,' said Harold, 'but the great secret is I never take anything that 'asn't come from a placed 'orse.'

SEVENTEEN

With the circus

The first visit abroad made by Glyndebourne Festival Opera was in 1954 in response to an invitation from the Städtische Oper, Berlin. Carl Ebert had been reappointed as its Intendant after a gap of twenty-one years, but would not be making a new production until the following year. He thought that it would enthuse the Berliners to have a foretaste of his qualities by giving them two performances of Rossini's *La Cenerentola* with the Glyndebourne cast conducted by John Pritchard in place of the unavailable Vittorio Gui. The Glyndebourne Rossini team was a revelation to Berlin and the performances were a huge success, not least for Ebert. What is more, the visit cost Glyndebourne not a penny.

We had to wait until 1958 for our next foreign outing, this time to Paris with *Falstaff* and *Le Comte Ory* to the Théâtre des Nations festival at the old Théâtre Sarah Bernhardt opposite Le Chatelet. *Falstaff* we had given first in the Edinburgh Festival of 1955; when we were to revive it for the Glyndebourne festival in 1957 I thought of Ian Wallace for the part. He was tempted and Gui, who was to conduct, was enthusiastic about the idea, as was Ebert, but Rodolfo Mele, Ian's singing mentor, was adamant that he did not have the right *tessitura* for it. With a heavy heart Ian declined my offer, which was then transferred to Geraint Evans. (Interestingly, two years previously Geraint had declined the part of Ford in the same opera because *his* singing teacher had said that he was not ready for it.)

Geraint's Falstaff, every inch a Tudor though Sir John was not a Welshman, fitted the role as if it had been written for him, and his facial appearance filled the Lancaster sketches for the character as if Osbert had had Geraint in mind from the start. The one problem was Falstaff's obesity. Geraint had not in those days, nor I should add in fairness has he now, a Falstaffian girth. The wardrobe staff made him massive padding to wear under his costume, but Osbert rightly insisted that fat men have fat legs, fat arms and wrists – though rather delicate hands and fingers – and a fat neck, all of which meant padded tights, sleeves and even wig down over the nape of the neck. The kapok padding for Corena was lightened to foam rubber for Geraint, but though the weight was less the heat retention was greater. The opening performance at Glyndebourne on 29 June was a sweltering hot night, one of those when, in the absence of air conditioning, the auditorium doors had to be propped open and the audience sat fanning themselves with their programmes whenever the tension allowed.

It was a triumphant evening and everyone acquitted themselves most nobly, not least Geraint. By the finale, after he had been rolled about the stage by the citizens of Windsor he was exhausted, and how he got through the final fugue neither he nor I know. What I do know is that he virtually passed out after his curtain call and his dresser Harry Kellard (who was really the property manager but who always insisted on doubling as dresser to his favourite singers) and I literally carried him to his dressing room. There we stripped the padding off him and gave him salt tablets and other suitable treatment. After this unhappy experience Harry used his skills as a property maker to construct a wicker body shape for Falstaff, which solved all the problems and which Geraint wore not only at Glyndebourne and in Paris but, I understand, continued to wear for the part long after.

It was warm in Paris too, but Geraint was at the height of his energetic powers. He took the city by storm and was lionized at the many parties that our supporters threw for us. He certainly had no difficulty in filling in his idle hours, like Falstaff himself, 'dalle due alle tre'.

John Christie came over to stay with Sir Gladwyn and Lady Jebb at the Embassy. Lady Jebb, having been told by someone of whom she enquired that John invariably ate porridge for breakfast, found her chef not only unable to provide the necessary oats but ignorant of the very art of porridge making. In desperation the Ambassadress sought help, which was readily forthcoming, from the NAAFI at the British Army headquarters outside Paris and the porridge was duly produced. John, unaware of the efforts that had been made, opted for croissants. He delighted the Parisians by wearing his Coke hat, that curious flat-topped bowler invented by Coke of Holkham, and generally living up to the expected standards of English eccentricity.

There was no doubt some sense of relief in the Embassy when he left after a brief two days. Shortly after he arrived back in Glyndebourne there was an urgent call to the Embassy to the effect that he had left an important key in a drawer in his room. A search was made and an old-fashioned wrought-iron key with a large linen handkerchief knotted into its ring was found. The key was that of the strong-room at Glyndebourne and the handkerchief was to prevent its being forgotten.

Great though the *réclame* for this visit was – and it gave me particular pleasure to see my name on the bill outside Sarah Bernhardt's theatre, in which her dressing room was kept intact, in the capital city of my forebears – it proved to be very expensive. The takings were not what we had been led to hope, partly because *Ory* didn't get full houses but also because we had not been warned of the large number of Parisians who, by one form of privilege or another, got in for nothing. The British Council met a third of the deficit and support from sponsors had been good but not sufficient. All in all John Christie saw no reason to lose his suspicion of the 'Frogs', but he did not, mercifully, hold it against me personally.

Glyndebourne's third and most extensive visit abroad was to Scandinavia in 1967. Negotiations for it began in 1962 and the tour was originally planned for 1966. The moving spirit behind it was Norman McKenna, then chief representative of I.C.I. in Scandinavia. Based in Gothenburg, but with a cottage in the wilds of Norway, a country to which he was particularly attached, this music-loving patriotic Briton took upon his own shoulders the implementation of his dream – to get Glyndebourne Festival Opera to Stockholm, Oslo, Gothenburg and Copenhagen.

Once again modest aid was given by the British Council, but it was nothing like enough. Norman made a most thorough job in each of the three countries of enlisting the support of all the companies and individuals who had interests in Britain and the arts. After two years of effort he asked for a one-year postponement, to enable him to attend a little more assiduously to his own affairs. We were not sorry to agree as this would materially improve the suitability of the operas we could take, adding the new *Don Giovanni* from the current year's festival to *Il matrimonio segreto* from two years previously.

We opened in Stockholm, not in the opera house but in the wonderful little eighteenth-century theatre attached to the Queen's summer palace at Drottningholm a few miles outside the city. The story of the rediscovery of this theatre in 1912 – cocooned exactly as it had been left when a flush of Swedish prudery closed it down – reads like a fairy-tale. It had been shut up in the candle-lit age, before gas came along to increase still further the likelihood of consumption by fire. (This fate has at one time or another befallen pretty well every theatre ever built, except the post-war concrete monoliths which unhappily are likely to last far too long.) The care with which the restoration has been made and the strict rule that nothing should be done for modernization's sake alone, except the reproduction as far as possible of original lighting effects by electricity and the installation of an automatic fire prevention system, stands as one of the successes of contemporary conservation.

The first time I went to Drottningholm was in the winter of 1954 when I was visiting Stockholm with Jani Strasser to audition singers. We heard many, including Elisabeth Söderström with whom I immediately opened negotiations for her to sing in the 1956 festival. On a bright crisp Sunday morning I was taken by the director, Dr Hilleström, to see his beloved Drottningholm. As I stepped out of the car, full of wonder at the glitter of the snow and the pale colours of the stucco palace, I was suddenly bombarded with snowballs thrown by the accurate hand of Elisabeth herself, there with her Naval husband. So began a friendship with both of them, each having different interests of mine in common, which I am happy to say continues today.

I was not, however, quite so pleased with her husband, Sverke Olof, when a few months before rehearsals were to start Elisabeth announced that she was pregnant and couldn't sing that year. She came to sing the composer in *Ariadne auf Naxos* in 1957, then had another year off for personal production before returning in 1959 to sing the Susanna in *Le nozze di Figaro* that she should have given us three years before. Since then she has sung in ten of the twenty seasons up to 1979. Not all her missed years were taken up with procreation, for she restricted herself to bearing three splendid sons. Sverke distinguished himself in June 1958 by turning up at Glyndebourne with some of his crew in Swedish Naval uniform, having arrived in a nearby port in command of the sail-training ship H.Sw.M.S. *Falken*. As he said at the time, he came just to leave Elisabeth's card so that we should not forget her. As if any of us ever could.

Some years later, when discussing the setting for the new production of *Ariadne auf Naxos* with John Cox, who was to direct it, and Michael Annals, the designer, the question came up of where the prologue was to be set. Productions all over the world have sought different solutions. Messel at Glyndebourne had put it in a great hall not unlike the Organ Room at Glyndebourne. John Cox thought of the dressing rooms and corridors of a small eighteenth-century court theatre. Suddenly the Swedish öre dropped. 'Have either of you ever been to Drottningholm?' I asked. 'No.' 'I think it's all there, so when can you both go?' They were duly packed off and came back with the most beautiful evocation and workable set for the prologue, based on an amalgamation of the understage area, the little dressing rooms and the wonderful old capstan-like machinery of wood and rope that controlled, and still controls, transformation scenes of great complexity.

To perform our two operas at Drottningholm was both a pleasure and a challenge. We could not use our own scenery, for the size and nature of the stage with its permanent wings, multiple borders and steep rake precluded that, even if the conventions of the house would have allowed it. I was given a catalogue of the scenery they had in stock, all of it eighteenth-century, wings, borders and backcloths, and invited to choose what we should use. It was a lovely game, like being given a No.100A set of artistic Meccano. The Drottningholm people didn't mind how we mixed up their stock and were prepared to, and did, repaint one or two backcloths that had almost disintegrated with age.

With *Don Giovanni* the problem was that Luzzati's very original costumes hardly went well with genuine, albeit Italian-inspired, eighteenth-century sets. However, I found some strongly painted scenes of Hell and some good streets and palazzo interiors, and the result was not bad. *Il matrimonio segreto* was easier, as the costumes fitted well and there were delightful pastoral cloths and rustic interiors to draw upon.

The biggest difficulty was in the orchestra pit. Conductor and orchestra at Drottningholm had to appear in eighteenth-century costume, often with incongruous modern spectacles and countenances somehow foreign to white wigs. John Pritchard did not quite see himself in the gear, and the players of the London Philharmonic were even less keen. The Swedish authorities pressed the point, however, and said that they had an ample supply of wigs and costumes to kit everyone out and would we please send measurements. These we did, the measurements being, I am afraid subtly doctored so as to make them difficult to comply with. Whether this ploy was successful or not I don't know, but at the last moment the Swedes told us that unfortunately their own orchestra had accepted engagements elsewhere during our tenure of the theatre and they felt obliged to play these engagements in costume. Though their stock of costumes was large they could not, even more unfortunately, manage to meet our requirements from their spares.

Would we therefore mind if we were the first orchestra and conductor to break the tradition and play in modern clothes? John Pritchard said he minded, but gave way with a suspiciously ready grace; the orchestra sighed with relief.

Oslo was utterly different from Stockholm but equally enjoyable. The theatre left a lot to be desired externally, but inside the facilities and acoustics were excellent and we were able to give performances nearer to our norm than amid the exotica of Drottningholm. Hospitality was even more formal but no less lavish and punishing. From there we went to Gothenburg, where we found ourselves in the small but modernized nineteenth-century Stora theatre, and then on to Copenhagen.

Here we were housed in the huge Falconer Centret, which catered for anything from motor shows to opera and ballet. It was much too big for us but its ebullient director, Blicher-Hansen, did his best to accommodate our demands for concentration and to conceal the fact that the audience was sitting on top of the ice-rink. In Oslo Crown Prince Harald had come to *Don Giovanni* and been more than kind at the reception afterwards, though perhaps more ready to talk sailing than opera. In Copenhagen King Frederick came to *Il matrimonio*, having been supplied with a score, at his own request, for previous study. He sat with his Queen in a box to one side with a lit lectern before him, his head immersed in the score and his right hand doing its best not to conduct too vehemently.

In 1969 we took *L'Ormindo* to the beautiful Cuvillièstheater in Munich. The first performance was on a Thursday and, as it was early May and rehearsals were in full swing at Glyndebourne, I flew home after the last rehearsal on Wednesday and planned to return for the last performance on Sunday. Anne Howells was singing the principal role of Erisbe. After the first performance she and a few others of the company went out to supper together. On Friday almost all of them became ill, obviously with some sort of food poisoning. I was told of this in Glyndebourne early on Friday morning, and immediately got in touch with April Cantelo who had sung Erisbe with the Touring Opera the autumn before and who was on stand-by for emergency. April said that she could go to Munich that Friday evening so as to be ready to sing the next performance on Saturday if, as medical opinion felt was likely, she were needed.

The only problem was her costume. Both Anne and April were, and still are I trust, beautifully proportioned, but they were not

replicas of each other and the costume was tight-fitting, the bodice
being more or less a corset. April might have been squeezed into
Anne's costume but she certainly could not have sung comfortably
in it. Her own costume from the previous autumn was in the wardrobe at Glyndebourne and to get it, together with her wig, tights,
shoes and other necessities, would not be difficult except for one
thing, the Customs regulations. These obliged anyone sending
theatrical costumes abroad to itemize every article on the right
forms in triplicate and involved them in a lengthy process of
checking. There was only one way round it and that was to take
them as personal baggage, but there was no hope of getting the
costume to April, who was flying direct from Manchester, in time.
I therefore resolved to return to Munich on Saturday morning and
to take her costume with me among my personal effects. I would
arrive in Munich in the early afternoon in good time for the
evening performançe

I asked my good friend Tony Ledell, in charge of the wardrobe,
then as now and I hope for a long time to come, to let me have the
necessary items in my office first thing on Saturday morning. I
packed my own belongings into a large suitcase, leaving room as I
thought for the costume to be added, and went to Glyndebourne
to have my usual morning meeting before departing for Gatwick.
Imagine my horror to find not the carefully folded costume wrapped
in tissue paper and ready to go into my suitcase which I had en-
visaged but a very large cardboard dress box, splendidly corded
and labelled 'Erisbe costume, wig and accessories by hand of
Moran Caplat to Munich'. I rang up Tony, who was adamant. The
skirt was all prepared, ironed and laid out; in no way could the
frock (his word) be bundled up and made to rough it with my
sponge bag and dress-shoes. There was no time to argue so off I
went, dress box and suitcase together. The English Customs were
of course not interested, for nobody was searching outgoing luggage
in those peaceful days.

On arrival I retrieved my luggage and thought what to do. This
was before the days of green and red doors and all incoming luggage
was liable to be searched for contraband, particularly coffee. I
found a trolley and loaded it, then noticed that there was an alternative exit gate specially provided for wide loads, so I reloaded my
trolley with the dress box athwartships, pulled my trilby to a
jaunty angle, gave a flick to my whiskers, moved my umbrella to
the slope position and, with the other hand, steered my trolley for
the wide gate. I sailed through, to be met by a young Customs

Guard who enquired what was in my box. Producing my British passport I replied, 'Kostümfest'. He gave me an odd look but let me through. Had he opened the box he might have wondered what sort of a fancy-dress ball I was going to, but then again his being a pink-cheeked young German and I a middle-aged and obviously dotty Englishman, he might not.

At the end of the tour we sold all the scenery and costumes to the Munich opera, where they must have wondered why the inventory showed only one Erisbe costume when they actually got two for the same price.

Sadly for me, because I love the city, none of the attempts to get Glyndebourne to Venice came off. Like so many other plans, they foundered for lack of financial support. Glyndebourne could never afford to take risks; profits we did not seek but we did not like to come home poorer than we went out, to the detriment of our home operation. The British Council, always ready to help, could never do more than prime the pump, and so we were dependent for the success of any attempt to take us out of our home base not only on the determined enthusiasm of one man such as Norman McKenna but also on his ability, and that of his committees, to raise firm guarantees. Alas, in Italy this has not yet been possible.

Among many exploratory visits to Venice one stands out in my memory. It was in early spring; the crowds had not yet arrived, but the chairs and tables had been put out in the Piazza San Marco outside the cafés. The weather was blustery: hot sunshine one minute and a squally shower the next. I was leaving by the after-noon flight. I finished my business in the morning, had an early lunch, went to do some last-minute shopping in the Merceria and then strolled past San Marco and by the piazzetta on to the Riva degli Schiavoni, admiring the beauty of my surroundings in the clean, fresh, spring sunshine with big fast-moving white clouds making sudden changes of light and shade. Looking towards the mountains I saw a black squall coming fast in my direction and hastened back towards the shelter of the arcades in the square. On an impulse I ran to the Campanile, bought a ticket and went up in the lift to the gallery round its top. My impulse was shared by a German, with a camera of course (I am not a photographer and have never since schooldays owned a camera).

We were just in time. The squall struck with a sudden fury almost like a tornado; it made me think of Tweedledum and Tweedledee's great black crow. The waters of the Grand Canal over towards San Giorgio Maggiore were whipped into steep

219

waves with white tops and flying spume, like an iced cake gone mad, the gondolas moored between their wooden posts tossed up and down like horses on a merry-go-round, the *vaporetti* scurried for shelter. Perhaps one of the great Venetian painters has painted such a scene, for it must have occurred virtually unchanged many times in the city's history, but if he has I have never seen it. On land the action was no less dramatic: the wind was sudden and strong, force 9 or 10 I would judge, the flags stood out like placards, chimney pots whirled, television aerials bent like saplings, and all the pigeons in the square took off and whirled away over the roof-tops. People in the square below ran for safety, their umbrellas inside out in an instant. The German's light jacket which he was wearing loosely over his shoulders blew first over his head, in-hibiting his camera work somewhat, then flattened itself against the protective netting round the gallery. I laughed, a wild exultant laugh it must have been because my companion on the platform gave me the most apprehensive look.

Then, with a last tremendous gust, the blue sky already showing vividly beyond the black, came the most dramatic effect of all. Down below me all the metal-framed chairs, and some of the lighter tables together with their cloths, took off and went scream-ing across the stone floor of the piazza to break like a great ocean wave on the steps of the far end. Then, as suddenly as it came, the squall had gone, exactly like a Rossini *temporale*. Life came back to normal: the chairs and tables were recovered – not without damage – gondolas were bailed out, the sun shone and Venice, steaming gently, became once more her tranquil self.

But Venice is always dramatic. Diana and I were guests at the wedding of Franco Enriquez, Gui's stepson, to the daughter of the Moncenigos in September 1958. It had been a bumpy flight out, and on arrival it was very hot. We were misdirected into a bus to find ourselves in Jesolo instead of Venice, which meant another long bus ride. We arrived hot and bothered at our hotel, where much was made up for. The head porter of the Hotel Danieli was a close relative of a bass who had appeared recently at Glynde-bourne, and we had been given a suite on the third floor of the beautiful old building overlooking the Grand Canal and straight across to San Giorgio Maggiore, at a special price and at a time of year when rooms in Venice were at a premium. We changed and went out into the piazza for a drink before going to a favourite restaurant of mine, the Malamocca, only to find the square crowded and the outdoor variety of bingo that is favoured there in full swing. I managed to get a table from one of the waiters who remembered me – beards were rarer then – and we sat down to play the game which we did unsuccessfully for a round or two. Then the noise and the crowd began to worry Diana, so we decided to go back to the hotel and have something to eat quietly in our room. This we duly did; a light and delicious meal and a bottle of cool, white Tocai was brought, and we turned in.

We had hardly fallen asleep when the most horrific racket broke out. It sounded as if the Turks had returned to take their revenge for all those years of Venetian domination, had sailed into the Basin and were shelling the Doge's palace to our right. Diana cursed, reached for her ear-plugs and let them do their worst. I leapt out of bed, rushed to the window, opened the shutters and was met by a stunning display of fireworks set off from a barge moored in the middle of the canal. I watched spellbound as rocket after rocket exploded and fell in a glittering chandelier over the water with the great church behind. I kept encouraging Diana to come and see; she groaned and begged to be allowed to go to sleep. Finally I persuaded her and she staggered unwillingly to the window, just in time to see the last rocket over San Giorgio and the thin trail of the spent cartridge and stick as they fell back into the water. Probably it was the most poignant moment of the whole display but hardly the most spectacular.

On the second day the wedding took place, not in Venice but in the ancestral home at Vescovana in the Veneto some miles away. At an earlyish hour a cavalcade of chauffeur-driven limousines set off from the Stazione in Venice and wound its way through the countryside until they reached the village and descended in the dusty square in front of the church. On either side of the path to the door the villagers were clustered, the women in traditional blouses and skirts, the men in shirts and trousers, brand-new and supplied by the estate for the occasion. In we went to the church, and here was near pandemonium.

First of all nothing was ready. The altar was covered in flowers which served as inadequate cover for the *papparazzi*, who were there in force for the wedding of the *famoso* actor–manager– director to a lady of the aristocracy. The chairs in the nave were being pushed about by a crowd of socialities who were treating the whole thing like a cocktail party, and all the preoccupations of Diana about the seemliness of hats and the ban on bare arms were quickly swept away. Chatter was intense. Towards the back of the church a staging had been built for the villagers out of old trestle tables or anything else that had offered itself, and on to this the populace crowded.

Amidst the general mêlée Vittorio Gui and a small string band drawn from the players of the orchestra at La Fenice were endeavouring to rehearse. In the absence of a playable organ Gui was seated at a harmonium and not looking his happiest. At last there was a hush and in came the groom, looking every inch the man of the year. General hubbub, another hush, and he was followed by the bride, looking, and no doubt feeling, ethereal. More hubbub, during which the priest tried to make himself heard to little effect, and a popping of flash bulbs from all around including from behind the altar and even from under the priest's raised arm as he pronounced them man and wife. The last straw but one came as one of the *papparazzi*, whizzing out from behind the altar to fight his way down the aisle and catch the couple as they turned to leave, stepped heavily on Gui's gouty toe just as he was on his way back to the harmonium for the wedding march. Vittorio's cry and stifled imprecation remain with me to this day. The last last straw was the collapse of the improvised staging for the peasantry at the back just as the procession reached them. With impeccable aplomb Franco, wilting bride on his arm, strode through the wreckage to the noonday sun outside.

Here another *coup de théâtre* awaited us. One of the carriages from the family collection in the stables was drawn up, but instead of horses the traction was provided by the men of the estate, some of them limping a little from the collapse of the grandstand, all dressed in their new clothes and suitably garlanded. The bride and bridegroom were embarked and the triumphant cortège set off at foot pace to the villa. This was not far distant, but far enough in the hot sun for the stiletto-heeled female guests who, though no doubt relieved by the airiness of their garments, leant moaning steadily in that effective Latin way on the arms of their sweating and formally attired escorts.

The villa stood in a wonderfully pastoral setting. The only formal garden, as I recollect, was at the back of the central block, but we approached along the side of one of the two great arcaded wings which made up all the outbuildings, stables and the like. Under the arcades hung swags of tobacco leaves drying in the September heat and below these were set long trestle tables already weighed down with the makings of a rural feast.

The guests of honour followed the bride and bridegroom and their respective parents into the ground floor of the house itself –

exquisitely suitable, grand and at the same time simple as only the Italians have managed to make their country houses. We filed past our hosts on the receiving line up the *scala nobile* to the *piano nobile* above. Here were tables set out for the feast in rooms on either side and an operatic chorus of white-gloved, liveried servants. Slowly all was sorted out, there was a clap of the hands from the major domo, and the banquet began. There must have been at least two hundred guests.

Course after course arrived, each one cleared and the next delivered at the sound of a hand clap. Mercifully, perhaps, there were no speeches; I doubt if anyone had anything left to say. Then, replete with the good things of the region, and not least the wine, we were shepherded down and had to parade along both wings. To the right were the male workers of the estate and villagers, to the left the female, both sexes having obviously indulged lavishly in the food, wine and, on the male side, grappa provided. They rose unsteadily to their feet and bowed or curtsied as the gentry tottered past them, nods and winks and more ribald pleasantries were exchanged, and I for one indulged in the old naval custom of stopping for a tot on the mess deck. I thought it only courteous for a foreigner to praise the quality of the local grappa. So back into the limousines and to Venice – quite a day.

EIGHTEEN

Under sail again

When I started at Glyndebourne I was hard up. Pay in the Navy had not been large and I had spent it up to the hilt. At Glyndebourne I had only my salary to live on, a wife and child to keep, and a mortgage to service; every penny counted. I did, however, keep up my membership of the Royal Ocean Racing Club for a year or two. The subscription was low and I used the club in St James's Place occasionally. But I had neither the time nor the money to sail regularly, and began to feel frustrated whenever I went to the club and heard others talk of races and cruises. So I resigned – and soon regretted it. Then as things got better and Glyndebourne began to fall into a pattern, the old passion reared its head again.

My first good sail for fifteen years was in 1954 when George Barnes, having just moved from running the B.B.C. Third Programme on radio to take over as head of television, invited me to join him for a week's cruising in the Solent. This whetted my appetite. I managed to squeeze in the time in May before rehearsals began – Glyndebourne didn't open until 10 June that year – and we moved house from Lewes to Barcombe only a few days after I got back from sailing.

After my sail with George and Anne things improved. First Leo de Rothschild asked me to sail with him in his X boat from the Beaulieu River. We went *en famille* to spend a long weekend in the Master Builder's House at Buckler's Hard. Also staying there, while fitting out *Gypsy Moth III*, were Francis and Sheila Chichester with their young son Giles. Leo then moved from X boats to Dragons and I got more invitations to race. Diana's cousin, also Diana, and her husband Tony Beaumont owned a delightful yacht, *Artemis*, designed by Robert Clarke in which I sailed in 1961 and qualified to rejoin the Ocean Racing Club. With them we met yet another Diana, Diana Avebury, and by her kindness became *intimes* of Lepe House. One Easter I chartered a twenty-foot boat and my son Marc and I sailed about in bitter winds and snow in the Solent. Then a distinguished surgeon lent us his yacht, a sister ship of *Artemis*, in which the family and friends sailed for two seasons. (The yacht had the delightful name of *Saphena*. It took me some time to discover that this was not a lesser nymph in Artemis's pony-club but the name of the vein to which his skill was principally directed.) Later John Vernon, who had come to Glyndebourne with B.B.C. Television, asked me to sail with him in his South Coast One Design. Thus, little by little, I worked my way back into the sport I like most of all.

In 1966 I was asked by the secretary of the Ocean Racing Club, Alan Paul, whom I had known in *Phryna* days before the war, whether I would like to skipper the club's yacht, *Griffin*, for a race at the end of Cowes week from Cowes to Lequeitio in northern Spain, not far from Bilbao. Of course I said yes, though I had not sailed down into the Bay of Biscay since 1939.

It was an honour and a pleasure to be asked. The principle was simple: the club offered the skippership to someone they thought capable; he could gather round him three or four friends, and the club appointed as bo'sun for the year a young man who stayed with the boat throughout the season and was given a pittance and his keep. In addition three or four young would-be members from a list of applicants were provided from the crew-list run by the greatest gift of Ireland to ocean racing, Hope Kirkpatrick, the assistant secretary. Everyone, except the bo'sun, paid his own way together with a fixed charge to the club – more of course for the full members and less for the qualifiers. It was a wonderful system, and it worked perfectly until by the mid 1970s the sport had become so demanding of expertise as well as enthusiasm that the running of a comparatively large and old boat became not only uneconomic but also unrealistic. The club, rightly I think though to my personal sorrow, decided that the days of cider and roses were over and that their job now was to administer the newer and harder wave of entrants and help with training rather than merely to provide a vehicle for qualifiers.

In my first *Griffin* crew were Bill Almond and Guy Gravett, both local friends. I asked Hope Kirkpatrick to find me a really good navigator and she produced Philip Halstead, who sailed with me regularly thereafter. His father Horace had been first oboe in the Glyndebourne orchestra before the war, but that was pure coincidence.

In succeeding years we raced each August after Cowes week or after the Fastnet race, down to the Bay of Biscay, to Lequeitio twice, La Rochelle many times, to Bénodet and La Trinité on several occasions, from Cowes to Cork to celebrate the bicentenary of the world's oldest yacht club, the Royal Cork in 1974. I did another Fastnet race in her and took her from Gibraltar to Malta by way of Spain, Ibiza and Bizerta. Beverley Cross, librettist of Nicholas Maw's 1970 opera for us *The Rising of the Moon*, came ocean racing with me for two years and a most delightful crew member he was: resilient, always ready to do his bit at sea and a wonderful shore-side companion.

One of the best moments of my first visit to Lequeitio was dancing with Eric Tabarly's father in the yacht club – a strange couple we must have made. I should say that the late Tabarly *père* was nothing like so austere a figure as his distinguished son. On our second visit, having dined well in a restaurant above the harbour, we made our way to a café on the quay and settled down for coffee and brandy. After a while Beverley and Guy Gravett began to swop folk songs, Beverley's rendering of 'The Holy Ground' being particularly touching. Eventually we got to Guy's show-piece of 'MacNamara's Band', though he was restrained from rendering it with descriptive action as he was wont to do. The others chimed in, though I kept my mouth shut as far as singing went. It was a relaxed occasion – indeed the local residents came to sit and listen, no doubt helping the café's trade. When we judged it time to return to the boat for the night we called for the bill. The proprietor told us that the Spanish family who had been sitting at the corner table all evening and who had just politely said good night and left had settled our bill themselves. There's hospitality for you; or was it perhaps a Basque family who had leapt to too ready a conclusion about the revolutionary nature of some of the songs?

All ocean races heading west out of the Channel are routed north of Ushant (the north-west tip of Brittany) and west of the Ar Men buoy, avoiding the inshore passage close to the mainland of France. Outside Ushant the tide runs strongly and the seas, particularly if the wind is blowing from anywhere south of west, can be uncomfortable, to put it mildly. Also there are two busy steamer lanes to negotiate, great tankers and container ships thundering on their ponderous and unmanoeuvrable course at frequent intervals, not able to bother about small craft in their way. In fog, which is also not infrequent, the turning of the corner can be particularly fraught. After Ushant the bit of water to the Ar Men buoy off that strange reef of rocks and islets that sticks out below the Rade de Brest is almost always rough, with too much tide and usually too much, or too little, wind.

Almost all the Biscay races of the R.O.R.C. are won or lost on that corner. We won one race to La Rochelle by anchoring in a flat calm some twenty miles north of Ushant in deep water; every piece of rope or cordage in the boat was bent on to the kedge anchor and it held despite the tide. We watched competitors round us try to kedge too, but fail to hold and then drift away into the deepening twilight to the east. In the first light of dawn we got a little breeze, and the entire crew, except me who naturally felt I should not leave the wheel, laid on to our motley cable and with a great deal of cursing got it in. The tide was now fair, and away we went with a comfortable lead.

Once round the Ar Men the whole world changes. Tides are virtually forgotten, the sea turns from dirty grey-green to the wonderful turquoise of Biscay, the temperature rises by noticeable degrees, the seas lengthen out and you feel you have broken free of the land at last.

If you are not racing, or are on passage back from the Bay, the in-shore channel is the greatest fun; but the tide must be with you. One evening, waiting for it to turn, we went in to Audierne just south of the Raz and picked up a mooring in the harbour. Hardly had we tied up before another yacht arrived alongside and then several more, until we were stuck like a queen bee in the middle of a swarm. A party was somehow generated. I had announced to my crew that we were going to be off at 2000 might come what may. At 1930 Philip said: 'You'll never get out of this mêlée. Why don't we leave it till the morning?' With the Naval tradition of 'the ship must sail' and the theatrical tradition of 'the curtain must rise' I pushed my glass to one side and said, 'We shall sail on time.' And so we did, leaving the rest to do their hilarious best to resecure themselves round the void we had left.

The wind was a strong south-westerly, the tides were at springs and we shot through the Raz between the rocks and past the lights that mark the passage at literally a rate of knots, so fast that Philip the Navigator nearly broke his neck whizzing up and down to the chart table with new bearings. 'You're f...ing well mad!' he said, but he didn't mean it and enjoyed the wild ride as much as any of us, except perhaps Guy Gravett, who was at the wheel and singing as usual. Guy is the only man I know capable of singing the entire way through Stravinsky's *The Rake's Progress* while at the same time steering a boat on a stormy night. Photographer, painter, yachtsman, he is a man of many talents and a rhymester to boot. One blowy day round the Casquets he delivered himself of the following masterpiece of observed ornithology:

> It's a difficult life for a gannet;
> He hasn't the leisure to plan it,
> But flies to and fro
> In one hell of a blow
> Screaming 'Christ, bloody hell and goddamit!'

After a rather slow Fastnet race we had little time to get the boat together in Plymouth before starting the race to La Rochelle. Alan Paul, the secretary, came on board minutes before we were due to shove off for the start and while much of the stores and personal gear was still lying about all over the place below. 'Would you mind,' he said, 'taking the Heneage Ogilvy trophy [the cup for the race] with you?' 'Not at all,' I said. 'We're going to bring it back with us anyway. Put it on the chart table.' Then I promptly forgot about it.

Somehow everything got cleared away and stowed and we made a good start. By lunchtime we were off the Eddystone and an agreeable Danish crew-member volunteered to make the lunch as we had not yet set watches. It was a good race and we arrived in La Rochelle in a spectacular burst of speed over the finishing line, having been through a most dramatic thunderstorm the night before. Once locked into the basin and securely moored we smartened ourselves up and prepared to receive boarders. They duly arrived, not the least welcome amongst them Alan Paul. After a glass or two Alan said, 'By the way, can I relieve you of the trophy.' 'Of course,' I replied. 'Now where did you leave it?' 'On the chart table.' 'Well, it must be in one of the lockers under it.' It was not. 'How was it packed?' 'In a lot of newspaper in a Harrods bag.' Through the boat went a thorough search. No such parcel, but in a locker in the galley we found the empty carrier bag. Then it came to light. Our Danish friend, peeling the potatoes for lunch off Plymouth, had found the plastic bag on the floor between the chart table and the galley half full, as he thought, of old newspapers. He had added his peelings and other refuse and then ditched the lot just off the Eddystone, keeping the bag for future use. The cup was too light to make him think there was anything other than rubbish in the bag. The insurance paid up and a Heneage Ogilvy trophy still exists, though not as pretty as the old one. Perhaps somebody diving by the Eddystone in years to come will find the piece and puzzle how it came to be there.

For several years I took over *Griffin* from David Seth-Smith, who skippered her for the Channel race and the two short races in Cowes week. I sailed with David for one of the short races, in order to catch up with the boat's current state and in particular with the bo'sun of the year. David and I had sailed together one way and another for some years and became good friends. He was sailing *Griffin* in the New York Yacht Club trophy race in Cowes week in 1973, and I was with him when we were dismasted and nearly cut in half by a German visitor who charged the solid wall of yachts coming down the starting line on the starboard tack at full speed on port tack. Why nobody was seriously hurt I don't know. A young Frenchman lying on the deck by the mast just where the German hit nearly lost a leg, and the back-stays went off like pistol shots and whipped about just over the heads of the girls sitting behind the cockpit. The boom missed me and David by an inch. Anyway, that put *Griffin* out of the race and out of the running for the rest of the year.

David, a retired regular Naval officer was, as the Irish say, a lovely man, though something of a reprobate. A story he told with some pride should I think be recorded. He set out one evening by car to pick up his wife from her place of business not far from Golden Square. She was not in the office, so he went to a little club where he thought he might find her or she might look for him. Whom should he meet there but a painter friend of his. Together they sat down to wait and meanwhile discuss the progress of Life with the aid of a bottle of whisky.

Time passed and David began to think that he was dangerously late for dinner, but the conversation was good and the whisky not yet too low in the bottle. At last he decided that he should brave the probable wrath at home. Francis Bacon, his drinking companion, suggested that David had better leave his car wherever he had parked it and take a taxi. David agreed that this would be only prudent and left. The club being on the first floor, he made his way carefully down the stairs and opened the street door. There, by a miracle, was his car, parked apparently by some fairy coachman right outside. Forgetting the taxi idea David stepped in and drove off easily and well into Regent Street.

He was proceeding happily along it when, as he later told me, without warning, one of the bollards on a traffic island came straight for him in a bows-on confrontation which brought him to a sudden halt. There wasn't much other traffic at that time of the night and nobody seemed interested until a policeman appeared beside him and enquired if he was hurt. 'No,' said David, 'just surprised.' 'May I see your licence, sir?.' David hadn't got it on him but produced from his wallet some document or other that stated his identity and showed him to have been a Naval officer. 'Thank you, sir,' said the policeman. 'I was in the Service myself and proud of it, but may I trouble you please to breathe into this little bag?' David complied, not feeling he had any option in view of the man's extreme courtesy. 'Ah,' said the policeman, 'I'm happy to tell you, sir, for the honour of the Service that this is the highest count I've ever registered. Would you mind coming with me to Saville Row station?' Chatting amiably and leaving the car to look after itself, they strolled to the station. Once inside a sergeant began to take down the details. 'Would you,' he asked David hospitably, 'like a cup of tea?' 'No thank you,' said David, 'but I'd love a large whisky and water.'

I never sailed with Francis Chichester, but then very few other people ever did so either. We talked sailing matters together and he and Sheila came to Glyndebourne. He did not like crowds but seemed happy to sit in my box and dine privately in the interval, and our friendship grew. When therefore in 1975, three years after Francis's death, his son Giles asked me to go with him in his father's last boat, *Gypsy Moth V*, on a race from Portsmouth to the Azores and back, I jumped at the chance.

I was the old man of the party. Giles had found two contemporaries of his and the four of us should surely be sufficient to sail the boat, which, though quite large, had been designed by Robert Clarke and rigged by him to Francis's requirements for single-handed sailing. Giles and his young friends were all vegetarians. I am omnivorous myself but decided that for the twelve or so days in each direction I would manage. Perhaps the experience might even do me good. Teetotalism was not required but we renounced spirits except in emergency and the boys decided they would lay off the beer. One of them actually did. I organized a good supply of duty-free Beaujolais.

It was a strange voyage for me because in some ways I was much more alone than I had been on previous ocean races. Then there were always three or four people awake and active at the same time and in the cockpit one was seldom alone; here the reverse was true. For the first few days two of the crew, including the owner, were seasick. We were going to windward in rough seas round Ushant and out across the top of the Bay of Biscay, so Martin Walford (who had been bo'sun of *Griffin* with me in 1968) and I took alternate tricks at the helm. The self-steering gear had been damaged before the start and did not work. We dismantled it and carried on steering manually by the big tiller. It was possible, however, to balance the boat well with the sails, and I rigged a device with ropes in the cockpit which was adjustable and would keep the boat on course for reasonably long periods. This device Giles christened Beaujolais, and it got suitably toasted at regular intervals.

The two sufferers could be got on deck for major sail changes and we adopted a routine for such events: I went with thankful alacrity to the tiller and the three youngsters did all the work. *Gypsy Moth V* had some large sails, and the two long aluminium poles used to boom out the big headsails used for running – she had no spinnakers – were heavy and unwieldy. How Francis managed all that on his own at his age I shall never cease to wonder. Apart from scalding my arm and my feet rather badly when a pot of boiling water in which I was about to plunge some spaghetti leapt off the stove during one of the wilder lurches, I came to no harm from our diet; but I had discovered a large bucket full of peanuts stowed in a locker under my bunk in the fore-cabin and became a secret peanut addict. Those and the vegetable stews, containing mostly onions and cabbage, in which Giles specialized when he had got his sea-legs, helped to ensure that neither the boat nor I was short of wind, though we did have one protracted twenty-four hour calm when she lay unmoving despite the crew's lusty and well-fuelled efforts to remedy the situation.

I occupied the big cabin forward of the mast, specially provided to accommodate Sheila in comfort whenever she sailed with Francis. It did double duty as a store-room. It had, surely the only one in any boat built for single-handed sailing, a dressing-table and mirror with a stool. Its large bunk was in fact a drawback when the boat was jumping about as it was difficult to wedge oneself in. When I was not on deck or eating I spent my time in my bunk reading. I had only one book with me as I was determined to try to read it through. It was the Old Testament. Even in just under a month I regret to admit that I only succeeded in getting to the second book of Kings, Chapter 4, 'the deadly pottage'.

We did well in the race, finishing a close third after two of the bigger multihulls. A few days were spent in Horta getting my scalds treated in the local hospital and drinking in the renowned Café Sport with Peter, its proprietor. Peter, who counted himself one of Francis's friends, was keen to do Giles proud. To this end he had encouraged the visit, from one of the more sophisticated islands of the group, of a young and merry widow. Giles did his best to rise to her challenge but his heart was not in it. She attached herself, however, and on the day when a twelve-mile race was to be sailed round the bay, she came with us. Of opulent charms, she was pleased to expose a generous part of them to the beauty of the day and the admiration of the crew. As I was supposed to be the most knowledgeable about racing round the buoys I was in charge for the race. We led all the way until overtaken on the last broad reach by one of the multihulls, but out in the Sound it was blowing a fresh force 5 and there was a good deal of movement. The lady's naturally olivine complexion turned several shades greener and a light dew appeared upon her brow and generous, slightly hirsute, upper lip but she continued to smile and bulge invitingly. Unfortunately for her, Giles wasn't feeling too good either, so nothing came of Peter's good intentions. Two days later we set sail for home.

The major difference in the return journey was that I had had to replace the Beaujolais with a local dry white from Pico in large demijohns. As on the outward journey, I caught no fish; *Gypsy Moth* either didn't go fast enough or she went too fast. I tried mackerel spinners and a larger hook, baited, in the absence of good raw meat, not with onions or peanuts but chunks of red plastic cut from one of O. M. Watt's carrier bags. The spinners disintegrated due to the high speed, but the large hook obviously attracted something as it and its bait were snapped off. Apart from a whale near the Azores and a few dolphins, marine life was not evident. Alas, plastic pollution and chunks of tar were too often to be seen even hundreds of miles from land.

Seven years later, in 1982, Giles asked me again to sail with him and the same two companions, to take *Gypsy Moth V* from the Beaulieu River to Santander where we would hand her over to Desmond Hampton. He had chartered her for the round-the-world singlehanded race which was to start from Newport, Rhode Island, a few months later. In order to avoid tax formalities the handover had to be made in a non-E.E.C. country, and northern Spain was the most convenient.

It was a nostalgic voyage, the Azores one in miniature, except that the 'boys' were seven years older and vastly more experienced. This time I did catch some mackerel and the voyage was so short that the diet did not pall. Once again I supplied the Beaujolais (an excellent wine for sea-going – the temperature of a boat's bilges is about right and it doesn't mind being bounced about) and, what is more, found that my old friend Beaujolais, the steering wizard, was still in operation despite, or perhaps because of, the thousands of miles *Gypsy Moth* had sailed in the intervening years.

When we left the Beaulieu River on 27 May I was conscious that Sheila Chichester felt she was saying goodbye to the boat. Desmond's trip would take a year and finish in Newport. Would *Gypsy Moth* ever come back to England? It seemed doubtful. She was already expensive to maintain, and it was likely that on completion of the round-the-world race she would find her way to the Caribbean and go on charter there. Of all Francis's boats Sheila loved this the best. In her relative, Lord Montagu's launch, *Cygnet of Beaulieu*, she followed us out of the river and down to the West Lepe buoy, before turning for home with a wave.

What none of us knew was that *Gypsy Moth V* was to be tragically lost on Gabo Island in the Bass Strait just short of completing the second leg of the race at Sydney. By a miracle Desmond survived, but *Gypsy Moth*, the valiant fruit of Francis's determination, Sheila's love and understanding and Robert Clarke's genius for designing graceful yachts, was so wedged as to be unsalvable. I imagine her wooden bones to be there yet, with the seas tearing through them but her skeletal frame indomitable. Perhaps she didn't want to end up carting boozy land-lubbers round the Caribbean. If that is the case it was bad luck for Desmond. But I hope it wasn't the fault of Beaujolais.

Half-way down the Bay of Biscay, somewhere in the latitude of St Malo and on the edge of the continental shelf where the greater depths of the Atlantic give way to the shallower waters of the Bay, on a misty night with little wind and poor visibility, I had just handed over the watch to Martin Walford as dawn began to break. I got into my bunk, and had dozed off when Martin shouted for me to come on deck quickly. Unable to imagine what the emergency could be I tumbled out and climbed into the cockpit. 'Look,' he said, pointing over the starboard bow. There, at the limit of our visibility, perhaps half a mile away in the grey light of dawn, was a destroyer, long and lean, and, though no doubt well aware of our presence, ignoring us. Just astern of her the huge sinister shape of a nuclear submarine was heaving itself from the sea slowly and reluctantly like some lethargic monster. I somehow expected to see its back covered in seaweed and barnacles. It was four times the size of my T class wartime boats, with a great sail, as they call the structure which replaces our conning tower and bridge, towering over a sleek hull that extended in both directions until it dissolved into the waves in a way that suggested untold lengths ahead and astern. Slowly, behind its escort, it crossed our bow, then they both made speed and were gone in the murk, no doubt heading for the French base at La Pallice.

The Falklands war was in its most crucial stage at the time, and this incident made a great impression on me. I had had a ringside seat for a brief moment at the beginning of the conflict. The Royal Navy is now largely, and very properly in my opinion, run by submariners. Admiral Sir John Fieldhouse ('Snorkers' to the trade) was nice enough to invite Diana and me and Captain John Coote and his wife to lunch with him at Admiralty House, Northwood. Beside submarines, we had sailing and an interest in opera in common. The invitation, issued some weeks ahead, was for Monday 5 April. On Thursday the first the news looked bad. On the second the Argentines invaded and the sending of a task force was announced. Obviously our lunch party would be off. Nobody rang to say so, but we assumed they must be too busy. On Saturday I rang Johnny Coote. No, he said, so far as he knew lunch was still on. On Sunday he confirmed that it had not been cancelled.

Accustomed to sail when ordered we duly presented ourselves at Northwood for lunch. It wasn't quite the small get-together we had been promised – informal, certainly, but the Fieldhouses apologized for the increased numbers due to the emergency. The carrier group of *Invincible* and *Hermes* had sailed at noon. We were joined by a handful of senior officers from different branches of the services coming from the operations rooms. The preponderance of males was relieved by a number of Wren officers and other ladies from the Staff. Diana and I felt that we were back in the world of (S9) at Dundee. So, I suppose, we were.

NINETEEN

On the bummel

Holidays abroad in Europe have been a series of pleasures and adventures. Usually they were combined with business in one way or another, but Diana and I tried to get away together once a year on our own.

We crossed to France in 1946 and spread our travels wider in succeeding years. Mostly we went by car and made great use of the air car ferries, alas no longer functioning, from Lydd in Kent to Le Touquet and Geneva. The planes were war-time conversions and for some reason it proved uneconomical to replace them when they became too old. To load with three other cars at Lydd in the not too early morning and be two hundred miles on from Geneva by a welcome dinner-time the same evening was a real luxury.

Often our first and last port of call was Eric Dunstan's house in Provence. At first it was the Moulin de la Mourachonne at Mouans Sartoux between Cannes and Grasse. This was converted before the war from its original use as a watermill for pressing olive oil to a most attractive villa with the old water-wheel, which still turned in a sluice at the side of the dining room, giving a delightful coolness to the interior. The river never dried up, even in the hottest periods, since it came from the high mountains in the interior. It provided an extensive system of irrigation, which made it possible for Eric to create an English-type garden with lawns and flowers not normally seen in those parts.

There was a small circular swimming pool hidden in a bamboo brake at the far end of the garden which one could retire to after a splendid lunch cooked by Cheméne, the cook. We were waited on by Sancuni, Eric's Indian manservant who, dressed in a sarong from the waist down, when serving would tickle – inadvertently of course – the lady guests' bare shoulders with his abundant and curly pectoral hair.

Eric was always generous with his hospitality and only took to locking his drinks cupboard when he found that his *bonne*, who came daily from a nearby hamlet by bicycle, was for some reason never able to get home without falling off. The lane to his house led from the village of Mouans Sartoux, of which Eric became honorary mayor, past the mill and on to the much larger village of Pégomas. One evening when leaving Cannes, Eric gave a lift to an Algerian who said he wanted to go to Pégomas. Some way short of the mill the man pulled out a knife, made Eric stop, stabbed him several times, and robbed him of his wallet. Bleeding heavily, Eric was just able to drive to the mill and blow his car horn. Sancuni came running to find him already unconscious but managed to stop the worst of the bleeding and call the ambulance. Fortunately none of the many wounds was fatal, but this happening persuaded Eric that in the unruly conditions following the débâcle in Algeria, the mill was too isolated. He moved into the middle of the Cap d'Antibes, where again he succeeded on a much smaller scale in creating a garden of outstanding interest.

Staying with Eric was always a highly social occasion, and there were two and sometimes three parties a day somewhere or other. One day, just as we were setting off for Greece, we went first to lunch with an aged lady who lived up towards Mougins in a large house with her own vineyard. I praised her wine, which was more an act of politeness than truth, and with the coffee she pressed upon us her own *marc*, made on the property. It was fire-water, but once again politeness prompted praise. As we left, the butler appeared with a box containing two unlabelled litre bottles of the stuff which the good lady insisted we put in the car.

Off we went to drive down Italy to Brindisi and take the boat to Patras. On long trips we normally picnicked at lunch-time and made up for that in the evening. I did take a nip or two at the *marc* but found it increasingly awful; only my dislike of waste prevented my pouring it away.

We arrived eventually at Navarino, or more properly Pilos, and decided to stay there for several days. There were next to no tourists, we had the best room in the hotel with a wide balcony right on the harbour and, luxury of luxuries, a private bathroom, though the plumbing was what some much travelled friends of ours call 'narrow gauge'. A few miles to the south was the ancient Venetian fort of Methoni, where there was a half-built skeleton of a hotel and a little *kapheneion* on the beach. But mostly we had the place to ourselves.

The only petrol available in Pilos was low-octane and our M.G. saloon did not like it at all. I was told that we could get better stuff at Kalamata some thirty miles away to the east over the mountains, so one fine morning we set off early with a nearly empty tank into which I had put the last of our spare can of good petrol. Clanking about in the boot were our two litre bottles of so-called *marc de Provence*.

The road climbed high into the mountains where it was quiet and beautiful; apart from a few flocks of sheep and goats, each flock with its attendant shepherd or shepherdess or small child, we saw nobody, and higher up the only moving objects were a few eagles soaring in the distance. At the top of the pass we stopped to admire the view beside a little shrine in which a small oil lamp flickered, showing that it was tended by someone. I decided to leave a votive offering and got out the bottles of spirit. There was also some bread and a piece of cheese left from yesterday's picnic. I arranged all this neatly in front of the shrine and we set off down the hill to Kalamata.

It was baking hot there; indeed the port has the reputation of being one of the hottest places in all the Peloponnese. We got our petrol and went down to the harbour to find a good *taverna*. There were several to choose from, all looking much the same, but we made our choice and went into the cool interior to go through the Greek ritual of washing our hands in public and then entering the kitchen to select our dishes. We chose some fine fat fish known as *kephali* from the cold box, to be grilled with fennel on the open fire, and asked for it to be ready in half an hour, which time we proposed to spend with *ouzo* and black Kalamata olives (the best in all Greece), snippets of octopus and *tiropitakia* – delicious little triangular cushions of thin pastry with cheese inside – at the restaurant's tables under the carob trees by the water on the other side of the road. I had parked the car in the shade of the trees hard by. We had just ordered our second *ouzos* when another car pulled up behind ours and out of it got a youngish, obviously Anglo-Saxon, curly-haired man who somehow looked familiar. He too disappeared into the kitchen and then reappeared and came to sit at another table. We exchanged 'good mornings' in that reserved Anglo-Saxon way and he began to read his Greek newspaper.

Suddenly Diana noticed that on his upper arm there was a tattoo of a double-tailed mermaid. Silently she drew my attention to it and the penny dropped. It was Patrick Leigh Fermor. We had only met once before at a party at Peter and Pat Rice's in Hammersmith but we had discussed Greece with him and Joan Monsell, his companion, and we had his recently published book *Mani* with us as a guide. He looked very different here in his shirt, fisherman's trousers and sandals, and no doubt so did we. He moved to our table and confirmed that we had chosen the right restaurant because, he said, it had the best *retsina* in the whole of Greece, a fact we were only too happy to confirm over lunch. There was an impressive array of those curious gold-coloured metal jugs, in which it is commonly served from the barrel, on our table a couple of lazy hours later.

This was the same restaurant at which Paddy, as he describes in his book, had lunched some years before with Joan and another companion. Finding the midsummer heat too much, they had picked up their iron table and chairs and stepped fully dressed into the sea to sit down again up to their waists in the cooling water. The waiter had not demurred and had himself waded out to serve them. The diners (it was a feast day and the place was crowded) were delighted and the three in the water were inundated with jugs of *retsina* sent down to them.

Leigh Fermor had come into Kalamata to get medicine for Joan, who was lying sick in their tent at Kardamyli where they were making a more permanent dwelling place. But for her illness we would have visited them; as it was we said farewell at the end of this unexpected meeting and returned over the mountains in the late afternoon light to Pilos. At the top of the pass we stopped again and looked at the shrine. Our offerings had gone, though still no one was anywhere near. Diana thought I had been unkind, but perhaps the *marc* made a welcome change from *ouzo* or *retsina*, and in some remote house that evening there may have been revelry for priest or peasant or both.

On another occasion we were staying on Corfu, for the second or third time. We had not come by car but had flown out and taken up temporary residence in a small hotel overlooking the old harbour in the town of Corfu itself. A few doors away at street level were two favourite calling places of ours, a bar named on the sign over the front The Spoty Dog, and a little eating place where all the grilling was done on the pavement under a ramshackle shanty attached to the premises behind. This we always knew, for good reasons, as Smokey Joe's.

Joe presided over the grill in an aura of wood-smoke redolent of herbs of all kinds, grilled fish and grilled meat – his baby lamb on the spit was a gourmet's delight. The proprietor stayed inside and looked after the kitchen range on which the usual mixture of weeds and pasta, that no respectable Italian would ever touch, bubbled away. Here too was the cold cabinet, dependent for cooling on a huge block of ice renewed daily, from which one chose the *pièce de résistance* of one's meal, which then either went to Joe to be grilled or to the kitchen for other simple forms of cooking.

Diana and I were greeted by the owner, whose English was ambitious if not expert. 'Oh, sir and lady,' he said, 'I have something special today. Mines,' and he drew from the box a large tin dish. 'Mines?' we said, and pondered over what more than usually explosive dish he could be referring to. 'Yes, yes, mines,' he repeated excitedly. 'Small meat mines.' We looked into the proffered dish, expecting to see little rissoles or something of that sort. What met our, until then, hungry gaze was a slippery mass of grey amorphous matter slopping about in what looked like washing-up water. Suddenly Diana twigged it. 'Brains,' she cried in triumph. 'Calves' brains.' 'Yes, yes,' the proprietor agreed in triumph. 'Minds.' ('Small meats' was the standard translation for veal. Meat meant beef only. Pigs' and sheep's meat was usually named as the animal itself and lamb invariably came out as lum ('Lang may your lum reek', as any Scot might have commented on my mother-in-law's wartime attempt at smoking 'macon'.)

From the window of our room and its balcony, four storeys up with a tiny, groaning, antique lift as the means of ascent, we could not only smell the delights of Smokey Joe's but also see the whole bustling life of the unsmart part of town and harbour. To our left was the entrance to the market, and from the quay below us came and went all the *caiques* and local traffic. We decided to take one of the regular inter-island *caiques* and spend a night or two on Paxos, then undiscovered by tourism. The island lies a few miles south of Corfu. We found that a *caique* would leave for Paxos the next morning at eight o'clock, paid our fares in advance, the equivalent of eight shillings each, and had supper in Smokey Joe's where Christo Vlachopoulos, a local artist in love by correspondence with an English girl, the daughter of a cathedral dignitary, found us and over a lot of *ouzo* assured us of the delights of Paxos.

Next morning dawned bright and clear. I went down to the market to buy some provisions to see us through the four or five hour trip: a loaf of coarse, dark bread, black olives, cheese, fruit, a bottle of *ouzo* and a bottle of wine. Taking only a small grip each we joined the *caique* at the quay. She had already loaded her cargo and the rest of the passengers and promptly set off. The big saloon aft, the passenger accommodation, had the usual Greek complement of priests, peasants of both sexes, babies and goats, together with all their paraphernalia of baskets, boxes and bundles and chickens tied by the legs. It was pretty crowded but we, as first-class passengers (we had probably paid at least twice the fare charged to the others), were proudly given two rickety deck-chairs set up on the hatch cover just forward of the bridge. The sun shone and our vessel sedately bonked its diesel way out of the harbour past the castle and into the wider waters dividing Corfu from the mainland.

Once we were round the headland and heading south-east, things changed a little. The sun still shone out of a cloudless sky but a fresh head wind got up which caused short steep waves to develop. The bluff-bowed *caique* plodded on but the motion became rather pronounced and soon spray was being thrown up and on to us on our deck-chairs. The captain was in the wheelhouse looking down on us. He grinned now and again, a rather piratical leer, and lit another cigarette, but our only means of communication was through the deck-hand who spoke a kind of Italian. The entire crew was four: captain, engineer, deck-hand and a boy.

Diana is not a particularly good sailor. I explained that where we were was probably the most comfortable place in the vessel with the least movement, just about in its centre of gravity, but we were beginning to get wet and had brought no protective clothing. The deck-hand, whose name was Niko, suggested we move inside to the saloon; he would oblige its occupants to clear a space for us. One look inside and one sniff convinced Diana that that was no place for her. *Mal de mer* had overcome most of its inmates, including the goats, and the windows had been battened down against the spray. So up to the poop we went. Behind the saloon and wheelhouse, it was protected from both wind and spray, a space just big enough for our two chairs and sundry bits of cargo that had been secured to its pretty bright blue-and-white painted ornamental rail. High up in the stern of the pitching vessel, it was rather like being on a switchback at a fairground; but the view was splendid – brilliant blue water with little white wave-crests, the perfect blue of the sky, the length of Corfu on the starboard side and the high ground of the mainland just in sight to port. We pitched and rolled along, making slow but definite progress. By eleven-thirty, not having got as far as I thought we should have done, I broke out the *ouzo* (which I had intended as iron rations in the unlikely event of Paxos proving inhospitable). Niko provided the necessary beakers and some rusty-looking water which, without the *ouzo*, I should have felt extremely chary of drinking. A libation was sent to the wheelhouse together with a few olives.

By twelve-thirty the situation was reappraised, by me anyway; the sun still shone but the wind also continued to blow, and rather more fiercely. It was now up to a good force 7 and still rising. As we began to draw level with the southern tip of Corfu the head sea increased and we were now nearly out into the Ionian sea itself, which no less a sailor than Ulysses had found choppier than he cared for. By two o'clock it was clear that we were getting nowhere, just 'going up and down in the same hole', a phrase that no doubt Ulysses himself invented. The motion on the poop had changed from the simple switchback, via the great dipper, to more like an express lift with an eccentric operator. On occasions the deck-chairs actually left the deck and hung suspended in space until the deck came up to meet them again. Diana was unhappy.

I noticed that we had changed course a little. We were now heading more to the eastward and taking the seas on our starboard bow rather than dead ahead. This gave us a rather worse motion, a sort of corkscrew progress which brought wails and bleats of dismay from those in the saloon with any squeak still left in them. Niko came aft to inform me that *il capitano* had decided to go into a little inlet on the mainland still some hours' steaming away and wait there for the weather to moderate before proceeding to Paxos. Diana thought that a good idea and so did I for a different reason. After a drop or two of *ouzo* Diana had forgone any other nourishment except a few grapes. I on the other hand had had most of the bread and all the cheese; there wasn't much *ouzo* left, thanks to the help I had received from Niko, *il capitano*, the engine room, and the bottle of wine wouldn't last past tea-time.

On we corkscrewed until at last, as evening was beginning to make its coming obvious, the *caique* dodged behind a headland. Suddenly we were putt-putting steadily up a small fjord with a few houses and a little quay at its head. We tied up. Niko announced that *il capitano* had decided he would not go on until first light next morning; meanwhile all passengers were welcome to sleep aboard, or ashore if they could find anywhere. He would give a toot on his siren half an hour before departure.

Where were we, demanded Diana? Moultou, replied Niko. Where was that? About twenty kilometres down the coast from Igoumenitsa, the ferry port on the mainland opposite Corfu. 'I've had enough,' said Diana. 'Let's drop the idea of Paxos, go to Igoumenitsa and take the next regular ferry back to Corfu.' 'Right,' I said. 'I'll go ashore and ask when the next bus goes.' Niko came to help. 'Bus!' they exclaimed, in the little bamboo vine-enveloped *kaphenion*, a real pull-in for caique-men. 'There is no bus.' 'Right,' said I, 'what about a taxi? Anyone here with a car who will drive us to Igou?' 'No cars.' 'A couple of donkeys,' I said in desperation. 'Perhaps, but not tonight. There's no road out of here. It takes at least two days to walk to Igou. Maybe, if he feels like it, the owner of that fishing boat will take you in the morning.' 'Where can we sleep tonight? Is there a hotel here?' 'No, there is a *taverna* up the road where you may get a meal tonight but you'll have to stay on the *caique* unless the lady in that house over there will let you have a room.' I explained all this to Diana who had recovered from the sea but not yet recaptured her holiday euphoria.

We walked over to the house, which was on the water's edge with a field of maize behind it. The rest of the village was out of sight up the valley of the little river that ran into the inlet at the quay. It was a typical Greek farmhouse, white-washed with a flight of stone steps that led up to the main house door and the living quarters, which were on the first floor. We knocked and a cross-eyed peasant woman in the inevitable black appeared. By sign language we indicated that we wanted a bed for the night. Impassively she led us back down the steps and flung open the wooden door of the ground floor under them. We entered, to find a large earth-floored room with two shuttered windows overlooking the little harbour, and the sea washing against the outside wall. The room was bare except for two single iron bedsteads and an iron stand with a tin basin and ewer on it. There were straw palliasses on the beds and sheets made out of flour sacks sewn together. They were washed and clean but the printing on them was still visible and they felt far from dry.

Stranded seafarers can't be choosers, and we had noted the letters D.D.T. and a recent date painted roughly on the outside of the house. We agreed to pay the ridiculously small number of drachmae indicated on her fingers. We dumped our bags on the beds and put on some warmer sweaters, while she filled the ewer from the well outside with good fresh water, not at all brackish as one might have expected. She then beckoned to us to follow her again and led the way upstairs into her quarters. There, with pride, she flung open a door facing the entrance and showed us the loo, a wooden cupboard with a bench with a hole in it which gave directly on to the sea below just beside our bedroom window. Diana said she'd prefer the maize field and after dark stuck to her resolve. I too did not feel inclined towards that noisome and draughty lodgement.

It was now about seven o'clock and we were hungry. We indicated this to our landlady; she called her husband who, equally unsmilingly, beckoned to us to follow him up the village street which was no more than a stony track. Most of the houses were in ruins and the whole place looked like a village wrecked by war, as indeed it was. One of the roughly repaired houses was clearly the village *taverna* and hubby, having indicated it with a wave of his hand, made off back down the road.

We went in and the proprietor appeared. We opened negotiations in sign language and tried pidgin Italian as well as English, of which the fellow had a few words. Eventually he indicated that at half-past ten, in four hours' time, we could have something good and hot but what it was to be we couldn't understand except that it was to include chips. There was no point in waiting there so we walked down the street again to the little café where most of our shipmates and a few fishermen and loungers – no women, of course – were already gathered. Little cups of coffee and glasses of *ouzo* were forthcoming but the service was very slow. There was a large basket of olives from which one could help oneself, otherwise nothing. The gale was obviously still blowing as by now we could see big clouds whizzing by over the tops of the surrounding cliffs, but it was calm enough down there. We tried to read but the light got too bad and the café's one pressure lamp didn't shine far enough to light us properly. By eight-thirty it was dark and lightning had begun to flicker in the sky inland behind the village. We debated and decided that the tavern keeper must have meant an earlier hour than ten-thirty, which was very late for rural Greece.

One fisherman, who for some reason had only one shoe, the other foot being bare and horny, spoke a little Italian. From him we gathered that he was from Parga lower down the coast but had come in to Moultou because his engine had broken down. He had been there a week already, unable to get to Igoumenitsa to get the necessary spare part because he had no money to pay anyone to take him and there was no way overland, particularly I suppose with only one shoe. However, he said, the biggest of the fishing boats in the harbour belonged to a *capitano* who might be persuaded to take us. If so could he come too? He went off to speak to the *capitano*, who he said was in bed with a lady not his wife somewhere up the valley. He returned to report that the *capitano* would make no promises but if he felt like it in the morning he might consider taking us the ten or twelve miles round the headlands to Igou.

With this we had to be satisfied. At nine, the little *kaphenion* emptied and we decided to go back to the restaurant in case we had made a mistake and the owner had meant nine-thirty. Half-ten in a lot of the world, including parts of our own country, can mean half an hour before ten rather than after.

There was a bit of moon between the clouds which now seemed to have slowed down, and the flicker of distant but increasingly frequent lightning helped to light our way up the rutted track. The *taverna* was full when we got there. Our *caique*'s crew and the priests who were passengers, together with most of the café's previous customers, were sitting playing backgammon, smoking – and eating! The tavern keeper rushed to greet us and quickly cleared a table, but he looked at his watch, shook his head and quite clearly pointed to half-past ten. Those who were eating were devouring large platters of that terrible pasta. We settled down to some more *ouzo* and watched the backgammon. We were offered a game but felt we didn't know the local rules well enough. A couple more shots of *ouzo* and I thought it politic to go on to the local *retsina* which certainly would not have won a prize in Kalamata.

Around ten the storm broke, the thunder cracked, the lightning became almost continuous and then the rain came down. Despite the babel of conversation the noise of the storm was predominant, and every now and then a wet figure with an empty sack over its head would stagger through the door to be greeted with cries of merriment. Diana was the only female present, though whether this inhibited conversation I was in no position to judge; there were several priests there, after all.

At exactly ten-thirty the door to the kitchen was opened with a flourish and out came a boy bearing a large tureen with steam arising from it. Our table was quickly covered with the usual damp cloth; large soup plates, cold, and spoons together with a basket of bread were put down, and while everyone in the room watched with awe the tureen was put before us. It contained *avgolemono*, chicken soup with rice and lemon juice and the little yolks of what looked like pullets' eggs bobbing about poached in it. It was delicious. We had two or three plates each with lots of the good coarse bread. The only other course we knew we could expect was chips, of which incidentally there had been no sign on any other table. Beaming at last we sat back as best we could – it is extraordinary how uncomfortable Greek *taverna* chairs are – and waited for the potatoes. Though we liked the pungent Greek olive oil in a salad we were less happy about it as a cooking fat and had been nervously discussing the likely quality of the chips.

What appeared, however, was a large boiled chicken dismembered on a bed of rice with a lemon sauce and plates of those weeds known in Greece as *horta* or *radikia*, boiled, allowed to cool and swamped in oil. The chicken was delicious, if a little tough. The local *retsina* seemed to have improved and we ordered more, also for our friends around us. Compliments were paid to the proprietor and the chef, who turned out to be the same person. We finished up with grapes, coffee and brandy, by now friends with all the world.

But where were the chips? Not that we cared. All was now explained, for our means of communication had magically improved. The long wait was because the tavern-keeper had no food good enough for such distinguished guests. He had therefore to go to the hen-run and despatch one of its fattest ladies. She had to be plucked and prepared, and all the as-yet-unlaid eggs withdrawn to go into the soup that her boiling provided. Because, though plump, she was not young the boiling took some time and even then he could only hope that the exquisite flavour had made up for a slight toughness. 'And the potatoes?' we asked. '*Patates*?' Alas, no, there were none in Moultou at the moment, shipping difficulties, etc. 'Chips, we thought you said.' 'Chips? No chips – cheeps!' Roars of laughter and more brandy. He did not know the English for *kotopoulo* but what a *kotopoulo* said was universal language wasn't it? (Our elder daughter later christened our canary Arnold, not after Matthew as her literary bent might imply, but after Wesker and *Chips with Everything*.)

About midnight we felt we ought to go. I paid the modest bill and the door was opened for us to depart. The wind had dropped and the thunderstorm passed on out to sea, where it could be heard rumbling away, but the rain was still falling and running at full spate down the road to the harbour. At once a piratical figure stepped gallantly forward with a large and dilapidated umbrella which he held over our heads as he escorted us to our lodging. Dressed in rags, with his rubber boot soles flapping and a black patch over one eye under an old yachting cap, he was too bizarre to be true but, far from being dangerous, he courteously and with dignity refused my tip as he left us at the door of our seaside apartment.

The night was short. We slept suitably clad on, rather than under, our damp flour-sack sheets with our grips as pillows. Our only light on going to bed had been a candle which had attracted a few mosquitoes, but on the whole the D.D.T. application had obviously done its stuff. The light began to come through the shuttered but glassless windows and then suddenly there was a long and reverberating toot from the siren of our *caique*. *Il capitano* was living up to his promise of giving half an hour's warning of his sailing for Paxos. Diana was absolutely clear about one thing: she had no intention of continuing our voyage in a southerly direction. We heard the *caique* start its diesel and depart and then arose, stiff and a bit hung-over, to see whether *il capitano* no. 2 was sufficiently refreshed after his night's pleasures to take us to Igou.

After we had made guarded visits to the maize field we repaired to the *kaphenion* for breakfast of coffee and peaches. Our one-shoed friend was there. Good news – *il capitano* was in high spirits, the morning was fine and clear and we would go to Igou 'very soon'. After another hour, but still in the freshness of the early morning, a rumpled, red-eyed, handsome young Greek arrived, looking rather like a matador on the morning after a successful *corrida*. A few drachmae changed hands and we were off to Igou; not only the two of us and 'one-shoe', but several others who were glad of the free ride. They could obviously depend on the captain's sexual urges to guarantee them a return trip.

It was a nice little boat and the day was glorious. We thumped along under the high cliffs and skirted small islands rather like those on the west coast of Scotland. I learnt from the captain, who became quite talkative in the sort of Esperanto I was getting used to, that Moultou had been used as a secret naval rendezvous by one side or the other in the war and that it had eventually been shelled by someone, he thought the Albanians, which had caused the damage I had seen. Greece was not then keen to restore so remote a place and Albania was not paying reparations – as we British well knew after the loss of our destroyer to Albanian guns in the straits of Kassiopi in Corfu. So there Moultou was, as lonely a settlement as if it had been in Alaska; more so, perhaps.

Our little saga in classical waters was not yet over. Having arrived in Igoumenitsa at about nine in the morning we found that the next ferry for Corfu would not leave until two p.m. Igou town is not very exciting so we decided to walk along the beach to the south and swim and read and then make our way back to lunch in a *taverna* on the quay before departure. We strolled perhaps a mile away from the town before finding a beached *caique* that we could use for shade on an otherwise empty stretch of sand and shingle. We changed into bathing costumes, Diana into a shapely one-piece and I into shorts (Greece in those days did not encourage anything less), swam and lay down in the shade of the boat to read.

Soon, shambling over the shingle, there appeared an aged crone in black draperies who eyed Diana with intense admiration, giving me not a glance. After silent inspection she withdrew, only to return shortly after with a grubby-looking but no doubt freshly washed piece of linen which she held by the four corners and slyly, rather than shyly, offered to Diana. 'What's the old thing want?' Diana asked me. 'She wants to give you something. You must never refuse Greek hospitality so you'd better take it.' The kerchief contained two wizened figs and a miserable apple. Diana took them gracefully and put them into her bag as if for later consumption. The crone beamed, her two teeth showing to advantage in the sunshine against the sinister burgundy red of their setting.

Then, ignoring me still, she beckoned Diana to follow her. Diana, not wishing to offend, rose and went after her. I was amused but stayed where I was, thinking that Diana was probably being taken to look at the orchard from which the fruit had come. I was just beginning to think it was time to see what was going on when Diana came running, and with a cry of 'My God!' plunged into the sea. I followed her and she told me that the old witch had led her to a filthy cabin in the reeds behind the beach into which she had invited her. After a step into the interior Diana had turned in a state of near panic and fled.

As we returned to the shore the black figure reappeared, hobbling over the crest of the shingle towards us. 'We can't stay here,' said Diana. Indeed it was now nearing noon and lunch was calling, so we started to dress. The old woman, silent but grinning as always, moved steadily closer and took up station squatting on the beach below us so that, as Diana modestly worked off her bathing dress beneath her towel and replaced it by her normal undergarments, she was enjoying what might be termed a worm's eye view. 'Filthy old thing,' said Diana and flung one of her own figs at her. The old woman just cackled. As we made off towards town I advanced my theory that the poor dear was either an expatriate from the far distant island of Lesbos or, more probably, that she was simple-minded and had imagined that Aphrodite had once more arrived ashore.

So, after some grilled mullet for lunch, it was back to Corfu and the civilization of Smokey Joe's, The Spoty Dog, and Christo's romantic conversation.

Another year we flew from Athens to Sofia for our first visit there as official guests. Looking down from the plane was a great pleasure as we flew over the Aegean and Mount Atlas, past Thasos, over the Rhodope mountains and ancient Thrace to Sofia itself, the city of Saint Sophia.

Our Bulgarian friends, in particular Michael and Anny Hadjimischev but also, without exception, all the Bulgarian artists who came to work at Glyndebourne, have always been wonderfully warm and welcoming people and I have been back to Bulgaria on a number of occasions. On this first visit we had not yet made many of these friends and we went formally through the proscribed procedure. The first mistake was our own. We were not prepared for the considerable drop in temperature in late September between Athens and Sofia and had insufficient warm clothing. We had been touring around for some three weeks in a still balmy Greece. Then we were stranded for a while at the airport. No one seemed to speak English and the official representative of the concert agency had not yet arrived. Eventually she turned up, clutching a regulation posy of wilting flowers for Diana, and whisked us off to the huge hotel built in the Russian Soviet style which towered over the ruins of a little Byzantine church sunk in a pit in the ground under its walls. A vast hall and wide corridors, all of an unprepossessing décor, led to our suite on the sixth floor. First there was a windowless entrance-hall-cum-ante-room with two uncomfortable-looking single beds and little else in it, which we erroneously at first supposed to be our bedroom, then a large sitting room pompously furnished and suitable for a conference of twenty people. This had a single, small, round window, too high to see out of. Opening off this was our bedroom, equally large, equally pompously furnished with one large and one single bed, equally ill-fenestrated and poorly lit at night. The bathroom was like the ante-room, square with no windows and seemingly no ventilation either. The bath was large and, like the wash basin, plugless, the loo was in a sort of cubicle within the bathroom. Duckboards covered the concrete floor which had a gurgling drain in the middle down which all the effluents, except mercifully those from the loo, found their reluctant way.

We were staggered. Used as we were to rural simplicities, the mixture of the grandiose and the naïve was overwhelming. Subsequent enquiry from those prepared to comment revealed that we had been given one of the suites reserved for visiting political dignitaries, and that the beds in the ante-room were not for the children we hadn't brought but for our equally absent bodyguards. Furthermore, the absence of plugs had nothing to do with a shortage of rubber goods in the Iron Curtain bloc but to a widely held Eastern European belief, to me easily understandable, that it is a nasty habit to lie about in one's own dirty water and that all washing should be done in running water. The fact that the water, like the heating, was unpredictably scalding hot or freezing cold, and that washers anywhere in the plumbing acted as no more than inhibitors to the leakage of liquids, had to be put down to efficiency not yet having caught up with ambition.

On subsequent visits I stayed in less grandeur but much cosier comfort in the Balkan Hotel down the road, past the mausoleum where the saviour of his country lay in state, wrapt in an odour more of formaldehyde than sanctity and guarded by some impressively uniformed heyducks. The hotel was not far from the opera house and closer still to the unfrocked cathedral of Santa Sophia, with its collection of ikons and Thracian treasure.

Private hospitality more than made up for a rather distant treatment from the top brass, but the change of climate gave us both heavy colds, and after a stay of four or five days we were not too heartbroken at being homeward bound by way of Vienna. Our take-off was marked again by the late arrival of the official representative who came panting over the tarmac just as we boarded the plane, clutching yet another bouquet of red roses, flowers that in Bulgaria grow particularly well but which seem to wilt quickly in hot bureaucratic hands.

In Vienna, in Sacher's Hotel, in a large and comfortable bed with a lace coverlet, with heart-warming nineteenth-century paintings in heavy frames on the damask walls, a luxurious bathroom with plugs so that we could wallow to our hearts' content in hot and scented water, and delicious food and drink brought to us by smiling servitors, we relaxed in warmth and began to enjoy our colds.

In the winter of 1960 Jani Strasser and I, auditioning singers in Rome, were invited to the studio – extremely ornate and over-decorated with somewhat doubtful statuary in marble and alabaster – of a fashionable voice teacher to hear a new young basso said to be of great promise.

A tall youngish man, good-looking in a classical Roman way, patrician but not decadent, with slightly curly hair laid neatly round his skull, presented himself and sang two or three arias in a way which impressed us, even if he seemed nervous and gauche. As was, and still is, usual in Italian auditions he was not alone but accompanied by a dark, well-dressed, intense-looking lady, certainly not younger than he but equally certainly not his mother. The atmosphere was a little bizarre but Jani and I came away thinking that perhaps we had made a discovery.

There was no immediate opening for him, as is so often the case. However, just as rehearsals were about to begin for the revival of *Il barbiere di Siviglia* a few months later it happened that the singer engaged for Basilio was obliged to withdraw. Jani and I remembered Carlo Cava, our auditionee in Rome, and he was summoned. He turned in a splendid performance, one of the many that I can remember in this rewarding role. What is more, the impression he made was sufficient to get him engaged for the following season, this time as Bartolo in *Figaro*, which was perhaps not surprising, and, more significantly, as Seneca in *L'incoronazione di Poppea* in which, in Rennert's strong, dramatic production of the scene of his death, he scored a great success.

Carlo Cava came in fact not from Rome but from Le Marche. His father and mother were at this time the much respected mayor and mayoress of the small but beautiful town of Ascoli Piceno up in the hills, some twenty miles inland from the Adriatic coast between Ancona and Pescara, where they owned and personally conducted the local Fortnum and Mason's. Carla, the dark lady in his life, was herself a fine violinist and a Sardinian (whom Gui called 'a sardine', just as he called a lady of Semitic extraction 'a juice'). As befits a Sardinian she exhibited very possessive feelings, and Carlo's performance as Henry VIII in Donizetti's *Anna Bolena* at Glyndebourne, while in every vocal and most histrionic ways admirable, was rendered a little cold in the passionate love scene with Jane Seymour by the baleful dark-eyed laser-beam projected from the wings by the 'sardine'.

On our way to Greece Diana and I, at the pressing invitation of the Cavas, stopped at Ascoli Piceno. We found ourselves ensconced in the Jolly Hotel. For whatever reason, probably a surfeit of Venetian seafood ingested on the way down, Diana was not feeling all that hot and on arrival went straight to bed. We were, however, bidden to dine at nine o'clock in the apartment of the senior Cavas nearby. This was an invitation which obviously could not be refused.

Accordingly we presented ourselves, Diana groaning inaudibly, at a modern block of flats and found our way to the penthouse on the eighth floor. We had put on the best of the clothes we were travelling with but were still underdressed by our hosts' standards. Carlo and Carla we knew well, but this was our first meeting with

Mamma and Papa and it was all very formal. Mamma was encased in a garment of the utmost elegance, a sort of black and silver carapace. Papa wore a tie of dazzling magnificence and a shirt of hand-laundered linen that gleamed a perfect white in his bright blue mohair suit. Carlo and Carla were in 'black tie' and a long slinky black dress respectively. The equally formally aproned maid had shown us into the drawing room and we sat on richly upholstered but not particularly comfortable chairs, Diana and I gazing with astonishment at the ornamentation around us and the catholic taste of the pictures on the walls. A *carozza* was wheeled in, one of those gilt trolleys that contain a whole cocktail bar full of bottles, glasses, ice buckets and those gadgets, usually in the form of something else, without which no well-run establishment can be presumed to exist.

With true hospitality we were offered our own English drinks, at about triple the quantity even an Irishman would pour out. Conversation was a bit stilted, for the senior hosts had no English. Carlo and Carla had some, Diana and I some Italian, but Diana was inhibited by the fact that she felt mouldy and the room was over-heated. Two maids appeared with delicious hot things on salvers. I was rather hungry and tucked in, Diana nibbled politely. More and more varieties of *antipasti* appeared and we concluded, with a certain feeling of relief, that this was to be the evening and soon we could return to our hotel.

How wrong we were. An hour after we had arrived, when we were already sated with food and drink, a third serving woman appeared, obviously the cook, and announced that dinner was served. The mayor leapt to his feet, pressed a button set as I recollect in the navel of a small but highly nubile alabaster statue of a nymph and, as if by magic, one wall of the room complete with its numerous adornments rolled slowly aside to reveal a dining-table groaning – louder even than Diana – with silver, napery, cut-glass and every conceivable condiment. '*A tavola, a tavola*' was the cry and to table we went. Course followed course. Because Diana really could not eat anything by now, I felt obliged to eat for two. The food was magnificent, the best of *casalingo*, and the wine started with a Verdichio di Cupramontana with the *spaghetti alla pescatore* which came after a *prosciutto crudo* of exquisite quality, went on to Piceno Rosso with the pigeons, switched to Vernaccia di Serrapetrona with the *zuppa inglese* (trifle! – another well meant gesture to us) and finished off with a superb grappa, and coffee such as only the Italians can make.

The next day began with a walk round the town and a visit to the shop, where Mamma was already behind the cash desk. Papa in a backstage holy-of-holies, with the help of a youthful acolyte, was producing the day's fresh *pasta*. Everything was immaculately clean, the machines of gleaming stainless steel, both celebrants dressed from head to foot in spotless freshly laundered white. They laboured silently in a ritual that made one realize the importance of *pasta* in the Italian way of life. The pastes were carefully blended, the shapes and whirls lovingly produced; all was of the purest. In the next room, a kitchen, the stuffings of various kinds that were to be enfolded in the *ravioli*, the *cannelloni*, the *gnochhi*, were being prepared by two stout females. Anyone buying the Cava *pasta* in whatever shape or however garnished knew that it was fresh as the day itself.

We were then taken on a tour of the town, through the beautiful Piazza del Popolo, a miniature Piazza San Marco, and to the market where, to our embarrassment, everything we looked at with admiration was immediately purchased. But no parcels could be carried by such distinguished citizens as the Cavas or such renowned visitors as ourselves; a small boy was hired and tailed along behind with the shopping.

Next we went up the nearby Colle San Marco to admire the view ('*molto suggestivo*', in that charming Italian phrase which is more inspiring than salacious) and to down a Campari-soda or two before returning to the apartment for a light lunch of Papa's *pasta* and the *branzino* (sea bass) which we had admired on the slab in the market.

After lunch, by now members of the family, we were taken upstairs to the roof of the apartment house to see the kitchen. On the flat roof of the modern block was a kitchen as simple as any in Italy could have been centuries ago. The grill on which our fish had been cooked was fuelled from a stack of logs, an electric fan to force the draught replacing the older bellows. The stove was brick with a thick, black, iron top. The pots were iron or copper and the large room was hung about with garlic, onions, peppers and herbs. With pride we were shown the raw materials for our dinner that evening: enormous rib steaks from a young steer destined to be *bistecca alla Fiorentina*, delicious-looking *funghi*, tomatoes, basil, and '*per il dolce*', the eggs and sugar for the *zabaglione*.

We retired for the siesta. Mamma and Papa had to reopen the shop at four, but Papa was insistent that we present ourselves at eight so that we could inspect his *cantina*, a cellar he had had specially constructed in the bowels of his apartment block. We were fetched and driven the two hundred yards to the building. Diana had recovered but I felt that I was on a slippery slope. I knew what was to come. Papa proudly led us with much unlocking of doors down to a level below the underground garage to the cellar itself. Here was a room with a hefty table and wooden chairs. The walls were lined with casks of wine and bins of bottles, the ceiling was hung with hams and salami, dried fish and meat of many sorts; there was a big cache of tinned tunny, cans of tomato purée and flagon after flagon of rich, dark green olive oil.

'Ah,' said our host, 'we had a hard time in the war. Only those with foresight fared well and I am not going to be caught out in the next. If necessary we can sleep down here, Mamma and me, and we shall not starve or die of thirst.'

Next morning, extremely over-eaten, we made the valid excuse of having a long drive to catch our boat from Brindisi to Corfu and left at crow-pee. However, the hospitality was not yet over. Returning two weeks later we drove to Rome, to stay in our favourite hotel, the Victoria, near the Porta Pinciana. On our arrival the concierge told us that he had a heavy package for us. I went into the baggage room to inspect it. It was a wooden crate, a good deal larger than a case of wine, and it had clearly come from Ascoli Piceno. With difficulty, but no reluctance, we made room for it in the boot of an already overburdened car. By the time we got back to Lydd airport we had acquired our legal limit of duty-free wine – *poire Williams* from Geneva using up our spirit ration – and I felt it necessary to say to the Customs officer that I had no knowledge of what was included in the presentation case which he could see amongst our baggage. 'I'm sorry,' he said, 'but if you can't tell me what is in it I must look,' and with a jemmy he prised up the lid. Inside were two enormous hams of *prosciutto crudo*, four salami of various kinds, and four litres of *grappa*, on which last I paid up not unwillingly.

Another bass to be hospitable was Paolo Montarsolo, who lent us his seaside villa at Foce Sele for two successive summers. The villa was small but well equipped. It had a tiny walled garden and was only a few yards through a pine wood from the great sweep of sandy beach that stretches from Salerno past the Greek ruins of Poseidon's temple at Paestum to the charming little town of Agropoli. The river Sele is a slow-moving, muddy stream for most of the year but it drains the hills between Eboli and Potenza and is subject to sudden floods. At its mouth, the *foce*, it is famous for its eel traps

253

and indeed the two small *trattorie* which were the only eating places within walking distance of the villa served virtually nothing else. *Anguille in umido* (stewed) was the speciality of one, *anguille arrosto* (roast) of the other. Both were excellent, but alternate dishes in alternate restaurants on alternate nights did get rather boring. The alternative to eel in both was chicken, miserable stringy birds which responded badly to any method of cooking.

Besides eels, the other gastronomic glory of the place was the *uova di bufalo*, the egg-shaped dumplings of Mozzarella cheese made from buffaloes' milk. The buffaloes lived in a swamp at the end of the lane that led to the villa, and a few miles away there was a communal dairy where the cheeses could be purchased fresh, swimming in a plastic bag of buttermilk. When taken home, split open, still dripping wet, and anointed with dark green olive oil, salt and freshly ground black pepper, they were ambrosian fare indeed. Did the Greeks, I wondered, while at Paestum building their temples to Poseidon and Demeter, live on eels and buffaloes' eggs, and what did this do for their love life?

The first year we flew to Naples, hired a car and stayed a night with Montarsolo's parents in Salerno, after which his mother accompanied us to the villa to hand it over. Paolo's sister and her husband followed in their car and they took us to our first eel-feast for lunch. At the end of the day they left us to ourselves; apart that is from the gardener-caretaker, who had the disconcerting habit of appearing from nowhere at varying times and who spoke only a local patois so strong as to render our knowledge of Italian practically useless.

The next year we went to Brussels for the Flanders festival and from there by train to Rome. From Rome we drove down to Foce Sele. We found that the river had recently flooded and inundated the surrounding low-lying land, causing the *cantina* under the villa to become a large tank which the gardener was engaged in bailing out. Then he had to re-lay the tiled floor, which involved chipping away all day with a hammer and chisel in the cellar just under our feet. It didn't seem to matter as we were going to be out a lot and our siesta hours would be the same as his.

On the journey down we had taken a sleeper from Brussels to Milan and there changed trains for Rome. We found in our compartment a nun and a small child, whom she was accompanying with much solicitude, particularly as the child was very fractious. We spent as much time as we could in the dining car and mercifully they alighted in Florence. A day or two after we got to the villa

Diana began to feel ill and came out in a rash. She took to her bed. My God, I thought, has she developed an allergy to eels? If so, life was going to be difficult. She refused to see the local doctor, who had treated her the previous year and whom she had found neither sympathetic nor efficacious, just very expensive in a land where all else was cheap. I nursed her as well as I could myself, which, as anyone who knows me will know, was not very well. She wasn't interested in food, except for grapes and one particular sort of biscuit, and wouldn't come out into the sunshine as she was all one hot flush anyway. I went out betimes, doing what is now known as 'jogging' along the miles of beach, interspersed with swimming. Usually I saw no one and managed to get home without having got my bathing trunks wet. Antonio the gardener went on chipping away, which drove Diana mad. I made frequent attempts to get him to stop; he would agree and be silent for a while, but inevitably started up again.

After about a week Diana began to improve. By this time her rash had led to peeling, like the effects of sunburn, and her temperature was down. Home in Barcombe she consulted our doctor and friend of many years, Dick Caldwell. 'It's quite clear what you've had,' he said. 'Scarlet fever. I expect you got it from that child in the train. Probably the nun, and certainly Moran, had had it and were immune.' I suppose it was mere coincidence that we had been staying in the house of another of the great Don Basilios of our time, and that the scarlatina episode is one of the highlights of that part.

TWENTY

In the shop

It goes a long way to explain the now deeply rooted traditions of Glyndebourne and the standards it retains, that in all the years to the end of my tenure it had fifty-one different conductors in the pit but only four musical directors, and these were no less than Fritz Busch, Vittorio Gui, John Pritchard and Bernard Haitink. It also had twenty-seven directors but only five directors of production (to use a convenient omnibus title) – Carl Ebert, Günther Rennert, Franco Enriquez, John Cox and Peter Hall. Of designers one could list twenty-nine, but those who had the biggest influence at Glyndebourne itself were Oliver Messel, Osbert Lancaster, Emanuele Luzzati, Hugh Casson, John Bury, David Hockney and Maurice Sendak. The various amalgams have produced a continuity of style, or rather of styles, blending slowly from one to another which has made Glyndebourne like no other opera company in the world.

In terms of my artistic achievements, if any, in the profession that chose me I liken myself to a *chef de cuisine* who markets with care and pleasure, plans his menus with imagination, enjoys the act of cooking, of blending the right amounts of the right things, sees that the sauce does not curdle, that no subtle flavour is overwhelmed, turns the heat up and down as necessary, prepares the table and the surroundings for the meal and then, when it is ready, tastes each item briefly and leaves the enjoyment to others. Such a chef eats plainly himself and seldom goes to another restaurant except to steal an idea or find a new comestible. So it has been with me. I can count on the fingers of one hand, out of the hundreds that I have attended in other houses, the performances of opera that I have enjoyed totally. I have never been able to sit through one of the productions for which I have been responsible after the last dress rehearsal, but I have spent many, many happy hours in rehearsal at all stages of development.

When abroad I seldom saw the whole opera; usually I had come to hear one or two particular singers and knew which scenes were the most important. I could quickly take the temperature of the house and make my opinion of the quality of the conductor, director and designer, and I never met a fellow Intendant who failed to appreciate, or was offended at, the fact that a particular scene or two was all I needed to see. As my hypothetical chef might, having presented the meal to his guests, go to the opera for his release so I, having tasted the opera, invariably repaired to my favourite restaurant in whichever city I happened to be.

The two conductors with whom I shared the longest stretches were Vittorio Gui from 1948 to 1965 and John Pritchard from 1947 to 1977. Gui died in 1975 at the age of ninety. My time with him was spent in his maturity; he was sixty-two when I first met him and eighty when he conducted at Glyndebourne for the last time. His talents may never receive proper acclaim. He made relatively few gramophone recordings and little evidence remains for those who did not have the luck to be at one of his performances.

First and foremost was his authority and taste in the works of Rossini. He seemed to understand perfectly that composer's wit and pleasure in the joyful things of life. More than Beecham, because he was a deeper man, and more than any other Rossini conductor I have heard, he could make you feel the warmth of Italy, the sunshine after the rain of the little storms and the exact pace of the music surrounding the Italian language, and he timed the musical jokes to perfection. The orchestra loved him and he them. I think that Gui's reading of Beethoven's Pastoral Symphony, without being in any way sentimental, was the most lyrically beautiful that I ever experienced; and as for *Die Zauberflöte*, I know that no one at Glyndebourne in my time has ever constructed that marvellous, perfect arching bridge of music, starting from the appearance of the Armed Men through the trials by fire and water up to the end of the finale, with such sure architectural strength and grace.

I visited Gui often at Fiesole and spent many happy hours with him and with Elda his second wife, who continues to live in the villa overlooking their beloved Florence below, making daily sallies down into town to coffee-houses with her friends and seeming to get to every concert, operatic or theatrical happening of any consequence in that busy city.

Talking over future productions occupied many days and, luckily for me, called for regular visits. Gui would dart from piano to bookshelf and from reading lectern to telephone; he kept in constant touch with his colleagues and seemed to know all the latest talents arriving on the scene. You have only to study the lists of Italian artists at Glyndebourne in his time to realize that, in the majority of cases, those now world-famous names were comparatively unknown when they arrived in Sussex.

When in residence at Glyndebourne Gui could be found every morning after breakfast and before rehearsal sitting under the old mulberry tree reading *The Times* from cover to cover. His interest in politics was great. Though at one time he was considered in Italy to be too far to the Left, and certainly he was an anti-fascist, he was in fact a patrician Liberal. Sometimes it would be hard to get him to rehearsal before he had fully discussed the import of the day's leading article. Some of the members of the orchestra would be only too keen to enter the discussion, which might continue in the break or even afterwards. He ate and drank frugally but with relish – indeed the celebrated violinist Giaconda da Vito once said that she could not think how such a good musician and cultivated man could make such ugly noises with his soup.

He loved risqué jokes and plays on words. On one occasion Diana and I went to stay with him by way of Eric Dunstan in Antibes. Eric had given me a cutting from the English-language section of *Nice-Matin* which had the following misprint: ' . . . the bride wore oyster-satin and carried a bouquet of lilies and orchids, the bridegroom was in a grey morning coat with a white gardenia in his bottom-hole.' Gui was vastly amused and made suggestions as to the appropriate tempo for the wedding march. I asked him what button-holes were called in Italian. *Asole*, he replied, and he was quite right, but then the joke had to be re-examined. He loved it and told everyone.

At Edinburgh in 1954 Ian Hunter announced that he would like to give a party for the Glyndebourne company. What would I suggest? That year we had the vivacious Hungarian soprano Sari Barabas with us in *Le Comte Ory* and I knew that she loved making goulash. The weather was suitable and Ian, who was not yet married, willingly gave her the run of his kitchen. A telephone call had to be made to Mr Weiss, the proprietor of the Hungarian Csárdás restaurant in Dean Street, who immediately put a large supply of the best paprika on a passenger train to Edinburgh. Much shopping was done and after the performance of *Così fan tutte* that evening we all repaired to Ian's house. Diana and I arrived with the Guis and Ian was at the door to greet us. Smiling most welcomingly he tried his best Italian. '*Ben vento, maestro,*' he cried, (omitting the '*u*' in *venuto*). '*Sì,*' said Gui, '*dopo la goulash ungherese.*' His evening was made still further when, after the goulash, Ian offered him *'Chiesa, maestro?'*

Early in 1953 I went to Venice to hear singers and to talk over plans with Vittorio, who was conducting Cherubini's *Medea* with Maria Callas singing the title role. She was already established as a big singer, and big indeed she was. A few years later, when she had slimmed down to the glamorous figure which is now remembered, I found it impossible to believe that such a metamorphosis could take place. We were all staying in the Bauer Grunewald Hotel and I well remember walking the short distance to La Fenice behind Maria, who was rolling along on the arm of her small husband, Battista Meneghini, like a ship-of-the-line in the Bay of Biscay. What particularly fascinated me was that I could distinctly hear the susurrus of one massive silk-clad inner thigh passing over the other in perfect time as the stately ship sailed on. She had a great success as Medea and earned endless applause. Gui himself was out of the theatre and back in the hotel while she was still taking solo curtain calls.

In the late morning after the first night I was sitting with Gui in the hall of the hotel when the Meneghinis appeared from the lift and came over to join us. Coffee was brought and the conversation was general until Maria suddenly said to Gui: 'Maestro, I wish to ask you a favour for the next performance. At the end of my first aria there are some few bars of music which prevent my audience from applauding as I know it wants to. I must ask you therefore to cut these bars and resume the next section after my applause.' Gui did not approve, any more than John Christie did, of applause breaking into the flow of music, and in addition, as he told me later, he thought Callas was getting, or rather taking, too much anyway. He replied that he was quite unable to make this cut, as Cherubini had deliberately provided those few bars to modulate from one key to another and he could not be such a butcher. Callas pleaded. Meneghini sat silent, as did I. Gui remained obdurate, Callas became more insistent, and suddenly Gui, normally the best mannered of men, appeared to lose his temper, leapt to his feet, brought his fist down on the table with a bang which made the cups jump in their saucers and with a *'No! Mai!'* which echoed round the hall, strode off to the lift.

There was a shocked silence and then Maria turned to me and said in her Chicago-accented English: 'You know Mister Cap-la*t*, I don't pretend to be Gard but when I say something I *am* right.' I rather weakly said, 'I don't quite see the difference,' and then her angry face broke into a smile and the incident was forgotten. The bars remained in subsequent performances.

I left Venice with the Guis and we shared a gondola from the side door of the hotel to the railway station. The first gondola to arrive was sent away by the hall porter as not being smart enough for the Maestro and replaced by another, rowed, so the concierge said, by the champion of last year's regatta. Gui gaily hummed a few snatches from Rossini's well-known song on the subject and we embarked. We threaded our way through the narrow canals past La Fenice (surely the only opera house in the world, including that in Sydney, where the scenery comes direct to the stage entrance by water), crossed the Grand Canal and were taking another watery lane towards the Stazione when, on rounding a corner, we came into head-on collision with another gondola. There was a loud bang, and much swearing from our man; the other gondolier fell in with a great splash, and Gui put up his umbrella. To add the final touch of comedy the man overboard had no need to swim, he just stood up to his waist in water while our champion explained to him the reasons why his parents had been unable to spawn a worthy gondolier.

Gui's home, the Villa San Maurizio, has its own private chapel with a small side door under the stairs of the house itself. In the chapel are the relics of the saint and beneath the floor now lie the tombs of Vittorio and his first wife. Whenever one visited the chapel Gui would point to his eventual resting place beside his beloved first wife. Elda, his no less beloved second wife, one day said: 'But once you are in, there will be no room for me.' 'Yes there will,' he said. 'You can lie sideways at our feet.'

Our first arrival at the Guis' seaside villa at Maratea in Calabria was a little drama in itself. It was late September and we travelled by train from Naples along the coast through Salerno. By the time we reached the shores of the delightfully named Golfo di Policastro not only was night falling but a monumental thunderstorm was building up over the sea, as they so often do at that time of year. We arrived at the station at Sapri where we expected to be met by Elda (Gui never drove, he only conducted). It was there that the drama erupted. The storm broke over the land and the rain came down in those Mediterranean bucketfuls which always look like a film where the effects men have got out of control. To make matters worse, we did not know that Sapri was a half-length platform, that the front half of the train would disgorge its passengers and then pull ahead to let those in the back half off. We were in the back.

As soon as the train stopped we got out on to the tracks. We had a lot of luggage as we were on a long trip. There were no porters and the rain was teeming down on our unprotected heads and shoulders. The train pulled away, to stop again, maddeningly, in a position where we could have descended under cover. We stumbled over the sleepers along the ballast between the rails, humping our luggage, our way lit by the savage and luckily almost constant lightning.

By the time we had reached the station the train had gone and so had any other passengers. The station master looked surprised to see us. Was there a car waiting, I asked? No, he said. Well, we'd wait for a while, after all in such weather conditions anyone had a good excuse for being late. After half an hour or so, while we steamed gently in the dirty little waiting room and the storm continued unabated, I thought it was time to telephone to the Guis. There was no telephone in the station, I would have to go to the post office a couple of hundred yards away. Off I went, getting wet again and leaving Diana sitting on the baggage in a station which was due to close at any minute after the next up-train. The post office seemed to be manned day and night but not well manned; its unwilling concierge, appearing from the snug of her living room, agreed to try to get through to Maratea, but alas the line was unusable. No doubt the storm was responsible for the appalling crackles and hiccups which made any contact impossible.

It was now about 9.30 p.m. With difficulty a local taxi was found, promise made of payment of a sum equal to, if not greater than, our combined train fares from Rome, and off we went, subject to a small delay which I put down to a hurried visit to church on the part of the driver to request divine aid. We certainly needed it. The twelve or so miles of that coast road are set on the side of and usually half way up precipitous cliffs, which tower above one on one side and drop directly to the sea on the other. The road twisted and turned and at every bend and every lightning flash and clap of thunder – both very frequent – the driver crossed himself when in fact both hands were urgently required for the wheel. We passed a place appropriately called Acquafredda, a name I spotted momentarily lit by the headlights and lashed by the stair-rods of rain, then came more terrifying climbs and bends to Ogliastro and thus to Maratea, or rather to the big hotel down in the bay; the village itself is a steep climb up in the hills behind. The hotel directed us to the Guis' villa about a mile back up the road we had come by, and so we found ourselves at our hosts' house late and wet but, to everyone's relief, safe.

It transpired that Elda had gone to meet us at the little station of Maratea near by, only to see the train go roaring past as it did not normally stop there. She seemed to feel that we ought to have been able to oblige it to do so. We however had been informed that we must alight at Sapri and assumed she knew this.

As always in Italy, or so it seems, the storm subsided at once, we slept and awoke to the most perfect morning. We took a short climb down to the rocks to bathe in the limpid blue sea, where Vittorio was splashing about in great good humour in a pair of open-legged shorts that left no doubt of the old boy's endowment.

John Pritchard also stayed with Gui at Maratea and the photograph of the two of them in a rubber dinghy remains one of my more cherished possessions. John and I met frequently abroad and I have happy memories of many good meals together as well as shared jokes. Only rarely did we travel together for a specific purpose; one such occasion, however, was in 1974 when we went to Florence to discuss with Franco Enriquez a proposal that he should return to Glyndebourne after a lapse of three years. We flew to Pisa where we picked up a hire car. For the first day or two it rained hard and Florence was not at its best. Franco was fraught with rehearsals and the atmosphere was not conducive to a confident view of the future.

On the third day, a Saturday, we finished our business by lunchtime, repaired to the hotel and, not being required to report at Pisa until mid-afternoon on Sunday, decided that we would drive into town. There we would split up to shop – John to add to his vast, though no doubt freely distributed, collection of Swiss Army penknives, digital watches and other gadgetry and I to buy yet another pair of grey cotton gloves for the retired Jani Strasser and yet another set of straw table-mats for myself – and then meet in one of the two big cafés in the Piazza della Republica.

At six o'clock we drove down, only to find that parking was a problem. However, I found a space amongst other cars, which encouraged a feeling of safety, and we parted and met again as arranged. We were on our second round of drinks, listening to the aged tenor serenading the café with strangulated Puccini arias and Neapolitan love songs, and commenting idly on the passing populace when I said on an impulse, 'I hope the car's all right.' At that instant John looked up from the immediate foreground. 'No, there it goes,' he said. Sure enough, on the top of a double-decker transporter towed by a police jeep was our bright red Fiat, unmistakable with its hired car insignia on the rear window. We dined

262

well and took a taxi back to our hotel.

On collecting the car the next morning, we were fined heavily for the parking offence and charged not only for the carting away but also for garaging the car. Yet the lunch at the Buca di Sant' Antonio in Lucca made up for it. Sunday luncheon in a first class Italian provincial restaurant is a major pleasure. A trip that failed in its primary purpose and was costly in penalties, paid its way in amusement, entertainment and companionship.

Of Bernard Haitink I can truthfully say that working with him was unalloyed pleasure, not only because everything went so smoothly but because of the genuine warmth between us. Though he presents a somewhat austere appearance he is not so much a shy man as a man shy of wasting his time on profitless diversions. The Dutch word *stoor* is often used in a pejorative way to mean blinkered to the extent of stupidity, but it could well be used to describe the power of concentration that this eminent Dutchman, who loves England, so powerfully demonstrates.

I first met Bernard in a coffee bar in Wigmore Street in the mid-fifties when Ian Hunter, by then installed in Harold Holt's, asked me to come round the corner from my office in Baker Street to meet a young Dutch conductor who was rising rapidly, who had no operatic experience, but whose talent Ian thought was the kind that Glyndebourne knew best how to nurture. We had a pleasant meeting and I formed an impression, which was never to change, of a man of taste and culture in whom there ran a sense of humour akin to my own. There was no immediate opportunity to engage him but through Ian I was kept in touch with his progress and went to hear his second essay in opera-conducting in Amsterdam, *Don Carlos* in the Holland Festival of 1966.

In 1970 Bernard took over as chief conductor of the London Philharmonic Orchestra from John Pritchard. Two years later, as the orchestra was firmly involved in its ninth year at Glyndebourne after succeeding the Royal Philharmonic, what was more natural than to ask its musical head to conduct an opera in the season? So *Die Entführung aus dem Serail* became Bernard's third opera. He became Glyndebourne's musical director in 1978, since when he has established himself as one of the leading conductors of opera in the world.

Carl Ebert was a fine actor in the old-fashioned actor-manager school, a fact that I well recognised and respected. I would not describe him as deeply humorous but he had the actor's feel for comedy. He could demonstrate to the singers what he wanted much more easily than he could describe it. Most of his rages in rehearsal were carefully orchestrated for effect; much of his flattery and the laying-on of his abundant charm was just as calculated – very necessary attributes in an actor-manager.

One evening during rehearsals Carl asked us to dine with him and the German conductor Wolfgang Savalitsch and his wife at a local restaurant. Invitations from Carl were rare and this one we felt could not be refused. Peter Ebert and his wife were also bidden. Carl decreed that we should go straight to the table and order from there. This we did, and sat down in the German fashion, husband beside wife rather than separated. The menus were passed round and the orders given. The waiter asked what we wanted to drink. Since Carl showed no interest in the proffered wine list we ordered wine by the individual glass.

The meal proceeded merrily enough, operatic shop being the order of the day. We came to the dessert, which was plentiful and rich, it being a Swiss cuisine, and belatedly Carl ordered a bottle of sparkling wine and eight glasses. The end came with coffee and a brandy for some of us, I think only Savalitsch and myself. The waiter came to make out the bill. 'In one?' he said. We all looked at Carl. 'In four,' he said, 'but put the bottle of wine on mine.' I looked at Peter. I was in half a mind to accept the whole bill for the honour of Glyndebourne but then thought, why should I? Peter looked discomfited. 'I'd like to pay for the Savalitschs',' he said. 'I've been their guest in Germany.' So the bills were made out as three, of which Peter had the largest, and we paid up. The receipted bills came back on a saucer. Carl then calmly pocketed them, saying they would be useful for his income tax returns. Matheson Lang or Donald Wolfit could not have done better.

Günther Rennert was a different man, much more reserved, but beneath the surface he seethed with pent-up passions of many kinds. Ambitious for power, which he exercised as Intendant of Hamburg in bringing that opera house back like a phoenix from the ashes, a ruthless director, one might say dictator, he was quick on his feet and quick in his mind, with a sense of humour that had cruelty never far below the surface. One peculiarity of his was that in every production he had to have a whipping boy: one member of the cast would be singled out, and nothing he or she did could be right. He didn't want them changed, they were never bad enough for that, he just had to have someone on whom he could vent his own frustration. I grew to pity these people and did my best to explain matters to them, but they went through a hellish time.

Despite this I got to know Rennert well and to like him. I had a hard time, and was not always successful, in weaning him away from his favourite designers in Germany to work with British artists who were less subservient and ready to make concessions if they thought what Rennert wanted was incompatible with their own style. However *L'incoronazione di Poppea* in 1962 with Hugh Casson and *La pietra del paragone* in 1964 with Osbert Lancaster were successful collaborations.

Rennert left Hamburg about the time he became head of production for us and freelanced for some years, but he was never happy without his own full-time house and when the colossal job of Intendant at Munich came up in 1967 he jumped at it. This in turn took him out of our orbit because the Munich festival period clashed with Glyndebourne.

Rennert at the wheel of his car perfectly portrayed his whole personality. He drove big, fast cars, Mercedes or Citroëns; hunched over the wheel, his hands, white at the knuckles, gripping it in the ten-minutes-to-two position, head thrust forward with piercing eyes glaring straight through the windscreen. He was impatient to pass everything. Not a good driver, because he had little imagination or care for what the other fellow might do, his imagination drove him along faster and faster. A long journey beside him down the autobahn on a winter's night with driving rain and sleet was indeed something to remember.

Reading Peter Hall's *Diaries* I am struck by the similarities between his character, though not his way of working, and that of Carl Ebert. Peter was on the brink of accepting an invitation to join Glyndebourne as Ebert's assistant in 1955 when he was offered the Arts Theatre in London, an offer that he understandably preferred as he was to be his own master. It was fifteen years later that he came to Glyndebourne for Cavalli's *La Calisto*. He and Glyndebourne had been inexorably drawn together.

I have taken a particular pleasure in working with stage designers. Being the son of an architect and having been employed while a teenager on a variety of building projects I began with some idea of form and construction. Hamish Wilson was my guide to backstage Glyndebourne on my winter visits between 1934 and 1939, but by the end of the war he had faded from the scene. The arrival of John Piper, an acquaintance from my acting days, to design the Britten operas of 1946 and 1947 brought a new and more modern aspect, but it was the success of *Ariadne auf Naxos* in 1950 that confirmed Oliver Messel as the ideal designer for the Mozart and Rossini operas which were to be Glyndebourne's staple products in the following decade. In that period Oliver designed nine operas, including all the major Mozart operas except *Don Giovanni* and the one-act opera, *Der Schauspieldirecktor*, which Peter Rice designed in 1957.

John Piper's designs for the *Don* were so strong that it continued in the repertory until Rennert came to produce it in 1960 and wanted his favourite collaborator, Ita Maximowna, as designer. This was not visually a success, unlike her *Fidelio* of the year before. Oliver would have liked to do *Don Giovanni*, I know, but his highly decorative talents were better suited to the comedies and the *opera seria* of *Idomeneo*.

The 1954 season opened with *Il barbiere di Siviglia* designed by Oliver Messel. We were anxious to keep it in its original two-act form and avoid the long wait after the first scene which, in most productions at that time, turned it into a three-act opera. Oliver provided a solution. The curtain rose on the corner of a house in centre stage with streets in forced perspective leading steeply away on either side. At the end of the serenade, without pause or lowering of curtain, the chorus took hold of the house and opened it out, revealing a two-storeyed, full-size dolls' house within. Every night this got a round of applause.

Ebert had seen and approved the models in Oliver's studio but when he came to the first rehearsal and was faced with the completed set he was amazed. He came into my office, sat down and said: 'Moran, I can't use these sets. I didn't realize that the two streets were to be in such steep perspective that I can't send anyone up them. I can only use the wings and the house door for entrances. The interiors are in perspective too and that will make grouping difficult.' To me the whole idea seemed magical. I soothed him and assured him that the house effect would come off. Anyway it was too late now; I pointed out that he had passed the models. He went back to rehearsal and Oliver turned his charm on him: 'Carly darling, it's going to be beautiful!' Two days later I was in my office, which in those days overlooked the walled garden, and overheard Ebert, who was walking in the garden with a visitor, proudly expanding on his brilliant conception of the dolls' house and how well dear Oliver had carried it out. Of such is theatre made.

Working with Oliver was a never-ending amusement. He designed almost always directly into models, which he constructed himself with a small army of skilled assistants, and many and frequent visits to his studio were happily necessary. These ended in dinner downstairs in the basement kitchen presided over by Vagn Riis-Hansen and the Danish cook. The food and drink were always delicious. While Oliver, his assistants and the scene-builders and painters worked upstairs in the studio, Vagn would be in his sitting room stitching at a tapestry frame and watching Westerns on television; but once we were round the table with the iced schnapps Vagn came into his own. He was a fine raconteur with a great stock of stories and that curious quality, which only a few possess, of being able to use the most improper words and phrases in any company and somehow avoid offence.

Perhaps the least successful of Oliver's works at Glyndebourne was *Die Zauberflöte*, where his usually so impeccable sense of scale momentarily deserted him. His last work for us was *Der Rosenkavalier*. By then he was already in agony much of the time with crippling arthritis and he, with Vagn, finally deserted London's damp climate for the warmth and sunshine of Barbados. There he set up a cottage industry of interior design and decoration, and indeed architecture, and taught his skills to a new set of assistants. Although often invited I was never able to visit them there but I heard many accounts of the wonders of their establishment. The Scandinavian-born wife of a distinguished architect friend came back and reported that they had a large staff of black menservants and gardeners, all apparently members of the same family since they all answered to the name of Darling.

Oliver helped his nephew Tony Armstrong-Jones in getting started on his photographic career, and Tony photographed some of Oliver's work at Glyndebourne. When Tony got engaged to Princess Margaret, Vagn telephoned us with the news some hours before its announcement. He sounded incredulous but delighted. I think he may have had visions of himself following in Ernest Thesiger's footsteps as embroiderer-extraordinary to the Royal Household.

In 1953 Hugh Casson and Osbert Lancaster both came to work for Glyndebourne. Hugh did Gluck's *Alceste*. It was as a result of getting to know him at the time of the Festival of Britain, of which he was the head of design, that I proposed him to Ebert. He designed for this, his first professional venture into the theatre, some beautiful architectural sets, perhaps the most striking being the interior of the temple of Apollo with the lower part of the mutilated statue of the god, by Christopher Ironside, disappearing into the flies above and dwarfing the cast and chorus. Much to John Christie's relief, an early idea of Hugh's to have the architecture indicated in a formal way by constructing it in arrangements of aluminium piping, suggesting fluted columns and silhouetted against the cyclorama, was dropped as being more suitable for ballet than for opera. But the final compromise pleased everyone, being neither boringly heavy nor in any way flippant.

Hugh went on from *Alceste* to design two more operas for us: *L'incoronazione di Poppea* in 1962, and in 1979 Haydn's *La fedeltà premiata*, the first and so far only opera by this composer to be given by Glyndebourne. The scenery for *Fedeltà* has now alas been scrapped to make way for newer acquisitions, but I rescued one of the two larger-than-life-size statue groups of Diana and Actaeon as the stag and have erected it in a suitable place in our garden at home where it is much admired and is weathering well.

Hugh did not design his own costumes for the first two operas, but at last I persuaded him to turn dress designer too and he produced some ravishing Watteau-like confections which helped to make *Fedeltà* one of the prettiest operas that Glyndebourne has seen. Sadly a project in 1956 to get him to design *Die Zauberflöte* did not materialize. He prepared sketches for it to be done in a thoroughly *chinois* style and Mary Kessel made some exquisite costume sketches, but they were thought to be a little too daring for those days. Messel did the *Flute* instead, though his costumes too caused some excitement for he had the women's chorus as apparently bare-breasted Minoans. Though there was in fact a layer of gauze between flesh and fresh air, some of the ladies refused to look topless and others were wrongly endowed, either with too little or much too much.

Bosoms caused a disturbance too in Osbert Lancaster's first work for us, *The Rake's Progress*. Not only did he have advanced views about the amount of nudity he wished for amongst the ladies of the town in the brothel scene, but he made the fullest use of the expansive cleavage of Nan Merriman as Baba the Turk, and even the beard she was adorned with seemed only to accentuate her natural voluptuousness.

It took a long time, and Peter Hall, to get down to the naked truth at Glyndebourne. In *La Calisto* in 1970 the little satyr (Satirino) was deliciously acted and sung by Janet Hughes, topless except for a well-adjusted chest wig that did little to reduce the charms of the performance. She was balanced, if that is the correct assessment, by Hugues Cuenod as the elderly nymph Linfea, whose somewhat pendular appendages were given a lifelike form and animated movement by being filled with birdseed.

It was the next baroque opera, *Il ritorno d'Ulisse in patria*, that first got female frontal nudity on to the stage of that haven of sensuous delight in Sussex. It was Hall again. 'Human frailty' in the prologue sang and moved beautifully, dressed in no more than Melisande's wig. Nobody appeared to be worried, least of all the stage crew who stood by to take her off the descending lift at the end of her scene, though one of the girls who later took the part was upset when a critic commented on what he thought was a wrinkled body stocking. Life is more liberal now, and it would surprise me if exposure of one sort or another was not evident on the operatic stage with greater frequency. There are, after all, opportunities in most operas. What indeed could someone in the future make of Cherubino's dressing up, or down, in the Countess's boudoir? And how did Octavian get on in an age when female undergarments were seldom closed at the knee?

Osbert Lancaster designed five more operas after the *Rake*: *Falstaff*, *L'Italiana in Algeri*, *La pietra del paragone*, *L'Heure espagnole*, and *The Rising of the Moon*. *Pietra* was despised by almost all the purists and pundits and loved by the audience. Rennert himself had adapted the Rossini opera with libretto by Luigi Romanelli. John Pritchard conducted, faithful to all that Gui had taught him. It was very funny and only occasionally a little heavy in what Gui charmingly described as its 'comicity'. Gioacchino Rossini himself – one of the men I would most like to have known – would surely have told the carpers to sit back and enjoy themselves.

Osbert had splendid names for the critics, not all fully earned but at least partly deserved. Martin Cooper was of course Martin Carper; Philip Hope-Wallace, Abandon Hope-Wallace; Felix Aprahamian, Felix Apprehension; Gillian Widdecombe, Gillian Widdershins; Stanley Sadist, and so on. The most down-to-earth remark about a critic I ever heard was when I said to Vagn Riis-Hansen that a conductor known to us both thought his bad notices from a certain critic arose because he had rejected his amatory advances. 'Bloody silly thing to do,' said Vagn. 'He's the best f... in London.'

Emanuele Luzzati designed the best, and also the most magic, *Zauberflöte* I have seen – including David Hockney's – as well as five other operas all in his original and individual style: *Macbeth*, *Don Giovanni*, *Die Entführung*, *Così* and *Il Turco in Italia*. A delightful Genoese, a worker in ceramics, cartoon animator, children's book writer and illustrator, his period of design at

Glyndebourne faded with Enriquez's departure and the decline of Italian influence.

Of recent years John Bury has dominated the scene as Peter Hall's chosen collaborator. Bury works in a style tending to the massive, but is also able to give us the delicate beauty of his *A Midsummer Night's Dream*. Greatly supported by his wife Liz he is an all-round man of the theatre, practical about stage machinery and management, lighting and the use of materials, and will leave his stamp on our times in a significant way. Starting in 1970 he has designed seven operas for Glyndebourne and is currently on his eighth, with a number still to come.

I have often been asked how one copes with the temperament of singers. My reply has been that I have found them no more temperamental than anyone else in the theatre. Indeed, at times I have known stage carpenters more difficult than any prima donna.

That singers have special problems is a fact quickly learnt. An actor can go on with a cold and, though perhaps he may not give his most sonorous vocal performance, can still act to the top of his bent and even perhaps beyond it because he is conscious of his lack of vocal expression. A singer cannot do that. The greater part of his acting is with the voice, and if his vocal chords are too slack or too tense he is in danger of doing them irreparable harm. The girls have their own special regular (usually) problems which affect the voice. When I went to Vienna just after the war I was shown a chart on the wall of the administration office on which was shown the names and the ancitipated 'periods' of all the female singers. Each of those named had to hand in their chits as far in advance as they could and they would then not be scheduled to sing on the two or three critical days of the month. It was a standing joke that many of the older members of the company continued to fill out their chits long after there could have been any validity in their prognostications.

Things are tougher now, for dates of performances are set irrevocably several months or years ahead, and cancellations for lunar reasons are rare indeed; but pregnancy still plays havoc with pre-laid schedules. Only recently a singer at Glyndebourne had to withdraw at rather less than eight months' notice from a part which she much wanted and which had been set aside for her, because her baby was due on the first night. We have had a Queen of the Night in *Die Zauberflöte* who was so far advanced in her pregnancy that I nightly expected the baby to be born during either the first or second of her very acrobatic coloratura arias. Happily her costume not only concealed her state but would possibly have allowed for the birth to go undetected by the audience or anyone else until the truck on which she was standing had been rolled back out of sight.

Male singers are quite as difficult and temperamental as female, but then wardrobe masters are as touchy as wardrobe mistresses and the same goes throughout the theatre. Gérard Souzay came to sing the Count in *Le nozze di Figaro* in 1965 but was never happy. He took affront at the fact that Oliver Messel had given him only a short sword, little more than a dagger, to wear with his costume for the wedding scene: he took this to be a direct insult to his virility. He sang the first performance edgily and failed to get an enthusiastic reception. Half an hour before the second perform-ance, having arrived in his dressing room, he suddenly suffered a *crise des nerfs*, rushed out of the theatre back to his hotel in Lewes and within minutes was on his way to Paris.

We had a Spanish soprano who got through more whisky in an evening than most Scots drink in a week, yet never missed a note. And we had a carpenter who, every inch a male and usually bearded, took to going off sick for a month at a time during which period a lady would come to collect his pay. The lady and the carpenter turned out to be the same.

In one opera, which Michael Redgrave, himself not the least temperamental of producers, directed brilliantly, we had a real-life situation when the hero and heroine fell deeply in love off stage as well as on. So deeply indeed that, the heroine being physically more resilient than the hero, it was the latter who at the afternoon dress rehearsal fainted in the love duet – whether from emotion or exhaustion brought on by living his role to the full, I never dis-covered. I suspected the latter, and my limping translation into French for their benefit of the old quatrain:

> 'Uncle George and Aunty Mabel
> Fainted at the breakfast table.
> Children let this be a warning
> Not to do it in the morning'

did at least ensure that the first night and subsequent performances, though charged with passion, were sustained.

Hugues Cuenod came to Glyndebourne for the first time in 1954 to sing Sellem, the aucioneer in *The Rake's Progress*, as he had in the original Venice production. Nineteen years earlier he had been considered for the part of Monostatos but turned down on account of his height. Thirty years later in 1984 at the age of eighty-two he appeared in Glyndebourne's golden jubilee *Le nozze di Figaro*. A veteran indeed.

Cuenod is a gifted raconteur with an inexhaustible repertoire. One of his *contes* concerns the late Alfred Deller. Hugues is a great performer of early music himself and has a considerable range of voice, as those who have heard him know well. On one occasion he was attending a concert with Deller as soloist. Deller, a commanding figure with a beard, opened his mouth for the first time and out came not the baritone voice that one would expect from his appearance but the high-pitched, and some might say strangulated, tones of a counter-tenor. In the pause between items an old lady sitting next to Hugues turned to her companion and said in a loud voice: 'Good heavens, *how* does he make those extraordinary sounds?' The companion, confusing a counter-tenor with a *castrato* and obviously not wishing to shock the old lady, replied: 'There's an operation carried out in childhood that allows him to retain his boyish voice.' The old lady thought for a moment, looked at Deller again, and said: 'I suppose he's grown that beard to hide the scars.'

TWENTY-ONE

On the beach

When, on 1 October 1981, my sixty-fifth birthday, I stepped down from the bridge of Glyndebourne, I did it with a sense of relief, knowing that the ship and its company were in good nick to continue the long voyage, and that I was becoming too set in my own way of running things to adapt readily to the changing conditions, social, commercial and technological, that lay ahead.

I had handed over command not only to Brian Dickie, who assumed my title as general administrator and who already had many years of Glyndebourne and Wexford experience behind him, but, in overall responsibility, to George Christie himself. I had started as the young, some thought too young, man working for the old man John and had seen him and his generation, Busch, Ebert, Gui, Beecham, all move out of the realms of influence until I had become the old man of the crew. The passing of Jani Strasser left me with no colleague older than myself.

George was ten years old when I first met him and it was another ten years before he began to take a serious interest in the work. On Glyndebourne's and his twenty-fifth birthday (he is actually six months younger than the opera if you date them by their first public appearances) he took over as chairman from his father, who was then seventy-one, while I was forty-three, eighteen years George's senior. George (now justly Sir George) is today the oldest of the administrative team and its unquestioned leader.

I have found life since retirement, not surprisingly, both a relief and a frustration: relief from responsibility to an organization which demanded perhaps too much from my care for wife and family; frustration in no longer having the necessity, and pleasure, of making important decisions. But without retiring I should not have had the leisure to write this little chronicle, not the least amusing part of which has for me been the gradual uncovering of long-forgotten or even long-unknown, and possibly inaccurate, details of history.

I hope I have given the reader a few glimpses of my wife Diana's importance to me and my dependence on her strength of character and taste. I have not said much about our children, largely because their lives since their schooldays have been very much their own, though happily lived in close contact with ours. Simone married the elder son of my old friends Miki and Agi Sekers and I can truthfully say, having worked alongside Hungarians so often, that it is good to have one in the family. If nothing else they help to keep up the pleasure of uncertainty. Simone cooks to a proper standard and writes about it with a mouth-watering fluency. Marc bustles around this part of England draining fields with careful efficiency and at the same time trying to keep the conservationists happy. Marc's wife has enough to do looking after him, dogs, cats, the occasional horse and children. Dominique, our younger daughter, is the only person I know about whom I have never heard an unkind remark, nor have I been able to invent one about her myself. Before she married she spent some time as a secretary at Collins when they were in St James's Place, as well as working for the drug squad of Brighton Police. Her husband works like a lunatic for BBC TV; he learnt lunatic behaviour as one of the electrics staff at Glyndebourne.

Between the three they have so far produced five grandchildren for Diana and me: all, as far as I am concerned, quite acceptable after a certain age. It is now a matter of eager speculation whether another grandchild will make it before the first great-grandchild arrives on the scene.

'What is it like to be retired?' one is asked to the point of boredom. The answer is 'I don't know'. Three years is not enough. I do not hanker after my old profession, but I wish I had a new one. It's a bit too easy to say: 'I now have the time to do all sorts of things that I have wished to do before.' One has the time all right, but in many cases either the wish or the ability, or both, have lapsed and opportunity is, as they say, a great thing. As far as my favourite sport of ocean-racing is concerned I've perforce 'swallowed the anchor' and it sticks in my gullet a bit. But I am hopeful; like some old-time admiral on half-pay I feel that the great First Lord above will one day call me – and I don't mean to my eternal rest.

My life, however prosaic I have made it appear in these writings, has always seemed to me to be a wonderful succession of theatrical events, truly a comedy rather than a farce, and spent, a large part of it, on a bridge of one sort or another. But then life is a comedy and also a bridge between somewhere and somewhere, even if our beginnings and our endings remain intriguingly obscure.

274

Index

References to illustrations are set in bold.